D0754580

THE END

How American Incompetence
Created a War Without End

OF IRAQ

Peter W. Galbraith

SIMON &
SCHUSTER

London · New York · Sydney · Toronto

A CBS COMPANY

First published in Great Britain by Simon & Schuster in 2006
An imprint of Simon & Schuster UK Ltd
A CBS COMPANY

1 3 5 7 9 10 8 6 4 2

Simon & Schuster UK Ltd
Africa House
64–78 Kingsway
London WC2B 6AH

www.simonsays.co.uk

Simon & Schuster Australia
Sydney

A CIP catalogue record for this book
is available from the British Library.

ISBN-13: 978-0-7432-9505-5
ISBN-10: 0-7432-9505-6

Designed by Paul Dippolito

Printed and bound in Great Britain by
The Bath Press, Bath

For my Mother and Father

Contents

Death Speaks

There was a merchant in Baghdad who sent his servant to market to buy provisions, and in a little while the servant came back, white and trembling, and said, Master, just now when I was in the marketplace I was jostled by a woman in the crowd and when I turned I saw it was Death that jostled me. She looked at me and made a threatening gesture; now, lend me your horse, and I will ride away from this city and avoid my fate. I will go to Samarra and there Death will not find me. The merchant lent him his horse, and the servant mounted it, and he dug his spurs in its flanks and as fast as the horse could gallop he went. Then the merchant went down to the market-place and he saw me standing in the crowd and he came to me and said, Why did you make a threatening gesture to my servant when you saw him this morning? That was not a threatening gesture, I said, it was only a start of surprise. I was astonished to see him in Baghdad, for I had an appointment with him tonight in Samarra.

As retold by W. Somerset Maugham, 1933

Bring them on.

—George W. Bush, 2003

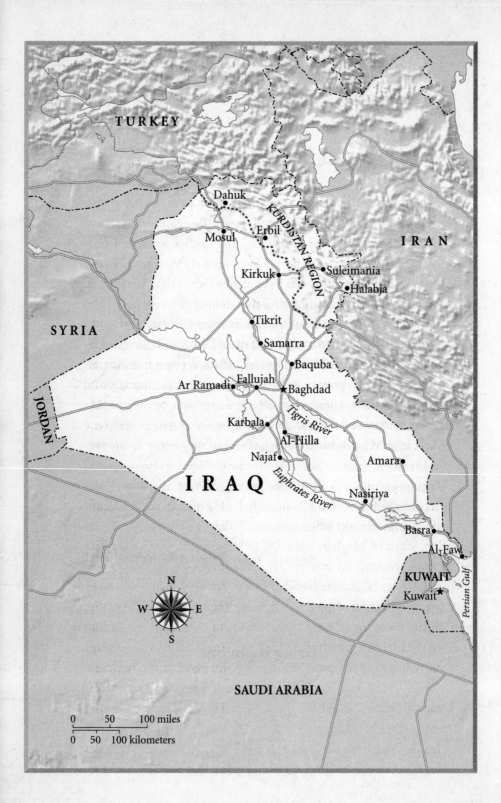

CHAPTER 1

The Appointment
in Samarra

Iraq's deadliest terrorist attack killed no one.

In the early morning hours of February 22, 2006, armed men stormed the Askariya shrine in Samarra, sixty miles north of Baghdad. They handcuffed the four guards, and left them in a side room. Working for several hours, the men placed several hundred pounds of explosives at strategic points under the shrine's golden dome. At 6:55 A.M., they detonated the explosives, probably with a cell phone. The dome collapsed and a shrine dating back to the ninth century was in ruins.

For centuries, Iraq's Shiites brought a saddled horse to the Askariya shrine. The horse waited for the return of Mohammed al-Mahdi, the twelfth and last Imam who went into hiding in 878 in a cave under the shrine. Still a child when last seen, the Imam communicated with his followers through an intermediary for seventy years before contact ceased. Shiites believe he is still alive. His return will usher in an era of justice to be followed by the Judgment Day. The powerful Caliph of Baghdad, the spiritual head of the rival Sunni branch of Islam, had ordered the Mahdi's grandfather, the tenth Imam Ali al-Hadi, brought to Samarra in a kind of house arrest. The Shiites believe that he had Hadi poisoned in 868 and that he ordered Hadi's son, the eleventh Imam Hassan al-Askari, killed six years later. The faithful hid the twelfth Imam to spare him the same fate.

Iraq's Shiite majority see the men who destroyed the Askariya shrine as successors to the Caliph's assassins, and with good reason. Almost certainly, the shrine was destroyed by al-Qaeda in Mesopotamia, the Iraqi offshoot of the organization that brought down New York's World Trade Center. Al-Qaeda seeks to restore the Sunni Caliphate and considers adherents to the Shiite branch of Islam as apostates deserving of death.

Within hours of the shrine's destruction, black-clad members of the Mahdi Army, a Shiite militia named for the twelfth Imam, took control of key points around Baghdad. Shiites then launched attacks on Sunni mosques around Baghdad. Intimidated by the Mahdi Army, the Iraqi Army and the U.S. military did not intervene. Some Iraqi police, the beneficiaries of a multibillion-dollar U.S. training program, joined the attackers while others looked on. Three Sunni Imams were killed that day in Baghdad. In Basra, a Shiite mob broke into a jail, seized ten foreign Arabs who had been jailed on suspicion of terrorism, and shot them. The next day, Sunni Arabs pulled forty-seven Shiites off buses near the mixed Sunni-Shiite city of Baquba and executed them. In order to keep people away from inflammatory sermons expected at Friday prayers two days following the attack, Iraq's Shiite-dominated government imposed a twenty-four-hour curfew on Baghdad. Even so, twenty-nine bodies turned up around the city. The victims had been handcuffed and shot in the head, an indication that they were Sunnis picked up by the police—or Shiite militia wearing police uniforms—and killed.

In the week that followed the Samarra bombing, 184 Sunni mosques were destroyed or vandalized. Sectarian violence killed more than one thousand Sunnis and Shiites. In predominantly Sunni neighborhoods, vigilantes warned Shiite families to leave while Sunnis were evicted from Shiite neighborhoods. Those foolish enough to ignore the warnings were killed. Baghdad's mixed neighborhoods became armed camps.

Atwar Bahjat, a thirty-year-old reporter for al-Arabiya, the Dubai-based Arabic television network, raced from Baghdad to her native Samarra on hearing the first reports of the bombing. Ten minutes after a live broadcast from near the shrine, gunmen abducted her along with cameraman Khaled Mahmud al-Falahi and soundman Adnan Khairallah, and shot them. Atwar Bahjat was born to a Shiite father and a Sunni mother. As if to underscore that there is no place in the new Iraq for Sunnis and Shiites to live together, Sunni gunmen attacked her funeral, killing one mourner and wounding several others.

As civil war accelerated, Iraq had only a caretaker government. In December 2005, Iraq had held its third national election within that single calendar year, choosing the country's permanent parliament under the constitution approved by voters the previous October 15. Intended to cap a year of transition to a new democratic Iraq, the elections served to intensify Iraq's religious and ethnic divisions. Shiites voted for Shiite religious parties, Kurds for Kurdish nationalist parties, and Sunni Arabs for Sunni religious parties or for Sunni Arab nationalists. Fewer than one in ten Iraqis had voted for parties that crossed ethnic or religious lines. Iraq's constitution is intended to foster consensus by requiring a two-thirds majority to form a government. But Iraq's three main communities—the Shiites, the Sunni Arabs, and the Kurds—do not have similar values, a common program, the same allies, nor even a commitment to the continuation of Iraq as a state. After the elections it took more than four months to find sufficient common ground to choose a President, two Vice Presidents, the Parliament's Speaker and his deputies, and to designate a Prime Minister—in spite of broad agreement that there should be a government of national unity that represented all three groups.

In Iraq's civil war, the United States is in the middle. Sunni Arabs believe the United States delivered Iraq to the Shiites and the Iranians. In the February 2006 pogroms, they blamed the U.S. military for standing aside while Shiites destroyed Sunni mosques. The Shiites accused the United States of having sided with the Sunnis in the period leading up to the attack in Samarra. Abdul Aziz al-Hakim, the leader of Iraq's most influential Shiite party, charged that the American ambassador to Iraq, Zalmay Khalilzad, had given the terrorists "a green light" when he criticized the human rights record of Iraq's Shiite-led security forces. Shiites refer to Khalilzad, a Sunni Muslim who is a naturalized American originally from Afghanistan, as "Abu Omar," a reference to the second Sunni Caliph, who, in the Shiite view, usurped the legitimate succession to the prophet in the seventh century. Moqtada al-Sadr, the radical Shiite cleric who leads the Mahdi Army, blamed the U.S. for the destruction of the Askariya shrine, saying the Americans were even worse than Saddam. According to al-Sadr, the United States invaded Iraq to assassinate the Mahdi, whose return, the Americans knew, was imminent.

As the horrific events unfolded in Samarra and Baghdad, I was staying in the Baghdad headquarters of Kurdistan President Massoud Barzani, putting the finishing touches on this book. Because of the headquarters' central location in Baghdad's fortified Green Zone, Iraq's leaders gathered there to discuss the sectarian fighting and the problems of forming a government. As they discussed the crisis over-taking their country, it was clear they saw it as a civil war, and many used that phrase in their conversations with me. As if to underline the point, three nine-foot Katyusha rockets landed in close proximity to Barzani's house while I was writing the preceding paragraphs. Fortu-nately, the closest one—some twenty yards from me—was a dud. Its unexploded warhead burrowed three feet into the asphalt of the park-ing lot, but did no other harm.

In contrast to the Iraqis, the Bush Administration appeared unable to recognize what was happening. Just a few hours after the destruction of the Askariya shrine, U.S. Secretary of State Condoleezza Rice ap-peared on Egyptian television. The interviewer, Mervat Mohsen, summed up the changes in Iraq from a Sunni perspective.

"Excessive meddling has brought the Shiites in Iraq to power. The neighboring Iranians are Shia. The Sunnis are compromised. America's trusted Arab allies are Sunnis. There is a civil war brewing in Iraq. *What have you done?*"

Rice insisted Iraq's political process was fully on track. "Well, I don't think there is a civil war brewing in Iraq. I think what you have in Iraq is a country that has thrown off the yoke of a horrible dictator, who by the way, created all kinds of instability in this region with his wars against his neighbors. Now that that dictator is gone, you have the Iraqi people, who come from many different sects, from many different eth-nic groups, trying to use a political process of compromise and poli-tics, to replace repression."

With regard to Iraq, President Bush and his top advisors have consistently substituted wishful thinking for analysis and hope for strategy. In July 2004, the Central Intelligence Agency prepared a National Intelligence Estimate (NIE) of the situation in Iraq. Representing the collective judgment of America's most experienced Iraq analysts based on the best intelligence available to the U.S. government, the NIE warned of the danger of civil war. When President Bush was asked about the NIE in September 2004, he shrugged it off: "The CIA said life could be lousy, life could be OK, life could be better. The Iraqi people don't share their pessimism."

On June 4, 2005, I attended the first session of the newly elected Kurdistan National Assembly in Erbil, northern Iraq. Among those attending was Iraq's president, Jalal Talabani. Talabani, a Kurd, is not only the first-ever democratically elected head of state in Iraq, but in a country that traces its history back to the Garden of Eden, he is, as one friend observed, "the first freely chosen leader of this land since Adam was here alone." While Kurds are enormously proud of his accomplishment, the flag of Iraq, the country Talabani heads, was noticeably absent from the inauguration ceremony, nor can it be found anyplace in Erbil, a city of one million that is the capital of Iraq's Kurdistan Region.

Anne Bodine, the head of the American Embassy office in Kirkuk, spoke at the ceremony, congratulating the newly minted parliamentarians, and affirming the U.S. commitment to an Iraq that is, she said, "democratic, federal, pluralist, and unified." The phrase evidently did not apply in Erbil. In their oath, the parliamentarians were asked to swear loyalty to the unity of the Kurdistan Region of Iraq. Many pointedly dropped the "of Iraq."

The shortest speech was given by the head of the Iranian intelligence service in Erbil, a man known to the Kurds as Agha Panayi. Looking directly at Ms. Bodine, he said simply, "This is a great day. Throughout Iraq, the people we supported are in power." He did not add, "Thank you, George Bush." The unstated was understood.

Thanks to the American invasion, Kurdistan has consolidated its status as a virtually independent state and in so doing has righted an historic wrong. Winston Churchill included the Kurds in Arab Iraq in

1921 when he was a cabinet minister in Lloyd George's coalition government, responsible for the Middle East. The Kurds rebelled against
this decision through much of the twentieth century. Iraq's military response to Kurdish opposition escalated over the decades, culminating
with Saddam Hussein's genocidal Anfal campaign of the late 1980s, a
campaign that included extensive use of poison gas on Kurdish villagers. Churchill considered the forced incorporation of the Kurds in
Iraq as one of his biggest mistakes, and it is perhaps fitting that the mistake has been undone by an American president who keeps a bust of
Churchill in the Oval Office.

As Agha Panayi indicated in his speech, Iran has emerged as the
major beneficiary of America's Iraq War. Ever since the Ottomans and
Persians agreed in the Treaty of Qasr-i-Shirin to a demarcation line in
1639 between their two empires, the line that is now the Iran-Iraq border has separated the Persians from the Arabs, and the Shiite-ruled
lands from the Sunni-ruled. But, since 2003, Iranian-sponsored Shiite
religious parties have run Iraq's nine southern provinces, known as
governorates, as well as Baghdad. The Shiite religious parties dominate
Iraq's central government and control the Interior Ministry, which has
enabled them to place Iranian-trained militiamen into the police. Iran
has substantial influence over Iraq's U.S.-created military, and is developing economic ties that will soon link the two countries' strategically
vital oil facilities.

There is no small irony in these developments. As he began to prepare the American people for war with Iraq in his January 2002 State of
the Union speech, President Bush denounced what he described as an
Axis of Evil between Iraq and Iran (along with North Korea). At that
time, there were no more bitter enemies than the Iran of the ayatollahs
and the Iraq of Saddam Hussein. Thanks to George W. Bush, Iran has
no closer ally in the world than the Iraq of the ayatollahs. This new
Tehran-Baghdad Axis could have revolutionary consequences for the
Middle East. Iraq is now the Arab world's first Shiite-ruled state, and
the Shiite victory in Iraq is bound to influence a Shiite-populated crescent that extends from southern Iraq into Saudi Arabia's Eastern

Province, into Kuwait, and to Bahrain. This Shiite crescent sits atop the most important oil reservoirs in the world.

As the United States entered the fourth year of occupying Iraq, it had 130,000 troops battling a Sunni Arab insurgency. Based in a community that is no more than 20 percent of Iraq's population, the Sunni Arab insurgents cannot prevail militarily. But they cannot readily be defeated either. The U.S. can clear insurgents out of Sunni cities, but it has insufficient forces to hold the territory. Pushed out of one area, the insurgents move to another and return when the Americans move on.

Insurgency, civil war, Iranian strategic triumph, the breakup of Iraq, an independent Kurdistan, military quagmire. These are all consequences of the American invasion of Iraq that the Bush Administration failed to anticipate. About some of these things, such as the Sunni Arab insurgency, the president and his top advisors have admitted they were surprised. About others, they are in denial. In his 2006 State of the Union address, President Bush said, "Hindsight is not wisdom and second-guessing is not a strategy." It is, of course, understandable why the president prefers not to look back. It isn't that he failed to consider *some* possible adverse consequences of the war, but rather that he missed *all* of them. In devising strategy, one can hope for the best, but should be prepared for the worst. The Bush Administration hoped that American troops would be greeted as liberators and that Iraqis would embrace democracy, yet it had no contingency plans to follow in case it didn't work out that way.

Some of the outcomes in Iraq are the inevitable result of the invasion. Iraq was cobbled together by the British at the end of World War I from three different Ottoman valiyets, or provinces: predominantly Kurdish Mosul in the north, mostly Sunni Baghdad at the center, and Shiite Basra in the south. The Arab parts of the country had a shared identity, but the Kurds wanted no part of the new state. The British installed a foreign Sunni Arab prince, Feisal of Hejaz, as Iraq's king in 1921. He and his successors ruled through a Sunni Arab–dominated bureaucracy and military. In 1958, the Iraqi military overthrew the monarchy (gunning down Feisal's grandson, the young King Feisal II) but continued the Sunni Arab domination of the country. In order to rule over the 55 percent of Iraqis who are Shiite and the 20 percent who are Kurdish, Iraq's Sunni Arab rulers used varying degrees of force to stay in power.

In 2003, the United States ousted the last, and most brutal, of Iraq's Sunni Arab dictators. It smashed Iraq's army and then legally dissolved the Iraqi military, security services, and Ba'ath Party. The army and secret police were the institutions that had enabled Iraq's Sunni Arab minority to rule for eighty years. With these repressive institutions gone, Iraq's Shiite majority took power through democratic elections in 2005 and asserted sectarian control over key institutions, including the police. In the constitutional negotiations in August 2005, the Kurds consolidated the independence they always wanted. The Sunni Arabs resented bitterly their loss of historic hegemony and violently resisted a Shiite-dominated new order. Civil war was always a possible, if not likely, outcome. The only remarkable thing is that it caught the Bush Administration by surprise.

The Bush Administration assumed the transition from Saddam Hussein's Sunni Arab dictatorship to a stable new order in Iraq would be easy—so easy, in fact, that no real planning would be required. Many of the United States's present difficulties in Iraq are the direct consequence of the failure to plan for the day after U.S. troops entered Baghdad. The professional military had wanted to send more troops to secure Iraq than the Pentagon's civilian leaders were willing to commit. But even with the troops it did have in Iraq, the United States could have protected Iraq's government ministries and its most important national institutions, including the archaeological museum, had there been a plan to do so. During eight critical weeks after Saddam fell, U.S. authority in Iraq ebbed away as looters demolished the capital city's public institutions and it became clear that the U.S. military was unwilling or unable to maintain order.

The catastrophe was followed by a fourteen-month occupation that was mismanaged from start to finish. The president did not decide whether to turn power over to an interim Iraqi government or to have the United States run the country in the manner of the postwar occupations of Germany and Japan. For a month after the fall of Baghdad the Administration pursued both policies simultaneously. When Secretary of Defense Donald Rumsfeld chose an administrator for Iraq, he picked a retired diplomat with no experience of the country and gave him two weeks to prepare for the assignment. The administrator, L. Paul Bremer III, decided after three days in Iraq that he, not the Iraqis, would run the country. The result was a bungled effort at nation-building that was characterized by ineffective administration, constantly shifting political direction, an inability to restore essential services (including electricity), economic decline, mismanagement of billions of dollars in Iraqi and U.S. funds, corruption, and a failed effort to build a new Iraqi military and police.

The Bush Administration's grand ambitions for Iraq were undone by arrogance, ignorance, and political cowardice. In not preparing for the collapse of law and order, the Administration ignored the warnings of experts and of Iraqis and seemed to assume that Iraq's police and bureaucrats would report for work the day after Saddam fell. This coincided with its unwillingness to take the politically difficult decision to deploy sufficient troops, and to give those it did send responsibility for maintaining law and order. While attempting a breathtakingly bold effort at nation-building, the Administration relied on the judgments of inexperienced and unqualified staff instead of those who actually knew something about the country. In my recent trips to Iraq, I have asked its elected political leaders where they thought the United States went wrong. All gave the same answer: when the United States became an occupier instead of a liberator, in short, when the Bush Administration decided it was more capable of determining Iraq's future than the peoples of the country itself.

President Bush speaks of Iraq as integral to a larger struggle for freedom in the Middle East. In the run-up to the war, Vice President Richard Cheney and the civilians in charge at the Pentagon—Rumsfeld, Deputy Secretary Paul Wolfowitz, Under Secretary for Policy Douglas Feith—advocated the war because it was central to their radical ambition to remake the Middle East into pro-Western, market-oriented democracies that would have good relations with one another and with Israel. Iraq was to trigger a "domino effect," with Iran and Syria the next to fall. For this to work, the Bush Administration's visionaries had had to make certain assumptions about how Iraq's Shiite majority would behave after taking power. Wolfowitz theorized that Iraq's Shiites would oppose a clerical state and develop a pro-Western polity that could actually undermine the ayatollahs in Iran. This scenario ignored some inconvenient facts: Iran has supported Iraq's Shiites for decades, funding their political parties and training and equipping their militias. Iraq's largest Shiite party, the Supreme Council for the Islamic Revolution in Iraq (SCIRI), was founded under Iranian auspices in Tehran in 1982. Its name provides a clue as to its political agenda. A war undertaken in part to undermine Iran's Islamic republic has given Tehran its greatest strategic gain in four centuries.

In justifying the war, President Bush proclaimed that the "United States of America will not permit the world's most dangerous regimes to threaten us with the world's most destructive weapons." Iraq did not have weapons of mass destruction (WMD). But, with U.S. attention and resources committed to Iraq, both North Korea and Iran have been free to pursue their nuclear weapons programs. As the U.S. made preparations in 2002 and 2003 for the Iraq War, North Korea expelled United Nations nuclear inspectors, withdrew from the Nuclear Non-Proliferation Treaty, and reprocessed previously safeguarded plutonium into material for nuclear weapons. The president loudly insisted that the United States would not tolerate a nuclear-armed North Korea and did precisely nothing.

At the beginning of 2006, Iran announced it would enrich uranium that can be used for a nuclear weapon. With U.S. forces tied down in Iraq, the Iranians could feel confident that there would be no American response. Moqtada al-Sadr warned, "If neighboring Islamic countries, including Iran, become the target of attacks, we will support them. The Mahdi Army is beyond the Iraqi Army. It was established to defend Islam." This is no idle threat. During a 2004 uprising against the U.S. occupation, the Mahdi Army so disrupted American supply lines in Iraq that Bremer nearly had to impose food rationing on the thousands of Americans working in his occupation government in Baghdad. The Mahdi Army is in 2006 at least twice as strong as it was in 2004, and Iran would have the support of other Shiite militias as well.

Thanks to the American invasion, most Iraqis may well be better off. Iraq's Shiite majority is liberated from eight decades of oppression. Even if their political preferences are not those the Bush Administration dreamed about, they have been able to decide their future democratically. Iraq's Kurds are on the cusp of achieving their own state, and it is satisfying to see one of history's underdogs finally come out on top. Iraq's Sunni Arabs think of themselves as worse off, but they are only 20 percent of the country.

It is, however, impossible to argue that the United States is better off. Although initiated to protect the United States from weapons of mass destruction in the hands of a rogue state, the Iraq War has left the United States more vulnerable to potential Iranian and North Korean nuclear weapons. And because of the Administration's planning failures, looters had free access to a wide range of dangerous materials from Iraq's defunct nuclear and biological weapons programs. Some of these materials may have ended up in Iran or in the hands of terrorists, leaving the U.S. more at risk from Iraqi WMD-related materials than it was before the war.

By enabling clerical Iran to achieve its historic ambitions in the Shiite Arab world, the war is a major strategic setback for the United States in the Middle East. The only "democratic fallout" from the Iraq War has been the elections of hard-line extremists in Palestine and Iran. American prestige in the Arab world is at an all-time low with polls in some Arab countries showing Osama bin Laden viewed more favorably than President Bush. The war has damaged U.S. relations with its closest allies in Europe. No American president in living memory is as poorly regarded in Europe as George W. Bush.

The Iraq War has failed to serve a single major U.S. foreign policy objective. It has not made the United States safer; it has not advanced the war on terror; it has not made Iraq a stable state; it has not spread democracy to the Middle East; and it has not enhanced U.S. access to oil. It has been costly. As of this writing, 2,500 American troops have been killed, more than forty thousand have been wounded, and $300 billion spent. Some economists have calculated that the total cost of the war, direct and indirect, could exceed $2 trillion.* Continuing the present course of action will not bring the United States closer to success, however it is defined.

This book does not seek to rehash the debate about whether the United States should have invaded Iraq in 2003. That is an important question but not especially relevant to what should now be done. I will argue that the policies we have pursued since Saddam fell on April 9, 2003, have been flawed conceptually and in execution. The main error has been to see Iraq not as it is, but as we wished it were. This led to an unrealistic and futile commitment to preserving the unity of a state that was never a voluntary creation of its people, and that has been held together by force. In making this case, I do not seek to score points with the proponents or the opponents of the war, or for that matter of the current American Administration. My purpose is to urge a course of action by which the United States can extricate itself from the mess in Iraq, including from escalating civil war. This strategy should be based on U.S. interests and reflect the reality that Iraq has broken up in all but name.

---

* Nobel Prize–winner Joseph Stiglitz and Harvard Budget expert Linda Bilmes estimate at least $1 trillion in total costs and possibly more than $2 trillion. Their calculations include lifetime costs of disabilities and health care for veterans, the economic value of lost lives, the impact on investment, and the impact on the federal deficit.

CHAPTER 2

Appeasement

At dawn on September 22, 1980, Iraqi jets bombed Iranian airfields and military installations. At the same time, Iraqi soldiers crossed into Iran's Kurdistan Province in the north and its predominantly Arab Khuzistan Province in the south, the latter a strategic prize where Iran's oil industry started in the early twentieth century, and the location of rich reservoirs. By mid-November, Iraq had taken the port city of Khorramshahr and surrounded the oil facilities in Abadan. Saddam Hussein, who had become Iraq's president the year before, had gambled that Iran's revolutionary chaos would enable his country to achieve a quick victory over its much larger neighbor.

The Iran-Iraq War lasted eight years. It consumed a million lives, wounded or maimed another two million, and cost more than $1 trillion. With its static fronts, trench warfare, and relentless shelling, the Iran-Iraq War resembled the First World War. Like that conflict, it quickly became a stalemate where neither side could win, nor could they agree to a truce. There was another similarity: beginning in 1983, Iraq made use of increasingly sophisticated chemical weapons to offset Iran's superior numbers. It was the first sustained use of these weapons since they were banned under the 1925 Geneva Protocols, a treaty that resulted from revulsion over the horrors of poison gas in the First World War.

The war was ostensibly fought over the location of a border in a river. Iraq's two great rivers, the Euphrates and the Tigris, converge in the south to form the Shatt al-Arab, which is Iraq's access to the sea.

South of Basra, once Iraq's main port, the Shatt al-Arab becomes the border between Iran and Iraq. The Iraqis, backed by the British, long insisted the actual boundary should be on the Iranian shore while the Iranians argued it was the thalweg, or the middle of the river's deepest channel. In 1975, at the margins of an OPEC meeting in Algiers, the Shah of Iran and then Iraqi Vice President Saddam Hussein agreed that the thalweg would be the border. In return, the Shah agreed to cut off support for a Kurdish rebellion in Iraq that he had initiated for the purpose of extracting this concession from Iraq.

In January 1979, the Shah was overthrown and the Ayatollah Ruhollah Khomeini became Iran's de facto ruler. Khomeini despised Iraq's Ba'athist regime. Not only was its secular and nationalist character antithetical to the values of the Islamic revolution, it repressed Iraq's Shiites in a land where they were the majority and that contained Shiite Islam's most important religious sites. Khomeini had lived for fourteen years in exile in Najaf, the southern Iraqi city that is the resting place of Ali, the first Imam and the founder of the Shiite sect (the Shiites are, literally, "the party of Ali"). Khomeini had witnessed firsthand the predations of the Ba'athists. He also had a personal grudge. In 1978, at the behest of the Shah, Saddam expelled him from Iraq, a decision that proved the Shah's undoing and nearly Saddam's as well. From his place of exile in the Paris suburbs, Khomeini directed the anti-Shah uprising as he could never have done from a police state like Iraq.

Once in power in Iran, Khomeini appealed directly to Iraq's Shiites to replace a corrupt secular regime with a just—that is, Islamic—state. Saddam knew this was fertile ground and he responded harshly. Using the pretext of a failed assassination attempt on Deputy Prime Minister Tariq Aziz by a Shiite radical, Iraqi security forces on April 1, 1980, arrested the Grand Ayatollah Muhammad Baqir al-Sadr, Iraq's most senior Shiite cleric, and his sister Bint al-Huda. While the ayatollah was made to watch, the sister was raped and murdered. The torturers then set afire al-Sadr's beard before driving nails into his head. A furious Khomeini called for Saddam's overthrow. On September 17, 1980, Saddam abrogated the Algiers Accord and defiantly asserted Iraqi sovereignty over the entire Shatt al-Arab. Five days later, he launched war.

Beyond the personal vendetta between Khomeini and Saddam and the territorial dispute that was its proximate cause, the Iran-Iraq War was a clash of ideologies and civilizations. Saddam saw himself as the embodiment of Arab nationalism fighting against the Persians. He even referred to the war as Saddam's Qadisiya, recalling the seventh-century battle in which Arabs defeated the Persians and brought Islam to Iraq. Khomeini saw the war not only as the defense of the nascent Iranian Islamic Republic, but as an opportunity to spread the Islamic revolution to his fellow Shiites in Iraq.

Although Iraq's initial blitzkrieg allowed it to take territory temporarily from its disorganized neighbor, the balance very much favored Iran. Not only was Iran three times more populous, but it had the advantage of strategic depth. Aside from the oil facilities at Abadan and Khorramshahr, Iran's main cities and critical infrastructure are far from the Iraqi border. By contrast, most of Iraq's people live in the eastern part of the country, within easy range of Iranian aircraft. Basra, Iraq's second largest city, is on the Shatt al-Arab. The Iranians shelled it heavily during the war. In the war's early days, Iran closed down Iraq's oil exports through the Persian Gulf, damaging its offshore loading facility at Faw.* Iran also had the advantage of a long coastline on the Persian Gulf and Indian Ocean. Bandar-e-Abbas, a major Iranian port and oil export facility, is five hundred miles from Iraq, and was not bombed until the later stages of the war.†

Saddam and Khomeini each appealed to the disaffected populations in the other's country. Both were disappointed. Saddam hoped that Khuzistan's Arab majority would welcome Iraq's troops as liberators. They did not, in part because they were Shiites with no desire to trade Persian rule for a Sunni tyrant. The Iraqi Kurds readily accepted Iranian support, and used the war to expand their anti-Iraq military activities. Khomeini had hoped that Iraq's Shiites, who made up the

---

* Iraq was still able to export oil from the northern Kirkuk oil field through a pipeline to Ceyhan, Turkey.

† Kharg Island, once Iran's principal oil export terminal, was bombed from 1982 onwards and put out of commission in 1986.

bulk of the Iraqi Army, would come over to the Iranian side. A few did but most fought stubbornly, if not enthusiastically, for Iraq through the eight years of war. In 2003, U.S. analysts looked back on this apparent Shiite loyalty to Iraq in the Iran-Iraq War as evidence that Iran would not have undue influence in post-Saddam Iraq. It was a wildly wrong misreading. Shiite soldiers fought for Saddam not out of love for Iraq or the regime, but because they were conscripts who had little choice. As we shall see, the analysts might have done better to examine the words and actions of Iraq's Shiite religious and political leaders.

In 1982, the Iranians counterattacked, expelling the Iraqis from Khuzistan and pushing into Iraqi territory. Khomeini fired up Iranian recruits with religious fervor, promising instant entry into paradise for those who died as martyrs against the infidel Iraqis. Boys as young as twelve volunteered to be human minesweepers, crossing no-man's-land chained together and carrying plastic keys to unlock the gates of paradise.* The Iraqis, with a conscript army mostly filled in the lower ranks by sullen Shiites and potentially rebellious Kurds, had no comparable commitment to self-sacrifice.

After the Iranian counterattack, Saddam Hussein proposed a cease-fire, and a return to the prewar boundary. Khomeini refused, insisting that Iran would only stop the war if Saddam were gone. In a direct appeal to Iraq's Shiites, Khomeini told them, "We are related by race, traditions, and religion . . . No other government or nation in the world has the right to be concerned about Iraq's future." About the same time, SCIRI formed an Iraqi government in exile in Tehran, headed

---

* In 1987, I visited some of the child soldiers who made it through the minefields at a special POW camp set up by the Iraqis at Ar Ramadi on the Euphrates. The camp was a showplace for the International Red Cross, and occasional visitors like me. The boys, by now young adults, engaged in a variety of purposeful vocational activities, including weaving rugs with the likeness of Saddam Hussein. These activities were, however, clearly staged for my visit, and many of the Iranian captives seemed to suffer from depression and other mental illness connected with interminable confinement. Some remained as POWs until the late 1990s.

by Muhammed Bakr al-Hakim, with the express goal of creating an Iranian-style Islamic republic.*

As Iraq's military situation deteriorated in 1983, Saddam deployed poison gas. From November 1983 to August 1988, Iraq's use of chemical weapons escalated both in quantity and sophistication. The first attacks involved mustard gas, a blistering agent first employed by the Germans in Ypres, Flanders, in 1917. By the end of the Iran-Iraq War, Iraq was using sophisticated nerve agents, as well as experimenting with "cocktails" of nerve gas, cyanide, and mustard gas.

The initial U.S. response to the Iran-Iraq War was muted. President Jimmy Carter was in what turned out to be his final months in office when Saddam launched his initial attack. Carter had no reason to be sympathetic to Iran, which was holding fifty-two American diplomats hostage. With U.S. support, the U.N. Security Council passed Resolution 479 on September 28, 1980. It called for a cease-fire, but without demanding that Iraq give up the territory it had seized. The Iranians were furious with the United Nations' one-sided stance, although they had themselves to blame for the ongoing hostage crisis that resulted in Iran's isolation. The outbreak of war diverted Iranian attention from negotiations aimed at ending the hostage crisis, and destroyed whatever slim chance may have existed for Carter to win reelection.

In 1981, the Reagan Administration continued its predecessor's hands-off approach to the war. But after Iran turned the military tide in 1982, the Administration became concerned about the consequences of an Iranian victory. It also saw an opportunity to move Iraq from its alliance with the Soviet Union into a closer relationship with the United States, a relationship that the more optimistic Administration strategists thought might actually replace the lost alliance with the Shah as a means for protecting American interests in the northern Persian Gulf.

Just as Iraq started using poison gas, the Reagan Administration

---

* Bakr al-Hakim returned in 2003 to Iraq, where he was assassinated in a Najaf car bomb attack. His brother Abdul Aziz al-Hakim headed the Shiite list in the January 2005 elections, and is arguably Iraq's most powerful politician.

began in earnest its courtship of Saddam Hussein. In staffing his administration, Ronald Reagan had passed over Donald Rumsfeld, President Gerald Ford's chief of staff and defense secretary. In 1983, as something of a consolation prize, Reagan asked Rumsfeld to be his special emissary to Saddam Hussein with the goal of reestablishing diplomatic relations, which Iraq had severed in 1967 in retaliation for U.S. support for Israel in the Arab-Israeli Six Day War. Years later, as he pushed the United States to war in 2002, Rumsfeld claimed that he had protested Iraq's use of chemical weapons, but he did not raise the matter in his two meetings with Saddam Hussein. Meeting with Saddam in December 1983, Rumsfeld discussed America and Iraq's common antipathy for Iran and Syria, U.S. efforts to stop arms going to Iran, and U.S. financing for an oil pipeline from Iraq to the Jordanian port of Aqaba. Even though the second meeting, in March 1984, took place after the State Department publicly expressed concern about Iraq's use of chemical weapons, Rumsfeld was silent on the matter with the dictator. He did tell Deputy Prime Minister Tariq Aziz that the international community took a dim view of Iraq's use of chemical weapons, but by raising the matter with Aziz and not Saddam, Rumsfeld clearly signaled that Iraq's use of chemical weapons was a secondary issue for the Reagan Administration.

In March 1984, the U.N. secretary-general submitted an experts' report to the Security Council on Iraq's use of chemical weapons. The Dutch and British representatives to the U.N. circulated a resolution condemning the use of chemical weapons (without specifically blaming Iraq) but the United States took no significant actions to support its allies. The State Department did meet with Nizar Hamdoon, Iraq's ambassador to the United States, to discuss how the Security Council might handle the issue in a way that would cause the fewest objections in Baghdad. The Iraqis did not want the Security Council to adopt a resolution on the matter (which could have been legally consequential) and asked instead for U.S. support in limiting any Security Council action to a statement by the council's president. The Reagan Administration obliged and the Iraqis got the outcome they desired. At the U.N. Human Rights Commission, the Reagan Administration went a step further and actively *opposed* a resolution condemning Iraq's use of chemical weapons.

In 1982, Ronald Reagan removed Iraq from the State Department's list of countries supporting terrorism, although there had been no significant change in Iraq's support for radical Palestinian groups that were the principal terrorist concern at the time. The Administration began providing guarantees from the government-controlled Commodity Credit Corporation for Iraqi purchases of U.S. agricultural products in 1983 and extended Export-Import Bank credits to Iraq in 1984. While these credits were intended to finance the purchases of U.S. agricultural and manufactured goods, they aided Iraq's war effort by freeing up other funds that could be used for military purposes. By 1988, U.S. subsidies to Iraq approached $1 billion a year.

In 1983, the Reagan Administration ordered the CIA to share battlefield intelligence with Iraq. Liaison officers provided Iraq with the locations of Iranian units, which enabled Iraq to anticipate and prepare for Iranian attacks. Assisted by American intelligence, Iraq was able to target Iranian troop concentrations with chemical weapons. The Administration certainly knew how its intelligence was being used. Thus, while the State Department publicly criticized Iraq for the use of chemical weapons, the Reagan Administration was working secretly to make them more effective.*

Ronald Reagan had good reasons not to want to see Iraq lose the Iran-Iraq War. If Iran prevailed, it would install in power like-minded Iraqi Shiites—men such as Bakr al-Hakim—who would give Iran de facto control over the vast oil resources of both countries. Reagan's strategists feared that Iran would emerge as the preeminent power in the Persian Gulf, and be in a position to spread its revolutionary Is-

---

* Some writers have accused the Reagan Administration of supplying Iraq with the chemicals to manufacture its weapons. There is no evidence that this happened nor would it have been as consequential as the assistance the United States did provide. Most of the components for chemical weapons have legitimate commercial uses, and are available from any of several hundred potential suppliers. But only the United States could provide the intelligence that made Iraq's chemical weapons effective.

lamic message to the Gulf's Shiite crescent, which includes Bahrain, Saudi Arabia's oil-rich Eastern Province, and Kuwait.

However, Reagan's courtship of Saddam was not just about blocking an Iranian victory in the war. The president and his team saw in Saddam Hussein a potential partner in the Middle East, both politically and economically. By seeing in Saddam what he wanted to see, Reagan overlooked, and then became an apologist for, gross human rights violations, the use of poison gas, and, ultimately, genocide.

In the summer of 1984, the Senate Foreign Relations Committee, for which I worked as a professional staff member, deployed a five-man staff delegation to look at U.S. interests in the Persian Gulf. After a week of meetings in Kuwait, the United Arab Emirates, and Oman, I and staff colleagues Casimir Yost and Graeme Bannerman flew to Baghdad. The Saddam Hussein International Airport was sparkling new—it had been built to accommodate world leaders slated to come to Baghdad for the 1982 Non-Aligned Summit*—but was mostly unused thanks to the war.

The Iraqis afforded us extraordinary access, with lengthy meetings with Deputy Prime Minister Aziz and Vice President Taha Yasin Ramadan; it was one of the first times Ramadan agreed to see an American delegation. My colleagues, very much caught up in the excitement of a new relationship with a country that some hoped might be the next Egypt,† peppered the Iraqis with questions about restoring diplomatic relations and a possible Iraqi role in the Middle East peace process.

I was skeptical. I asked Aziz about his use of poison gas on Iran, which he denied. Ramadan, dressed in green fatigues and with a pistol

* The summit was switched to New Delhi, India, after Iran threatened to bomb the venue.

† After the 1973 Yom Kippur War, Egyptian President Anwar Sadat switched his country from being a Soviet ally to American ally; he made his dramatic peace mission to Jerusalem a few years later.

on the belt, explained that the United States had not yet done enough to justify Iraq resuming full diplomatic relations, as if the United States should jump through hoops to meet the requirements of his despotic regime.

On the surface, Baghdad was a thriving metropolis. We stayed at the brand-new Sheraton on the banks of the Tigris. Every night swank wedding parties passed through its soaring lobby, and affluent Iraqis rode the glass elevators to the rooftop restaurant. In the pool below my room, several young women bathed topless, not a sight I expected in the Arab Middle East.

But there was much about Baghdad that was not normal. There were the ubiquitous portraits of Saddam Hussein—resplendent in his field marshal's uniform, in a dark suit waving a large cigar, in the turban of a Kurd, on his knees at prayer in a Shiite mosque. These reminded me of the Lenins, Marxes, and Engelses I had seen in every public space in the Soviet Union during a trip I took as a teenager. There was also the pervasive fear. I was warned not to take a picture from my hotel room, since it not only overlooked the Tigris, but also Saddam's Republican Palace. Guests, I was told, had been arrested for ignoring this prohibition, and I wondered how many secret policemen spent their days watching the hotel's windows. I noticed the nervousness of the minions to Iraq's top leaders. They were afraid of their bosses, scared of saying the wrong thing to us, and jumped at any chance to ingratiate themselves with the higher-ups. In his all-white office (white leather sofas, alabaster table, etc.), Ramadan pulled out a cigar and four aides rushed forward with lighters. (None of them worked.)

My unease grew when I visited the Tomb of the Unknown Soldier on the vast parade grounds not far from the presidential complex. Newly built to honor the dead of the still raging Iran-Iraq War, it was meant to resemble a sword (in the colors of the Iraqi flag) thrusting upward with a large shield. It is not great architecture. I would drive past it in 2005 with Iraq's Deputy Prime Minister Ahmad Chalabi, who remarked that it looked like a toilet cover and brush. No one dared describe it that way in 1984. Underneath the shield at the top of the monument was the soldier's metal coffin, with a wreath of pink plastic roses sent by North Korean dictator Kim Il Sung. In a museum below the coffin, I counted 144 poster-sized photographs, each of Saddam Hussein.

I wondered about a leader whose idea of a war memorial involved 144 pictures of himself. When I wrote the first draft of our staff report, I described the Stalinist features of Saddam Hussein's Iraq. My colleagues insisted that this be toned down or deleted. We had a battle over my characterization of Aziz's statement that Iraq had not used chemical weapons. I said he had lied. They did not dispute the fact of Iraqi use of chemical weapons, but objected to the inclusion of language that might derail the dream of a strategic partnership with Iraq. In the end, we simply reported Aziz's denial. Some of the objections came from the Reagan Administration, with whom the draft had been shared.

Our report, *War in the Gulf,* was published in August 1984. Just after Reagan's reelection in November, the United States and Iraq restored full diplomatic relations.

CHAPTER 3

He Gassed His Own People

I n 1985, the Reagan Administration bizarrely shifted strategy, and initiated a secret program to arm Iran. Robert McFarlane, the national security advisor, traveled to Tehran on a fake Irish passport with a Bible inscribed to Khomeini by Ronald Reagan, and a cake in the shape of a key.* Secret flights carried American weapons to Iran. Although the quantity of arms was not great, they were militarily important because Iran's arsenal was largely American—bought by the Shah in his oil-fueled spending spree of the 1970s—and Iran had been unable to get spare parts since the 1979 hostage crisis.

On November 26, 1986, this tilt to Iran began to unravel. The Lebanese newspaper *Al-Shiraa* published an article asserting that the United States had been providing weapons to Iran in exchange for the release of American hostages held by pro-Iranian militants in Lebanon. A month later, the story was picked up in the American media. It became a national scandal when it emerged that the proceeds generated by the arms sales to Iran had been used to fund the Contras, a right-wing paramilitary force fighting Nicaragua's Sandinista government. This circumvented U.S. law banning such assistance.

Congress set up a special committee to investigate the illegality, but

---

* The key seems to have been an especially inept effort to capture the symbolism of the key to paradise given to the young martyrs sacrificing their lives for the Islamic republic. Khomeini never got the cake, since it was confiscated—and apparently eaten—by the customs officers at Tehran's Mehrabad Airport.

the first hearings on the matter were conducted by the Senate Foreign Relations Committee in early 1987. Claiborne Pell, a Rhode Island Democrat who had become chairman after the Democrats regained the Senate majority in the 1986 elections, did not want to lose sight of the foreign policy implications of Reagan's decision to arm an implacable foe like Khomeini. As the committee staffer responsible for the Near East, my job was to organize the hearings. Not surprisingly, our witnesses—including Secretary of State George Shultz—all agreed that arming Iran did not make for sensible national security strategy.

The hearings did not attract much interest from the media, which was falling over itself to dig up new details about the scandal, but not much concerned with the strategic consequences. The Iraqi Embassy, however, followed them closely. Nizar Hamdoon, the Iraqi ambassador, concluded that I must be pro-Iraqi since I had orchestrated hearings with an anti-Iranian cast. He told me that if I visited Iraq he would arrange permission for me to go wherever I wanted.

In early 1987, Iran seemed poised to win the Iran-Iraq War, in part thanks to American help. Iranian Revolutionary Guards occupied the Faw Peninsula, from which Iraq had exported most of its oil before the war. In the north, Iranian-supported Kurdish guerrillas, known as the *peshmerga*,* controlled large swaths of territory, including the heights above Erbil on the Mesopotamian Plain. With assistance from the peshmerga, there was a danger that Iran might move its artillery within range of the Kirkuk oil fields.

As the Reagan Administration scrambled to undo the political and strategic damage of the Iran escapade, it tilted ever more heavily toward Iraq. Cut off from the sea by the Iranian forces in Faw, Iraq relied on Kuwait's ports for supplies. Kuwait also helped finance Iraq's war effort through the sale of its own oil. In its effort to cut Iraq's supply lines, Iran began to target Kuwaiti shipping. The Kuwaitis appealed to the Soviet Union and the United States for help and, in part to preempt Soviet involvement, the Reagan Administration in 1987 allowed

---

* *Peshmerga* translated literally from the Kurdish means "those who face death." After 1991, the peshmerga became the regular army of the Kurdistan Region.

Kuwait to reflag eleven of its oil tankers as American and began providing them with U.S. Navy escorts. Then, on May 17, 1987, an Iraqi warplane fired two French-made Exocet missiles at the USS *Stark* as it patrolled in the Persian Gulf. Thirty-seven American sailors died, but the Reagan Administration quickly accepted Iraq's explanation that it was an accident. The president blamed *Iran,* insisting it was "the villain in the piece." The United States was now engaged in a debasing appeasement of a dictator who quite possibly had intentionally attacked a U.S. warship.

Senator Pell became concerned that Reagan's forceful reaction to his own policy mistakes of the year before would draw the United States into a war with Iran. He introduced legislation to reverse the reflagging of the Kuwaiti ships and decided to send another staff mission to the Persian Gulf. Part of the team went to the Gulf states on the Arabian Peninsula, and I went to Iraq. Of course, I took Nizar Hamdoon up on his offer of unlimited access. I told him I wanted to go to Kurdistan.

In September 1987, Haywood Rankin, the political counselor at the U.S. Embassy in Baghdad, and I became two of the very few Westerners permitted to travel to Suleimania in eastern Iraqi Kurdistan. I suspect that, when he arranged our permissions, Hamdoon himself did not know what we would find.

In a dust storm that turned the capital a sickening yellow, Haywood and I left Baghdad, traveling through Baquba, a mixed Sunni-Shiite city that in 2006 would be on the front line of Iraq's civil war, and then Jalawla, the last Arab town before entering Kurdistan. At a checkpoint outside Jalawla, we waited several hours for a military escort that consisted of two army trucks, the first with six helmeted soldiers and the second with several men manning an anti-aircraft gun.

Less than a mile from the checkpoint, we reached what had been a large Kurdish town. Except for a small section on the west side that had not yet been leveled, it was just piles of rubble. Between Jalawla and Suleimania, we counted twenty-nine destroyed towns and villages, but clearly there were many more in the area. In some cases, bulldozers were still at work, parked near half-demolished buildings. Where the demolition was more advanced, the Iraqi Army had burned orchards and fields, blown up mosques, knocked over grave markers, and stripped wire from the utility poles. Closer to Suleimania, we passed through a landscape dotted with fruit trees but with no sign of human presence, not even a shepherd.

In the relative security of the valleys, we could see the ongoing construction of new towns laid out on a grid with wide streets (to facilitate easy access by tanks). In and near the new settlements, the army and security services were building well-protected garrisons from which the local population could be controlled. Euphemistically called Victory Cities, these new towns were only slightly better than concentration camps since the Kurdish inhabitants could not easily leave. There was virtually no employment in the Victory Cities, making families dependent on state rations for survival. Men had little choice but to join progovernment Kurdish militias, known derisively as *jash* (little donkey, or ass).

Although we didn't know it at the time, Rankin and I had stumbled on the *Anfal*,* the military campaign to destroy rural life in Iraqi Kurdistan. In March 1987, Saddam had made his cousin Ali Hassan al-Majid governor of the north, with the mandate of solving the Kurdish question. Al-Majid declared large areas of Kurdistan free-fire zones, where "the armed forces must kill any human or animal present within these areas." †

By August 2, 1990, the Iraqi government had eradicated more than 4,000 of the approximately 4,500 villages in Kurdistan. In eastern Iraqi Kurdistan, the army destroyed the cities of Qalat Diza, Halabja, and Sayid Sadiq. According to the Iraqi Kurdistan Front, al-Majid's decrees put 45,000 square kilometers of Kurdistan off limits to human life, out

---

* The term *anfal* comes from a Koranic verse that has been interpreted to give believers the right to plunder the property of the infidels.

† This June 1987 decree was part of a cache of fourteen tons of documents captured by the Kurds during the 1991 uprising and deposited in the files of the Senate Foreign Relations Committee in the National Archives.

of a total of 75,000. Kurds living in the prohibited zones were deported to southern Iraq, or executed. After Saddam's fall in 2003, the Kurdistan government minister for human rights, Mohammed Ihssan, led forensic teams that uncovered mass graves containing thousands of Kurdish corpses near Samawa in southern Iraq and west of the ruins of ancient Hatra in Salahaddin Governorate. The Kurdistan Government officially estimates that 182,000 died between 1987 and 1990 in the Anfal.

The Reagan Administration knew about Saddam's efforts to destroy Kurdistan. Rankin wrote a twenty-seven-page report of what we had seen; it circulated within the State Department and was shared with other government agencies. I described the destruction of Kurdish villages in the report that the Foreign Relations Committee published after our trip, *War in the Persian Gulf: The U.S. Takes Sides.* In April 1988, Kurdish rebel leader Jalal Talabani, secretary-general of the Patriotic Union of Kurdistan (PUK), visited Washington, bringing with him a thick white book listing more than three thousand Kurdish villages that had been destroyed as of that date. He gave copies to me, to Richard Schifter, the assistant secretary of state for human rights, and to Larry Pope, the director for Northern Gulf Affairs in the State Department's Near East Bureau. By then attention was focused on an even more dramatic aspect of the Anfal—the use of chemical weapons against the Kurds.

As they rallied support for their respective wars, both President George H. W. Bush and his son President George W. Bush emphasized that Saddam Hussein was a brutal dictator who had "gassed his own people." At the time Saddam was doing the gassing, the Reagan Administration adopted the same indifferent posture toward Iraq's use of these weapons on the Kurdish civilians as it had adopted toward the gassing of Iranian soldiers. Although the poison gas attacks on Kurdish villages began in March 1987—and were presumably known at least to U.S. intelligence agencies—neither U.S. officials nor anyone else in the international community said a word publicly.

On the morning of March 16, 1988, Iraqi warplanes flew over the small city of Halabja, on a plain east of the strategically important Darbandikan Dam in Eastern Kurdistan. The day before, Iranian Pasdaran (Revolutionary Guards) and Kurdish peshmerga had captured the city, but both forces withdrew, possibly suspecting an Iraqi attack. Three years later, I was in Halabja and the survivors told me what happened next. Planes with Iraqi markings dropped bombs that made soft detonations. There followed a smell that resembled burned almonds. Leaves turned brown, and people dropped dead. The corpses turned black. I was shown the basement of a house—still shut up for fear of the lingering effects of the poison—where forty-eight men, women, and children had taken shelter and died. The floor was littered with rotting clothes. At the graveyard, a man stuck his hand in a pile of dirt and pulled out two skulls. They were small, the skulls of children.

More than five thousand people died in the Halabja gassing. The Iranians saw a potential propaganda coup. They brought Iranian and Western journalists into the dead city. On a doorstep, a man wearing baggy Kurdish trousers and turban lay dead with the corpse of a swaddled baby in his arms. The photo of that scene was transmitted around the world.

World opinion reacted to Halabja with horror. In the U.S. Congress, Senator George Mitchell, a Maine Democrat, introduced a nonbinding sense-of-the-Senate resolution denouncing Iraq for the attacks. Reagan's tilt toward Iraq was running into trouble just when it seemed Iran might win the war. Although survivors described planes with Iraqi markings, the Reagan Administration suggested that both Iran and Iraq were responsible. It was an illogical lie—why would Iran attack its own allies—but one that successfully obscured the issue with the American media and foreign policy cognoscenti.

Over the next few months, the fortunes of war shifted sharply in Iraq's favor. Iraq retook the Faw Peninsula on April 17, 1988, in a thirty-five-hour amphibious operation that made extensive use of nerve gas. Video shot afterward showed the corpses of Iranian soldiers surrounded by syringes as they tried to inject themselves with atropine in a fruitless effort to administer an antidote. By the summer of 1988, the Iraqi Army had recaptured almost all the territory that Iran had taken since 1982. For six years, Iran had continued the war because Khomeini wanted Saddam Hussein's head. At last, Khomeini recognized that this was not to be. Iran accepted U.N. Security Council Resolution 598, which called for a cessation of hostilities and a return to the status quo ante. It was, said Khomeini, like drinking poison.

It was an apt metaphor. Poison gas was decisive to Saddam's survival, and the American help with targeting was invaluable. While I have found no evidence that the Reagan Administration provided Iraq with battlefield intelligence related to the Halabja attack, this cannot be ruled out. Even after Halabja, the Reagan Administration continued to provide intelligence that Iraq used to target its chemical weapons more accurately.

Iran's propaganda coup at Halabja backfired. The images shown on Iranian television were terrifying, and recruitment into the armed forces dropped precipitously. With massive international debts, Iraq was in no position to resist international pressure to stop using chemical weapons. By falsely suggesting that Iran was also responsible for the atrocity, the Reagan Administration helped make sure there was no such pressure.

On August 20, 1988, an armistice went into effect between the two countries.

On August 28, 1988, I was home in Vermont for a long Labor Day break. I had just completed my favorite early morning run, a three-mile loop past a series of beaver lakes, when I picked up the *New York Times*. On page A15, Alan Cowell reported that Kurdish refugees crossing into Turkey said their villages in Dahuk Governorate had been attacked with chemical weapons.

There could be no question as to who was responsible. These attacks were taking place after the Iran-Iraq War had ended, and in a part of the country that is close to Syria and Turkey, and far from Iran. I felt instinctively that this was an act of genocide. Flush with victory, Saddam, I concluded, now intended to solve the Kurdish problem by eliminating the Kurds from Arab Iraq altogether. Many factors went into this assessment—the destruction of villages that I had seen the year before; Halabja; Saddam's personal brutality; the mass killings; and the racist nature of his Ba'ath Party, which defined Iraq as an Arab state and thereby relegated the Kurds to an inferior status. But I also believed genocide is a progressive crime. Even in Nazi Germany, Hitler did not start with the death camps but rather built up to genocide by a series of acts against the Jews that went largely unchallenged by the international community. Even if Saddam could not be stopped, I did not want to see his genocide go unchallenged.

In Washington in early September, I laid out my concerns to Senator Pell. He accepted my suggestion that he introduce legislation imposing tough sanctions on Iraq, and urged me to write something immediately as there was almost no time left on the Senate calendar. In little more than an hour, I drafted a four-page bill that imposed on Iraq every sanction that I could think of. The bill prohibited the import of Iraqi petroleum into the United States, ended U.S. credit guarantees for Iraq, prohibited most U.S. exports to Iraq including all sensitive technologies, prohibited loans or financial assistance, and required the United States to oppose international lending to Iraq. The president could waive the sanctions only if he certified to the Congress in writing that "Iraq is not committing genocide against the Kurdish population of Iraq . . . and Iraq is not using chemical weapons banned by the 1925 Geneva Conventions and has provided reliable assurances that it will not use such weapons." I gave the bill the title "The Prevention of Genocide Act of 1988" in part to help win support but also because that was what it was intended to do.

Making use of an arcane parliamentary procedure explained to me by Majority Leader Robert C. Byrd's floor staff, Senator Pell got the bill on the calendar for an immediate vote. Among the bill's co-sponsors were Byrd, archconservative Republican Jesse Helms, and Tennessee Democrat Al Gore. The Prevention of Genocide Act of 1988 unanimously passed the Senate the day after it was written and introduced. I had never seen the Senate act so quickly on such an important issue.

Senator Pell asked me to go to eastern Turkey to collect evidence that might bolster the bill's prospects in the House, and, as importantly, help persuade President Reagan not to veto the bill. I asked Chris Van Hollen, then a junior Foreign Relations Committee staffer working on European issues (and now a Democratic congressman from Maryland), to join me. Robert Finn, a political officer at the American Embassy in Ankara, and Hamza Ulucay, a Turkish Kurd working for the U.S. consulate in Adana, filled out our team.*

We spent the week traveling the length of Iraq's border with Turkey, from the junction with Syria to the junction with Iran. It is a landscape of barren mountains, green patches of trees and agriculture, and stone villages. Into this remote terrain, 65,000 village Kurds had arrived, along with their donkeys and horses and such possessions as they and their animals could carry.

Using topographic maps provided by the Pentagon, we asked survivors to pinpoint the locations of their villages, and to tell us what happened. We identified forty-eight villages in Dahuk Governorate that Iraqi helicopters or fixed-wing aircraft had bombed with poison gas between August 25 and August 27. Because survivors sometimes dispersed in different directions after the attacks, we were able to compare accounts by refugees in different locations in Turkey of an attack on the same village in Iraq. (In this era before cell phones and Internet, there would have been no possibility of refugees coordinating their stories.)

Because the gas attacks did not produce the same symptoms from village to village, we concluded that Iraq had combined chemical agents in "cocktails" that varied, perhaps because the Iraqis wanted to test the lethality of different cocktails. In some villages after the attacks, the refugees reported seeing Iraqi troops wearing protective clothing. In many cases, they shot survivors. At Baze Gorge, the Iraqi Army machine-gunned at least a thousand men, women, and children on August 28 or 29.

---

* I later recruited Robert Finn to be my deputy when I was ambassador to Croatia. He went on to be ambassador to Tajikistan and the first post-Taliban U.S. Ambassador to Afghanistan.

Virtually every refugee was an eyewitness to the poison gas attacks, and many described seeing bodies. We thought the evidence that Iraq had in fact used chemical weapons was overwhelming.

In the village of Bergine, Iskender Ahmed was up at 6:20 A.M. on August 25 when six planes dropped eighteen bombs. He told us: "I saw twenty-four people die in front of my eyes. When I recovered a little, I got a scarf and put it over my nose and face. From my family, eight people died. From the village eighty died, in open spaces. I wish you could provide a plane so I could show you the dead bodies."

Iskender's son explained that "animals and children died. Blood came from their mouths and a yellow liquid from their mouths and noses. The noise did not sound like regular bombs. They would just drop and make a very weak sound and then this cloud. Always expanding, a yellow cloud." Behchet Naif described something similar in nearby Berkule: "At 6 A.M. on August 25, eight planes flew over our village . . . They dropped thirty-two chemical bombs. We counted them later. When they dropped the bombs, a big sound did not come out, just a yellowish color and a kind of garlic smell. Almost fifty women died. Some died who went to help their families. My brother died. My children are OK. I won't go back as long as Saddam Hussein is there."

Our team talked to hundreds of survivors. Chris and I were struck by two things: the passivity with which most described these horrific events and, second, the absence of physical trauma. Except for a few refugees with burn marks, no one seemed physically hurt. We later realized that the absence of other injury was in itself a "negative proof" that chemical weapons had been used. If the Iraqi offensive had been a conventional one, there would have been fighting between the peshmerga and the army. We would have expected to see survivors with gunshot and shrapnel wounds. No one had these injuries. It was, as Chris observed, like Sherlock Holmes's dog that didn't bark.

Chris and I wrote our report on the plane back to Washington, and Senator Pell released it two days later. It concluded: "To dismiss the eyewitness accounts, however, would require one to believe that 65,000 Kurdish refugees confined to five disparate locations were able to organize a conspiracy to defame Iraq and these refugees were able to keep their conspiracy secret."

As it turned out, no one in the Reagan Administration or the House of Representatives disagreed with our findings. But there was enormous opposition to taking any action against Iraq.

On the day the Senate passed the Prevention of Genocide Act, Secretary of State George Shultz met with Iraqi Deputy Prime Minister Saadoun Hammadi and publicly denounced Iraq's use of chemical weapons as "unjustified and abhorrent." Later that day, Charles Redman, the State Department spokesman, publicly confirmed that poison gas had been used but without revealing that the United States had intercepts of Iraqi pilots discussing dropping chemical weapons. Redman said: "As a result of our evaluation of the situation the United States government is convinced that Iraq used chemical weapons in its military campaign against Kurdish guerrillas." *

The following Wednesday, September 14, 1988, Redman called the Prevention of Genocide Act "premature." This raised the question as to when the time for action against Saddam would be appropriate, or "mature." If we waited until he killed all the Kurds, it would be too late.

For all George Shultz's personal outrage, economic interest and *realpolitik* prevailed. When I returned to Washington after the week on the Iraq-Turkey border, I found hundreds of yellow slips on my desk, almost all calls from special interests that would be adversely affected by the sanctions. Iraq was the largest purchaser of U.S. rice (grown in Arkansas and Louisiana) and a significant importer of U.S. grain. American agricultural interests strongly opposed the bill. A staff member working for Louisiana Democratic Senator John Breaux on agriculture issues wept as he told me that I was committing genocide against his state's rice farmers. In the American business community, there was a widespread belief that, with the end of the Iran-Iraq War, Iraq would now be spending billions on reconstruction. The plight of

---

* The Iraqis did not attack peshmerga camps, largely because they did not know where they were. The attacks were all on villages (which had fixed locations) and almost all the victims were noncombatants.

Iraq's Kurds was unfortunate but not a reason why U.S. business should lose out on the bonanza. No one seemed to notice that Iraq had debts totaling more than $100 billion, or that most of the U.S. trade with Iraq was subsidized by government credit guarantees. (When Iraq invaded Kuwait in 1990, the U.S. taxpayer picked up the bill for the billions of dollars in guarantees that the Reagan Administration and later the first Bush Administration had so freely extended to Saddam Hussein.)

Thanks to business lobbying and Reagan Administration opposition, the Democratic leadership of the House of Representatives refused to take up the Senate-passed Prevention of Genocide Act. Instead, the House passed a much watered-down version of an Iraq sanctions bill. Then, on the last day of the congressional session, the chairman of the House Foreign Affairs Committee, Dante Fascell, and the chairman of the House Ways and Means Committee, Dan Rostenkowski, secretly stripped the Iraq sanctions language from a must-pass tax bill in which House and Senate negotiators had previously agreed to include it. Administration opposition, special interests, and the rush to adjournment killed the Prevention of Genocide Act.

The Reagan Administration was willing to overlook Saddam Hussein's gas attacks on the Kurds because it continued to believe that the dictator's behavior might be moderated and that Iraq could yet become a strategic asset. Caught up in their dreams of what Iraq might be, the Administration's strategists never asked whether a regime that gassed its own people was capable of being a reliable partner to the United States, much less a force for regional stability and peace. The evidence of Saddam's character was there for all to see—the ubiquitous portraits, statues, and other symbols of self-love; the palpable fear of all Iraqis when any conversation turned political; the public executions; the destruction of Kurdish villages; the use of poison gas—but the Reagan Administration chose to ignore all of this in pursuit of the mirage of a strategic partnership.

On September 15, 2003, U.S. Secretary of State Colin Powell visited Halabja. He stopped at the museum, looked at the photographs of the victims, and promised the Kurds that "what happened here in 1988 is never going to happen again." When a reporter asked why the response of the Reagan Administration to Halabja was so weak, Powell took exception to that characterization of the policy he had coordinated as national security advisor. "At the time, Halabja was commented on by the Administration. And it was commented on both by the White House at that time, as well as by the State Department. Strongly condemned. And there was no effort on the part of the Reagan Administration at that time to either ignore it or not take note of it."

CHAPTER 4

The Uprising

Congressional efforts to impose U.S. sanctions on Iraq resumed in the spring of 1990, gaining new impetus after Saddam Hussein delivered a speech threatening to use chemical weapons against Israel. Senator Pell, along with New York Senators Daniel Patrick Moynihan and Alfonse D'Amato, introduced new legislation, the Iraq International Law Compliance Act, conditioning further U.S. subsidies on Iraqi compliance with its obligations under the Genocide Convention, the 1925 Geneva Protocols banning use of poison gas, and the Nuclear Non-Proliferation Treaty.

George H. W. Bush strongly opposed the legislation, and taking any action against Iraq. After taking office in 1989, he had doubled agricultural subsidies to Iraq, making it in effect one of the larger recipients of U.S. foreign assistance. On June 15, 1990, Moynihan grilled John Kelly, the assistant secretary of state for the Near East, at a Foreign Relations Committee hearing on Iraq's multiple violations of its treaty obligations. Kelly replied that he was not a lawyer. Far from being an American priority, genocide against the Kurds, Saddam's gassing his own people, and Iraq's efforts to acquire nuclear weapons were reduced to legal technicalities on which the U.S. government's principal regional policy expert was not qualified to speak.

Over the Administration's opposition, the Senate passed the Iraq International Law Compliance Act on July 25, thanks in good measure to the passionate support of Kansas Republican Senator Nancy Landon Kassebaum, who explained that, much as her Kansas farmers wanted to sell their grain, she "did not believe that any [American] farmer would want to send his product . . . to a country that used chemical weapons and tortured its children." Only twelve senators supported the president's position.

Among the many Iraq enthusiasts both in the Bush Administration and outside, there was the expectation that Saddam Hussein, now freed from the crushing burden of the Iran-Iraq War, would devote himself to meeting the long-deferred demands of the Iraqi people for a better life. In pursuit of Iraq's economic development, they hoped Saddam would be buying American. Sanctions, it was argued, would not punish Iraq but only send its business elsewhere. The enthusiasts forgot one not-so-small detail: Iraq was broke.

The Iran-Iraq War left Iraq overwhelmed by debt. It owed $65 billion to Western creditors and the Soviet Union, including billions to the Soviets for military hardware. In addition, Arab states, including Saudi Arabia, United Arab Emirates, and Kuwait, had lent Iraq some $80 billion during the war, and Kuwait was pressing for repayment. Saddam did not acknowledge that the war had resulted from his own folly, and viewed his Arab creditors as ingrates seeking money for a common defense of the Arab world that Iraq had paid for in blood.

Saddam now found himself in an acute financial squeeze. He needed more oil revenues to service Iraq's enormous debt, but as Iraq increased production, others—including the ungrateful Kuwaitis—refused to reduce theirs. Prices fell, defeating the purpose of increased production. In June and July of 1990, Saddam's rhetoric toward Kuwait became more bellicose.

On July 25, 1990, Saddam summoned April Glaspie, the American ambassador to Iraq, to a meeting. Saddam treated Glaspie to a litany of complaints about low oil prices, Iraq's war debt, "aid . . . which some Arab states still record as loans," anti-Saddam hostility among "certain cliques" in the U.S. government, and "the aggression of Kuwait." Glaspie, a highly regarded Arabist from the career foreign service, missed the threat against Kuwait. She stressed President Bush's desire for good relations, and the Administration's opposition to trade sanctions. She repeated an earlier U.S. government apology for a Voice of

America editorial that had compared Saddam's Iraq to the recently toppled communist regimes in Eastern Europe and she called ABC News' use of a Diane Sawyer interview with Saddam "cheap and unjust." (In fact, Sawyer had accurately portrayed the brutality of Saddam Hussein's regime, including the gassing of the Kurds.)

On Kuwait, Glaspie told Saddam, "We have no opinion on inter-Arab disputes, like your border dispute with Kuwait." She did not warn Saddam against attacking Kuwait, nor did she raise American concerns about Iraq's chemical weapons, its program to develop nuclear weapons, the plight of the Kurds, or its abysmal human rights record. The title of her reporting cable back to Washington, "Saddam's Message of Friendship for President Bush," reflected how gravely she had misread Saddam's intentions.

Glaspie was not alone. As the crisis built in the last week of July, the Bush Administration sent three messages to Saddam Hussein. One, delivered by a deputy assistant secretary of state to Iraq's ambassador to the United States, did warn against using force to resolve the border dispute with Kuwait, but a subsequent message from President Bush to Saddam Hussein contained only expressions of friendship. Naturally, Saddam placed greater weight on the communication from Bush, especially since the message was the one he preferred. Not sensing an imminent crisis, Glaspie flew out of Baghdad on August 1 for her summer holiday.

That day was Secretary of Defense Richard Cheney's last in Washington before a planned vacation in his native Wyoming. Secretary of State James A. Baker III was en route to Mongolia, where he planned to combine official meetings with his passion for big game hunting, this time for a rare Mongolian sheep. Then, a little after midnight on August 2, Iraqi troops crossed the border into Kuwait. Within twenty-four hours, they controlled the entire country, encountering minimal resistance from Kuwait's U.S.-equipped military.

After Iraq invaded Kuwait, the Iraqi government published a transcript of Saddam's meeting with Glaspie. Liberal critics of the first Bush Administration seized on the transcript to suggest that U.S. diplomacy bore some responsibility for the invasion, implicitly questioning President Bush's judgment as he decided to pursue military action to oust Saddam from Kuwait. The Arab media went further, suggesting that President Bush had deliberately encouraged Saddam to invade Kuwait to have an excuse to destroy the most powerful Arab state.

Viewed on their own, the Glaspie meeting and the subsequent messages to Saddam convey weakness, but cannot reasonably be seen as a green light to invade Kuwait. But Saddam did not evaluate these messages in isolation. He saw them in the context of American diplomacy toward Iraq since 1980. When he had invaded Iran, the U.N. Security Council, with President Carter's blessing, passed a resolution that did not demand Iraqi withdrawal from occupied Iranian territory. President Reagan authorized intelligence sharing and other concrete assistance to Iraq's war effort. Iraq started using mustard gas on Iranian soldiers in 1983, and shortly thereafter the Reagan Administration began providing Saddam's regime with hundreds of millions of dollars in subsidies. When Iraq attacked the USS *Stark* in 1987, President Reagan blamed Iran. And when Iraq gassed the Kurds in 1988, the Reagan Administration fiercely resisted congressional efforts to impose sanctions. A year later, the Bush Administration increased U.S. subsidies. Even on the eve of the invasion of Kuwait, the Bush Administration was defending Iraq against congressional efforts to impose sanctions.

It is not hard to imagine how all this looked to Saddam Hussein. American policy confirmed his view of his own importance. The United States had acquiesced in his past transgressions, including grave breaches of international law. Saddam probably assumed that the United States would condemn the annexation of Kuwait, but eventually would accommodate to the new reality. After all, the United States would still need Iraq's oil, and Kuwait's oil. Iraq was the leading Arab state (at least in Saddam's mind) and the most important counterweight to revolutionary Iran. Iraq certainly could still be the strategic and business partner Washington seemed to want. There was nothing in American policy—or in the messages from Washington in the final days of July 1990—that made him think differently.

• • •

Three days after Saddam's tanks rolled into Kuwait, Jalal Talabani called me from Damascus. Would it be a good time, he asked, for him to visit the United States? I thought the answer was obvious. Overnight, Iraq had become Washington's top priority. If there was ever interest in the Kurds, it was now. Not only did Talabani have insights into Saddam's regime, the Kurds were potential allies in the event of a war. Of course you should come, I told him.

Talabani flew into Washington on August 10 and we met for lunch at La Brasserie, a small French restaurant two blocks from the Senate. It was a beautiful summer day and we had a table outside not far from a shady mulberry tree. Talabani, a man with an evident appreciation for good food and a comparably large appetite for knowledge, greeted me with a big hug. He was accompanied by Dr. Najmaldin Karim, a Washington-area neurosurgeon who had been the personal physician to Kurdish leader Mullah Mustafa Barzani in the mountains of Kurdistan before redoing his medical training as a refugee in the United States,* and Latif Rashid, Talabani's brother-in-law, who represented the PUK in London.† We discussed whom Talabani should see and what message he should deliver. Karim, who had become a one-man lobby for the Kurds (and a very effective one), offered suggestions. I emphasized that the story of the Kurds was largely unknown and that he should consider his mission an educational one. Karim and I arranged meetings with key members of Congress, including Senator Pell, Senator Edward Kennedy, and Senator John Kerry—who took time out from his Senate reelection campaign to join Pell in Rhode Island, where he was in the midst of his own reelection campaign. Talabani met with the editorial boards of the major American newspapers, and received speaking invitations from Washington think tanks.

No one in the Bush Administration would see Talabani. During his

* As a resident at George Washington University Hospital in March 1981, Karim was on duty when John Hinckley shot President Reagan. Karim visited the president during his recovery, telling him about the Kurds.

† Rashid became Iraq's minister for water resources in 2003.

first visit to the United States in April 1988, I had asked friends at the State Department to see him. Larry Pope, then the director of the State Department's office that handled Iran and Iraq, had agreed to do so. Unfortunately, Pope's meeting with Talabani took place only a few days before Turkey's President Kenan Evren made an official visit to Washington. Evren, a general who had overthrown Turkey's democratic government in a 1980 coup, was a hard-liner on the Kurdish question, and his regime's brutal tactics in Turkey's Kurdish southeast had, in 1984, helped trigger a Kurdish separatist war that would last until 1999.

Although Talabani had no connection with the Kurdish rebels in Turkey (the PKK, or Kurdistan Workers' Party), and disapproved of their terrorist tactics, Evren had focused only on his ethnicity. When Evren met with Secretary of State Shultz, he asked pointedly why the State Department was meeting with Kurdish terrorists. Shultz, who knew nothing of the Talabani meeting (the secretary would not normally be informed of a meeting held by an office director), was embarrassed. He could have told Turkey's dictator that the U.S. government will decide who it meets, and that Turkey could not choose which Iraqis the U.S. heard from. Instead, Larry Pope ended up on the receiving end of one of Shultz's temper tantrums. When the Iraqis also complained, the State Department instituted a ban on all meetings with the Iraqi opposition, including the Kurds.

By this time, August 1990, Evren had been replaced by an elected president, Turgut Özal, who boasted of having a Kurdish grandmother. After the invasion of Kuwait, U.S. officials were presumably no longer concerned about offending Saddam Hussein. Nonetheless, the no-contacts policy with regard to the Iraqi opposition remained unchanged. The United States had lost an important source of intelligence. The policy would have catastrophic consequences for Iraq's Kurds and Shiites.

Saddam's invasion of Kuwait at last galvanized the Bush foreign policy team into action on Iraq. Defense Secretary Cheney persuaded Saudi

Arabia's rulers to agree to the deployment of U.S. troops on their soil. United Nations Ambassador Thomas Pickering secured passage of five critical Security Council resolutions ratcheting up pressure on Iraq. On November 29, 1990, the Security Council approved Resolution 678 authorizing the use of force if Iraq did not pull out of Kuwait by January 15, 1991. Secretary of State Baker, Bush's campaign manager and close friend, demonstrated his continued prowess at fundraising. Baker raised so much money from other countries through his "tin cup" diplomacy in the fall of 1990 that the United States actually made a profit from the Gulf War. Building on his personal ties with world leaders, President Bush directed the effort to assemble a military coalition of some thirty-five nations.

Wisely, Bush decided he needed congressional authorization for the war. Resisting the temptation to turn Iraq into a partisan issue, he waited until after the 1990 congressional elections before going to Congress. The relevant House and Senate committees held extensive hearings on the Persian Gulf crisis in November and December 1990. After the new Congress took office on January 3, 1991, there was a full debate on the floor of each house. In the Senate, the law authorizing the president to wage war passed by just five votes* while the margin in the House was a wider 250 to 183. Although a substantial minority disagreed with the outcome, no member of Congress complained of being misled. In spite of the close vote, the process made for national unity as U.S. armed forces embarked on the country's biggest military campaign since Vietnam.

When President Bush ordered allied bombers to begin military operations against Iraq on January 17, 1991, he was acting in accordance with international law and with the full backing of the United Nations. While the United States supplied most of the military forces, thirty-five countries participated in the coalition, and not just nominally. Those contributing significant numbers of troops included France, Britain,

---

* Senator Alan Cranston, Democrat of California, was recovering from surgery and did not vote. He would have voted against the authorization of force, making the margin just four.

Canada, Egypt, Kuwait, Saudi Arabia, United Arab Emirates, Oman, Bangladesh, and Syria. The French, British, Saudi, and Spanish air forces flew sorties against Iraqi targets. As a result of having built a real coalition, this President Bush emerged from his Iraq war with a much-enhanced global reputation that allowed him to broker an important breakthrough in the Arab-Israeli peace process and to manage the peaceful dissolution of the Soviet Union later in 1991. And, as noted, the entire war was at no financial cost to the United States. While many of the names in their two administrations are the same, the way in which President George H. W. Bush went to war against Iraq in 1991 was in every other way different from how President George W. Bush would go to war in 2003.

The first Gulf War lasted six weeks. Allied air forces demolished Iraqi air defenses in the war's first few days. Bombers and cruise missiles leveled Iraq's known WMD facilities within a couple of days (but missed a covert nuclear program based on chemical separation of uranium), shut down the electric grid, and disrupted communications. Tactical bombing destroyed Iraqi tanks and hit troops—mostly Shiite and Kurdish conscripts—in trenches in Kuwait. In response, Iraq made a brief incursion into Saudi Arabia and launched Scud missiles at allied forces in Saudi Arabia and at Israeli cities.

American technology overwhelmed the Iraqis and wowed viewers around the world. Around the clock, CNN broadcast videos of laser-guided munitions blowing up Iraqi targets and of the nightly explosions shaking Baghdad. The Patriot anti-missile missile emerged as the hero of the conflict. As air raid sirens announced incoming Scuds, television networks broadcast live shots from Israel and Saudi Arabia of the Patriots arcing into the sky and then of the flashes of light as they intercepted the Iraqi missile. (Or, so it seemed. After the war, it was revealed that the Patriots had not stopped a single Iraqi warhead.)

On February 15, President Bush paid tribute to Patriot, traveling to the Raytheon plant in Andover, Massachusetts, where it was manufactured. At the factory, Bush thanked the workers, stressed allied resolve, and then added:

And there's another way for the bloodshed to stop, and that is for the Iraqi military and the Iraqi people to take matters into their own hands and force Saddam Hussein, the dictator, to step aside, and then comply with the United Nations resolutions and rejoin the family of peace-loving nations.

In Washington, the White House reissued the president's statement, ensuring the widest possible audience. It was carried on the major television networks, around the world by CNN and the BBC, and in the Arab media.

In the memoir he wrote jointly with his National Security Advisor Brent Scowcroft, George H. W. Bush explains that he had "impulsively added" the call for the Iraqi people to overthrow Saddam Hussein. Scowcroft writes* in the next paragraph:

This impulsive ad lib led, unfairly in my judgment, to charges that President Bush encouraged the Iraqi people to rise against Saddam and then failed to come to their aid when they did. It is true that we hoped Saddam would be toppled. But we never thought it could be done by anyone outside the military and never tried to incite the general population. It is stretching the point to imagine that a routine speech given in Washington [sic] would have gotten to the Iraqi malcontents and have been the motivation for the subsequent actions of the Shiites and Kurds.

While the Raytheon speech may have been routine, George Bush was not a routine Washington politician. He was the president of the United States, a country leading an international coalition then at war with Iraq. The U.S. government broadcast his call for Saddam's ouster on the government-run Voice of America and on a CIA-run clandestine radio station broadcasting into Iraq. Iraq's Kurds and Shiites

* Although it is a joint memoir, each man wrote his own sections, and they are labeled as such.

thought the president meant what he said. Given what happened sub-sequently, it is understandable that Bush and Scowcroft would want to minimize their responsibility.

On February 24, the Coalition's ground assault began. The Iraqis had expected an amphibious assault on Kuwait City. Instead, U.S. forces crossed from Saudi Arabia into southern Iraq and western Kuwait in a vast encircling arc. Iraqi forces pulled out of Kuwait heading north on the highway to Basra. Just short of the top of a long incline, U.S. helicopters and tanks intercepted a convoy of Iraqi troops fleeing for home with their loot, and shot it up. Journalists arriving on the scene described a massacre, and the road quickly became known as "the highway of death."

Faced with press furor over what one American pilot inopportunely called a "turkey shoot," President Bush decided to halt the ground war after one hundred hours. It seemed a time chosen principally for its public relations value. As a result, some of Saddam's most formidable Republican Guard units emerged from the war largely intact. Three weeks later, I visited that stretch of highway. The first vehicles had been shot up, but many of the ones that followed were untouched. A lot of the cars were civilian, presumably looted from Kuwait. I did not have the impression of a massacre and it seemed that most in the convoy had escaped to the desert.

On February 27, Senator Pell and I chaired an Inter-Parliamentary Consultation on the Kurds in the Senate Foreign Relations Committee hearing room. The speakers included Talabani; Hoshyar Zebari, the foreign affairs spokesman for the KDP; Sami Abdul Rahman, a soft-spoken man of aristocratic bearing who headed the Kurdistan Popular Democratic Party; Kendal Nezan, the chairman of the Kurdish Institute in Paris; members of several European parliaments; and Danielle Mitterrand, the wife of the French president and the most prominent international champion of the Kurdish cause. At a private lunch with the Foreign Relations Committee senators, the Kurdish leaders emphasized the pro-American sentiment in Kurdistan and the likelihood of an uprising. That evening, at a dinner for the participants at the Washington Court Hotel, we put a television near the podium to watch President Bush announce an end to the war. Jalal Talabani told me that an uprising would take place and that he intended to go back to Kurdistan.

This was big news and I thought the Administration should hear it. I placed a call to Richard Haass, the National Security Council director for the Middle East and a classmate from Oxford. I did not reach Haass, but I spoke on March 1 to Sandy Charles, his deputy. She angrily accused me of meddling at a sensitive time. Taken aback, I asked, "But don't we want to get rid of this regime?" Sandy replied tartly, "Our policy is to get rid of Saddam Hussein, not his regime."

Nor was I successful in getting Talabani in to see the State Department's Near East Bureau. Richard Schifter, the assistant secretary for Human Rights, had worked behind the scenes with me to try to get sanctions imposed on Iraq in 1988. (Schifter had urged me to get Senator Pell to invoke an existing provision of U.S. human rights law that prohibited assistance to countries engaged in a systematic pattern of gross violations of human rights.) Figuring that his portfolio gave him more latitude to see human rights victims than the regional bureau enjoyed, Schifter agreed to see Talabani. However, when the Kurds arrived at the State Department, they were ushered out of the building to a coffee shop across the street. Instead of a meeting with Schifter, they were treated to coffee with two junior staff aides. A few months later, Schifter resigned from the Bush Administration. He campaigned for Bill Clinton in the 1992 elections.

The evening of March 1, Talabani asked whether I thought it would be useful for him to stay in Washington; Turkey's President Özal had invited him to Ankara. Turkish sensibilities being a main reason for the cold shoulder in official Washington, I said that of course he should go. Before leaving, he invited me to join him in Kurdistan.

On March 2, in Basra's Sa'ad Square, an Iraqi tank driver turned his turret toward a two-story portrait of Saddam Hussein and fired. The shell ignited a rebellion that spread from Basra up the Euphrates and Tigris river valleys, reaching the southern outskirts of Baghdad.

In Nasiriyah, crowds literally tore Ba'ath Party officials apart. Government offices, Ba'ath Party headquarters, and military installations were looted and burned. The intensity of Shiite feelings was encapsulated for me in an incident that I witnessed a few weeks later.

I was in a refugee camp on the Iraq-Kuwait border when a U.S. Army medic in a Humvee drove into the camp. Four children, he said, had been collecting tomatoes on the Iraqi side of the border when they stepped on unexploded American ordnance. It had detonated. Was there a doctor, he asked. I rounded up the only available medical person, a Kuwaiti medical student, and drove him into Iraq. Three of the children had been moved to an American field hospital. The medic pointed a pin light in a twelve-year-old boy's eyes. There was no response.

As I watched, the boy's mother came up the road, unaware that anything had happened. Then she saw her dead son, his knees torn open. As she ripped at her hair and clothes, the first words from her lips were "Saddam did this."

About ten days after the uprising began, Saddam consolidated his position sufficiently to move some Republican Guards south. Unlike the conscript army, the Republican Guards were mostly Sunni Arabs and their officers included many from Saddam's own Tikriti clan. The Republican Guards were the regime's last line of defense and Saddam had deliberately kept them out of battle in Kuwait. They were intact and not demoralized by military defeat.

In mid-March, American troops still occupied southern Iraq, holding positions not far from the cities and towns along the Euphrates Valley. The Iraqi advance on the rebellious Shiites arguably violated the cease-fire terms ending the Gulf War dictated by the U.S. theater commander General Norman Schwarzkopf, which Iraq had accepted on March 3. American troops in Iraq could have stopped the Republican Guards and saved tens of thousands of lives. But they had strict orders not to intervene.

Saddam's retribution was swift and terrible. Republican Guard tanks blasted apart ancient city centers. Shiite shrines became battlegrounds and then slaughterhouses as rebels, clerics, and unlucky civilians were massacred. The Republican Guard attached nooses to the gun barrels of their tanks, hanging Shiite men—several at a time—by elevating the gun. As all this took place, American soldiers looked on, many seething with anger because they were not allowed to stop the killings. Patrick Lowe was one of the soldiers who witnessed the atrocities. Years later, he heard me on the radio and sent me an e-mail describing what he had seen:

> I was a recon scout with the 1st Armored Division. I was responsible for graves registration and EPW's [enemy prisoners of war] for the Squadron. After the ground war I was assigned to an area on the Baghdad to Basrah Highway, about 3 miles outside of Basrah. I watched as Iraq helicopter gun ships flew into the city and gunned down everything in their way. I watched as troops were sent in and I can tell you, first hand, what was going on in Basrah.
>
> I was the one that had to process the civilian refugees that fled the town. They pleaded with me to do something, anything to stop this wholesale mass murder. I heard stories of women and children being burned alive, in their homes. Women being raped to death, men being chopped up alive. Civilians being used for target practice, mass hangings. I can hear their screams and wailing to this day on bad nights. I remember one day in particular. I had been pleading for almost 3 days with my chain of command to let me do something about what was going on. The Squadron Commander flew up to my position, and we had a face to face. He ordered me to do nothing without express orders. In 12 years of service that is the closest that I ever came to disobeying a serious direct order. I even went to the point of sending a patrol out to get closer to the killing fields to see if the Iraq soldiers would shoot at them so that I had a reason to engage and protect those innocent civilians. They did not engage and so we continued to sit and watch. I have never been more ashamed of our country's actions as I was at that point.
>
> To this day, the time I spent on the Baghdad to Basrah highways haunts me. I should have not just sat there and watched. I

should have fought for them. I should have done something, anything to stop the blood bath. We are sworn to protect and yet we sat, I sat and watched hundreds of thousands die in the most horrible ways possible.

Between March and September 1991, the Iraqi Army and security services killed as many as 300,000 Shiites. One mass grave near the city of Hillah is said to hold 30,000 bodies alone.

While George H. W. Bush's call for the uprising may well have been a careless ad lib, this is not how Iraq's Shiites saw it. They believe Bush encouraged the uprising and intentionally allowed Saddam to crush it because Bush wanted Shiites to be killed.

The Kurdish uprising began in a similar manner to the Shiite uprising, but ended very differently. On March 6, 1991, a mob attacked the Ba'ath Party headquarters in Rania, a town at the edge of the mountains in Eastern Kurdistan. By March 14, rebels controlled most of Kurdistan, and on March 21 the Kurds took over Kirkuk, the place some call Kurdistan's Jerusalem.

Like the Shiites in the south, the Kurds vented their fury against the regime. When the rebels took over the General Security Directorate headquarters in Suleimania, they caught the security agents about to execute the remaining prisoners. Instead, the security men were shot. An elderly woman threw herself on one of the corpses, biting and kicking it. As the crowd tried to pull her off, she explained, "He killed three of my sons. Don't I have the right to do this to him?"

On March 30, I was finally able to accept Talabani's invitation from the month before. A Kurdish medical student accompanied me from Damascus to Qameshli, a dusty town in Syria near the junction with Iraq, and Turkey. There, Kemal Kirkuki, a peshmerga commander, arranged with the Syrian authorities for me to cross into Kurdish-held Iraq. He assigned Abdul Karim, an engineer, to be my escort and driver. Karim proved unflappable, which was the only realistic option considering what happened.

From the Syrian bank of the Tigris, I could see, and film, Iraqi Army mortars exploding near the Kurdish peshmerga positions on the Iraqi side of the river. For reasons I cannot quite fathom now, I did not worry about the danger of being killed. I was, however, worried that the shelling could make it impossible for me to return to Syria in time for meetings scheduled in a few days. My absence might call career-ending attention to my presence in Iraq. I had been deliberately vague both with the U.S. Embassy in Damascus and with my bosses at the Foreign Relations Committee about northern Iraq being on my itinerary, although the U.S. ambassador to Syria, Edward Djerejian, understood that my interest in spending Easter in Qameshli had nothing to do with the place's intrinsic charms. Karim assured me I had nothing to worry about because the peshmerga were planning an operation that night to take out the Iraqi firing positions.

We crossed the Tigris in a small boat with an outboard motor and jumped into a captured Iraqi Army Toyota Land Cruiser waiting on the Iraqi side. There were two bullet holes on the driver's side of the windshield but I decided not to ask about them. At one point the asphalt stopped and there was an area where the road had been dug up. Karim and another peshmerga had an animated discussion as to which way to go and then carefully followed the ruts made by an earlier vehicle a few hundred yards to where the asphalt resumed. Only when we were back on the road did I realize we had just threaded our way through an Iraqi minefield. Our first stop was Zakho, a town of 100,000 on the Khabur River. In the town center, politicians gave speeches to enthusiastic crowds, and political banners were displayed everyplace. I had my picture taken under a banner written in English—"We librated [sic] Kurdistan from the aggressors"—and then we continued to Dahuk, a city of 300,000 fifty miles farther south.

Our vehicles were the only ones heading south. All the other traffic was coming north. Not only were cars and trucks full of people, but most also had suitcases and furniture stacked on the roofs. This was not a good sign.

By the time we approached Dahuk, night had fallen. I listened to the boom of Iraqi artillery as flashes of light from the tracer rounds crossed the sky. Just outside the city we passed a rocky escarpment, and, all of a sudden, the night air was white and smoky. A phosphorous shell had exploded on the road a few seconds before. Karim veered sharply to avoid the fire and smoke.

Inside the city's administration building, I found Jalal Talabani discussing rule of law and minority rights with about seventy city leaders. A teacher asked what would happen to the collaborators with Saddam's regime, making clear his preference for a peremptory approach to justice. Talabani insisted that there had to be a fair trial. An Assyrian asked about religious rights. Talabani replied that the protection of minority religions was an essential part of the program of the Iraqi Kurdistan Front. The back and forth reminded me more of a Vermont town meeting than anything in the Iraq I knew, and as the audience became more engaged—it was surely the first time they had ever been able to question a leader—I wondered if I was the only one also hearing the rumble of Iraqi artillery.

Talabani invited me to speak. Perhaps a bit grandiosely, I recalled Woodrow Wilson's promise to the Kurds of their own state, and how pleased I was to be the first American official present on soil governed by the Kurds themselves. As I spoke I was aware that I had nothing concrete to offer these people who clearly were in a dire situation, but they seemed to appreciate my remarks just the same.

After the meeting, we went for dinner to the home of Lizginn Hamzani, a *jash** commander who had switched sides to support the uprising. We were joined by Sami Abdul Rahman, back in Dahuk for the first time in years; Yacoub Yousif, an Assyrian leader; and Ahmed Barmani, a Kurdish political leader originally from the nearby town of Barmani. Hero Talabani, Jalal's wife, was the only woman present. She had left her young sons with family in London to spend years in remote Kurdistan valleys where she endured the hardships of the peshmerga while assembling—in her head, on paper, and in photographs—a

---

* The *jash*, as mentioned earlier, were the Kurdish territorial forces on the payroll of the regime. Many Kurds joined these forces because they provided the only available employment, especially in the so-called Victory Cities.

record of Iraq's crimes against the Kurds. I was fascinated and horrified by her detailed accounts of Iraqi atrocities. The proximity of the Iraqi Army gave these reports, which included much new information she had gathered since the uprising, an immediacy.

As we dined on a whole lamb, chicken, and an enormous fish, the shelling intensified. In an effort to be reassuring, Ahmed Barmani would tell me that a particular round was Kurdish counterfire, although, in fact, the Kurds had no artillery. At one stage, Hero and I had a discussion of the difficulty of photographing artillery attacks. Yacoub Yousif wanted to take me to Easter Mass in an ancient Assyrian church that had been closed by the regime and reopened after the uprising. As the shelling increased, the Mass kept being postponed, and it was never held.

Jalal Talabani took me upstairs to a child's room to discuss how to respond to an invitation from Saddam to negotiate. "If we have hope for outside help, we will never negotiate. If there is no hope, we cannot refuse to negotiate." I knew that for the Kurds to open a dialogue with Saddam would damage their reputation in the United States, but I could hardly disagree with his assessment. I could see no help on its way.

Well after midnight we left Hamzani's house for another part of Dahuk to spend the night. At 6:15, Ahmed Barmani woke me, softly asking if I was ready to go. A minute later, I was outside in the early morning drizzle. The uprising had collapsed and Iraqi troops were moving into the city. We sped north in our Land Cruisers, passing shuttered shops and empty streets. Once we got on the road to the mountains, the outlines of the catastrophe overtaking the Kurds emerged.

Along the side of the roads, refugees walked alone—or in small family groups. The walkers could carry only enough food for a day or two. Those lucky enough to have a car and gasoline stuffed as many family members as possible inside. Some even rode in the open trunk. Higher in the mountains, the trek was still an adventure for children who I saw playing among the wildflowers of an early Kurdish spring. A week later, some of these same children would die from diarrhea and exposure on the stony mountainsides of the border with Turkey.

I felt for Talabani and his colleagues. While the uprising had begun spontaneously, the Kurdistan political parties had moved quickly to take control. While the Bush Administration's repeated snubs ought to have alerted the Kurdish leaders as to how they were seen in Washington, they had continued to have a blind faith in the goodness of the United States and its leaders. They had thought President Bush meant it when he called on the Iraqi people to overthrow Saddam Hussein. Now the illusions were stripped away. The Kurdish leaders faced the final destruction of the Kurdistan revolution, and the possible obliteration of the Kurdish people in Iraq. On that Easter Sunday, no one imagined that the refugees fleeing to the mountains would return.

At Amadiya, a Christian town spectacularly situated on a tabletop mountain, Talabani and I said goodbye. He headed toward the Iranian border, while I had no choice but to try to return to Syria. Mohid, a young peshmerga who spoke reasonable English, was assigned to take me to Qameshli. East of Zakho, we passed one of Saddam's "Victory Cities," the quasi–concentration camps where Kurdish villagers had been forcibly relocated. I asked to stop. It was as grim as the places Haywood Rankin and I had seen being constructed in Eastern Kurdistan four years before. The inhabitants were now free, but they had nothing. As I walked around on the rutted and muddy streets, I came across a group of men carrying a fifty-kilo grain bag. It was grain that had been treated to be rat poison. The men planned to wash it in the hopes of making it edible.

Our original plan was to stay in Zakho until night, and then cross the Tigris under the cover of darkness. But with the Iraqis having taken Dahuk, further south, early that morning, panic was spreading in Zakho. Not knowing exactly how soon the Iraqi Army would arrive, Mohid decided we could not wait. But even in these circumstances, Kurdish hospitality trumped other considerations. Before we headed to the river, Mohid arranged a multidish lunch which we ate sitting cross-legged on a plastic tablecloth in the home of a local resident. (Our host acted as if he had all the time in the world, but he probably headed for the mountains shortly after we left. Feeding both peshmerga and an American would have marked him especially for retribution.)

Back at the Tigris, the shelling was much worse than the day before.

We sprinted through reeds to a sandbagged position on the river's grav-
elly edge. My peshmerga companions stood guard while I lay on the
ground. When they heard the mortar blast, they ducked down on top of
me. Afterward, we all stood up, and I filmed the plume with my Sony
video camera. The peshmerga shouted repeatedly for the boatman to
come from the Syrian side to pick me up, but he was obviously reluctant,
and for good reason. Iraqi artillery had found the range, and several
mortars landed in the river not far from the boat. Mine was the last
crossing. A sniper shot the boatman in the head on his next attempt.

In Damascus on April 1, I stopped in to see Tony Touma, a Syrian
Christian working for ABC's Damascus bureau whose expertise and
contacts were legendary. When I mentioned that I had home video of
the uprising's collapse, an ABC engineer asked to see it. I overheard the
engineers critique my camera work as they ran it through their dub-
bing machine (it was only the second time I had used a video camera)
but then they asked if they could send it to New York. That evening my
footage from Iraq led the *ABC Evening News.* Peter Jennings did an
on-camera interview from New York in which I described the humanitarian catastrophe overtaking the Kurds. At 4 A.M. Damascus time,
ABC in New York woke me at the Damascus Sheraton to ask if I would
narrate my film for *Nightline.* That evening Ted Koppel concluded his
broadcast with a five-minute segment from my film.

I had violated a cardinal rule of the Senate Foreign Relations Committee: staff should never be quoted in the press. But I was the only
Westerner who had actually gotten out of Kurdistan by April 1. Hundreds of thousands of lives were at risk. I also felt an obligation to those
who had gotten me out of Iraq alive, at considerable risk to their lives.
Also, as it happened, the committee chairman, Claiborne Pell, was in
Albania, a country possibly more cut off from the world than rebel-
held Kurdistan. I knew it would be a while before I faced the music.*

---

* In fact, Pell and the other senators were fully supportive of what I did. Senator
Moynihan made a generous—perhaps overly generous—speech in praise of my
trip to the Senate, inserting into the record a cover article I wrote about it for the
New Republic (the article being another violation of the rules).

I responded to every media request. From Jerusalem a few days later, I was a guest on another *Nightline*, this time with conservative commentator George Will and Republican Senator Alfonse D'Amato. I could no longer contain my outrage. I asked, rhetorically, how George Bush, who had compared Saddam Hussein to Adolf Hitler, could now allow a new holocaust while American troops were on Iraqi soil. George Will, in the uncomfortable position of defending the Administration, expressed amazement at my language but D'Amato cheered me on. Afterward, a producer asked incredulously if I still worked for the U.S. government. I later received letters from viewers all over the United States who had watched the broadcast and shared my anger.*

Over the next week, 500,000 Kurds walked across the mountain range that divides Turkey from Iraq, setting up camp on the steep mountains on the Turkish side. Without shelter or food in chilling rain, they began to die by the hundreds. President Özal refused to let them further into Turkey, but he did make a decision that would reshape the Middle East. He allowed television cameras to film the suffering. The CNN effect was born.

Televised images of Kurdish men burying the small wrapped corpses of their children were contrasted with the president on vacation fishing in Florida. It became too much—first for Özal, then for British Prime Minister John Major (America's most important coalition partner), and lastly for President Bush. After flailing for a solution, Bush ordered U.S. troops into northern Iraq to secure a safe area for the Kurds. The cowed Iraqi Army complied with a U.S. order to withdraw from a triangle formed by Zakho, Dahuk, and Amadiya. Not long after, the United States declared a "no-fly" zone at the 36th parallel and northward from which all Iraqi aircraft were prohibited.† American

---

* Over the years, I have done several thousand television interviews, including many other *Nightline* appearances. Very occasionally, I might get a single letter. Clearly, the Kurdish disaster, and America's role in it, struck a chord with many people.

† The no-fly zone did not cover all of Kurdistan. It protected Dahuk and Erbil, but not Suleimania. Mosul, being north of the 36th parallel, was included in the no-fly zone but was controlled by Saddam's regime.

and British aircraft patrolled the zone for twelve years, up until the invasion of Iraq in 2003.

Refugees streamed home in a matter of days, most of them bypassing a reception and feeding center set by the U.S. Army in a grassy field east of Zakho. The United States and its allies now protected the same area in Dahuk Governorate that Saddam had gassed in his final offensive in August 1988.

In Kurdistan's east, Iraqi forces took Kirkuk on March 28, Erbil on March 30, and Suleimania on April 3. But as an Iraqi tank column headed north from Erbil, a peshmerga force attacked it in a narrow pass near the village of Kore. The Kurds destroyed the three lead tanks and the column retreated. Just east of Suleimania, the peshmerga stopped the Iraqi Army on Aznar Mountain, which overlooks the city. This left a vast territory in the east in Kurdish hands. Connected to the American-protected safe area by treacherous mountain roads, the eastern valleys and the Dahuk Governorate became the nucleus of a self-governing Kurdistan. In September 1991, Saddam Hussein abruptly withdrew the Iraqi Army and civil administration from the main Kurdistan cities of Erbil and Suleimania, and imposed an internal blockade. Without funding from Baghdad, Saddam expected the Kurdistan administration would collapse, paving the way for the restoration of central government authority. But for the Kurds, there was no privation that was not preferable to resumed control from Baghdad.

When the March uprising began, American power and prestige within Iraq could not have been greater. In a matter of weeks, an amazing array of high-tech U.S. weapons—never before seen in combat—had smashed the largest army in the Middle East. Many Iraqis wanted to do whatever the United States wanted them to do. The American president said he wanted them to overthrow Saddam Hussein, and most Iraqis thought he meant it. When the uprising began, they waited for a sign of U.S. support.

There was no support. On the contrary, Washington seemed to indicate that it wanted the uprising to fail. Iraqi Republican Guards mowed down Shiite insurgents as American troops in the Euphrates Valley passively looked on. American commanders in southern Iraq rebuffed the desperate pleas of Shiite rebels and ordinary civilians for help. In Washington, Europe, and Damascus, U.S. officials refused to meet with Iraqi opposition leaders. Mowaffak al-Rubaie and Ali Allawi flew from London to Frankfurt to meet with me at the airport as I changed flights on my way to the Middle East. As Shiite leaders, they could not get visas to the United States.*

Helicopter flights were the clearest signal to wavering Iraqis that they should not join the uprisings. As a condition of ending hostilities on February 27, the United States prohibited Iraq from using its fixed-wing aircraft or helicopters. With the victor's swagger, General Schwarzkopf told the Iraqis on CNN, "You fly, you die." But then Schwarzkopf took no action when Iraq used helicopters against Kurdish and Shiite rebels to deadly effect.

Schwarzkopf later explained that the Iraqis had snookered him into allowing these flights. In the formal cease-fire talks held March 3 in Safwan in U.S.-occupied southern Iraq, Iraqi General Sultan Hashim Ahmad requested an exception to the no-fly rule for helicopters. According to Schwarzkopf's account, Ahmad asked "to fly helicopters to carry officials of our government in areas where roads and bridges are out." Schwarzkopf agreed, feeling, as he says in his memoirs, that he owed the Iraqis this one request since they had agreed to all of his. (He seems not to have realized that the defeated enemy did not have a lot of negotiating power.) Schwarzkopf not only granted Ahmad's request, but agreed that the helicopters could be armed.

When the Iraqis started using the helicopters for an entirely different purpose than transporting officials, the United States could have reimposed the no-fly order, but chose not to do so. Schwarzkopf says it

---

* In the government elected in January 2005, al-Rubaie became the national security advisor and Ali Allawi the finance minister. In a religious government both are moderates and al-Rubaie is an American favorite who has met President George W. Bush.

was a White House decision. Senior officials in Washington insist that they had not wanted to undermine the field commander. But in truth, the Administration did not welcome the uprising the president had called for. In their joint memoir, Scowcroft provides an insight into President Bush's thinking:

> Occasionally, he [Bush] indicated the removal of Saddam would be welcome, but for very practical reasons there was never a promise to aid an uprising. While we hoped that a popular revolt or coup would topple Saddam, neither the United States nor the countries of the region wished to see the breakup of the Iraqi state. We were concerned about the long term balance of power at the head of the Gulf. Breaking up Iraq would pose its own destabilizing problems. While Özal put the priority on Saddam and had a more tolerant view of the Kurds than other Turkish leaders before or since, Turkey—and Iran—objected to the suggestion of an independent Kurdish state. However admirable self-determination for the Kurds or Shiites might have been in principle, the practical aspects of this particular situation dictated the policy. For these reasons alone, the uprising distressed us . . .

In short, geopolitics was more important than the human consequences of a failed uprising. A successful uprising by Iraq's Kurds and Shiites—80 percent of Iraq's people—would upset "the long term balance of power at the head of the Gulf." Given the alternative, Bush chose to keep Saddam Hussein in power.

After the uprising collapsed the Bush team came under fierce criticism for having lost an opportunity to get rid of Saddam and for having recklessly encouraged a rebellion that cost hundreds of thousands of lives. In their memoirs and other accounts, the principals explain why their actions didn't matter. Bush, Scowcroft, Powell, and Cheney all insisted that the uprising could never have succeeded. However, the uprisings nearly toppled Saddam, and would almost certainly have done so if a part of the military had joined, or the Shiites of Baghdad rebelled.

There were elements of the Iraqi military who contemplated going over to the rebel side. Some were in direct contact with Kurdish and other resistance forces. But for any Iraqi military officer, the decision to participate in a rebellion against Saddam Hussein was a matter of life and death, not just for the officer but for his family. Before taking any overt action, he would want to know that there was a good chance for success. The attitude of the United States was decisive. Would it help? By mid-March all the signals were no. If there had appeared a greater chance of success, it is likely the Shiites of Saddam City (the large Shiite slum now renamed Sadr City) would have rebelled.

Schwarzkopf, naturally, wanted to play down the consequences of his decision on the helicopters. After blaming the White House for the decision, he argues in his memoirs that the helicopters made little difference to the outcome of the uprising. In fact the helicopters made all the difference, especially in Kurdistan. The helicopters enabled the Iraqi Army to target peshmerga units both from the air and by ground forces. But their major impact was psychological. During the Anfal campaign (1987–88), the Iraqis dropped chemical weapons from helicopters. In March 1991, Kurds panicked when they saw—or heard about—the helicopters. The peshmerga could make a stand in the mountains (as in fact they successfully did east of Erbil and Suleimania) but they had no ability to manage the panicked flight of hundreds of thousands of city dwellers. Panic precipitated the sudden collapse of the Kurdish uprising, and it was the helicopters that triggered the panic.

In the last analysis, the Bush Administration principals have tried to change the subject from their failure to support the uprisings to the separate issue of whether the United States should have carried the war to Baghdad. They have argued that going to Baghdad would have exceeded the mandate of the United Nations Security Council to liberate Kuwait, and that it would have been unwise. As Cheney put it in an interview he gave after leaving office in 1993, "Now you can say, well, you should have gone to Baghdad and gotten Saddam, I don't think so. I think if we had done that we would have been bogged down there for a very long period of time with the real possibility we might not have succeeded."

The Persian Gulf War ended on February 27, 1991, settling the issue of whether U.S. troops should have continued to Baghdad. The uprisings only began on March 2, and it was not until mid-March that rebels controlled both the north and the south. The United States did not need to send in troops to help the rebels. It merely needed to enforce the flight ban and to order Iraqi armored units to stay in place. At most, this would have entailed the reengagement of the U.S. Air Force, although it is quite likely an ultimatum alone would have done the job. Unable to suppress the uprising, Saddam almost certainly would have toppled, and with him the rationale for a second Iraq war.

Ironically, it was Bush's failure to help the uprising that produced the breakup of Iraq. The Kurds created their de facto independent state when the president was forced to establish the safe haven for them. America's indifference to the slaughter of Iraq's Shiites drove them into the embrace of Iran. In the final irony, it is George H. W. Bush's son whose presidency is unraveling because of a civil war that can be traced in part to the failed uprising with American troops bogged down in Iraq, just as Cheney predicted.

With the creation of the U.S.-protected safe haven, it became relatively easy, as a Senate staffer, to visit Kurdistan. The U.S. Army flew Black Hawk helicopters regularly from Diyarbakir in southeast Turkey to northern Iraq. At the request of the Foreign Relations Committee, the Army laid on a flight for me on September 4, 1991. I met up with Jalal Talabani in Sarsanq, a village not far from Turkey where Saddam had had a palace set in a several-hundred-acre walled garden. After a lunch with the U.S. military mission in northern Iraq, the Black Hawks flew Talabani and me across a landscape of tabletop plateaus, deep ravines, and broad valleys. Five months before, ordinary Kurds would have been executed for entering this territory, which was part of the prohibited zone proclaimed by Anfal architect Ali Hassan al-Majid. Now,

Kurds were slowly returning to the land. Shepherds were the first back and as our low-flying helicopters scattered their flocks they waved enthusiastically. We landed on a high ridge in Eastern Kurdistan where PUK Land Cruisers waited to take us to Talabani's temporary home in the nearby resort town of Shaqlawa.

That evening, Talabani told me about documents the Kurds had captured. When we were at Lizginn Hamzani's house in Dahuk on March 30, Hero Talabani had described how the Kurds now had much new information about the Anfal and other atrocities. In the confusion of that evening, I had not fully grasped what she was explaining, and then I assumed that any evidence would have been lost in the panicked flight to the mountains.

Jalal Talabani now gave me the full story. During the uprisings, the Kurdish political parties overran the local offices of Iraq's General Security Directorate, General Military Intelligence Directorate, and the Ba'ath Party. Inside they found tons of files. Some were lost when angry crowds set the buildings on fire, but most were saved. The PUK peshmerga had taken roomfuls of documents to the mountains on the border with Iran, where they now were.

If the documents remained in Iraq, they risked being recaptured. I told Talabani that this unique record of the genocide against the Kurdish people should be moved to safety. I proposed that he give the documents to the U.S. government for safekeeping. "Absolutely not," he said. "I don't trust President Bush. Dear Peter, I will give the documents to you."

Although I didn't know what I would do with them, I accepted. I told Talabani that the documents should remain the property of the Kurdish people. I suggested that the documents be made available both to historians and for the purpose of bringing a genocide case against Iraq. Talabani did not want Iraqi agents to see the documents, nor did he want them used by those American Middle East experts whom he considered pro-Arab or anti-Kurd. I said I would find sympathetic researchers. He said he would leave this to me but insisted that I have sole control over access to the documents. I knew I would have a major logistical task organizing the transport and storage of the documents when I returned to Washington, but I first wanted to take advantage of the opportunity to move freely around Kurdistan.

I traveled north one day to Rawanduz, a town nestled in the mountains not far from the Iranian and Turkish borders. At a hotel that he had converted into his headquarters, I met for the first time Massoud Barzani, president of the Kurdistan Democratic Party. He was reserved as compared to the gregarious Talabani; I detected then the steely resolve that would serve the Kurdish cause so well. As the March uprising collapsed, Barzani's peshmerga had dwindled to a few dozen men. He had refused to join the flight to Iran, and instead joined the battle in the mountains north of Erbil. He told me he would rather die in Iraq than be a refugee again. We had a long and inconclusive talk about whether the Kurds should try to make an agreement with Saddam or rely on an uncertain commitment from the United States. On my way back to Shaqlawa, I passed a wedding and was invited to join the dancing.

The Iraqi Army still surrounded Erbil and Suleimania, Kurdistan's two largest cities. Within the cities, Saddam's Iraqi authorities coexisted uneasily with the Kurdish political parties and the peshmerga. Kosrat Rasul, a PUK peshmerga commander with a reputation for bravery, gave me a pair of baggy Kurdish trousers and wide cummerbund to wear. So disguised, we passed through the Iraqi Army checkpoints to visit Erbil. With peshmerga on one side of the street and Iraqi soldiers on the other, Erbil was positively surreal. I asked Kosrat if I could talk with the Iraqi soldiers, and he obliged by having his peshmerga detain several that I could question. The soldiers I interviewed had been in Kuwait but said they had gone AWOL rather than wait for the American attack. Apparently many other soldiers had done the same thing. From this admittedly small sample, I got the impression that one reason the hundred-hour ground war had gone so smoothly is that there were far fewer defenders in Kuwait than the Allies thought there were. This experience also helped confirm what my Kurdish and Shiite friends were saying: Saddam Hussein's regime rested on an increasingly fragile foundation.

Everywhere in Kurdistan I encountered Saddam Hussein's legacy. Jalal Talabani and I drove on dirt tracks through the lush Balisan Valley where, in 1987, Iraq first used chemical weapons against the Kurds. Five years before, it had been full of villages and farms. In 1991, it was hard to tell it had ever been inhabited. In Eastern Kurdistan, I visited the ruins of Qalat Diza, the city of 100,000 that Saddam Hussein ordered destroyed in 1989. Every building had been dynamited or knocked down by tanks. Some former residents had returned and were living in makeshift shelters. I visited with one family of at least twenty that was living in what had been the second floor of a school, now partially collapsed. With a concrete floor at an angle to the ground and a roof that was five feet above, their home more resembled a cave. It was, I imagined, like living in central Berlin in May 1945. In Halabja, I interviewed the survivors of the 1988 chemical weapons attacks and visited the cemetery. Halabja was also mostly ruins, with pancaked buildings and a mishmash of iron reinforcing rods pointed in all directions. After gassing the city in March 1988, the Iraqi Army had destroyed it.

To enter Suleimania, I again crossed Iraqi lines, this time not bothering to disguise myself. Our first stop was the General Security Directorate. In a smoke-darkened room, a peshmerga showed me where naked prisoners had been suspended by their arms from hooks attached to a ceiling pipe. In the back of the building, I was taken to a trailer full of girls' garments. It was the raping room.

In addition to documents, the Kurds had found scores of videotapes in the building and I was shown some of them. A video of an execution showed blindfolded Kurdish men tied to stakes as a Ba'ath Party official read out the death sentences to the applause of the assembled crowd. A volley of gunfire followed. Then, each Ba'ath Party official present emptied his pistol into the corpses. Several bodies were so bullet-ridden that they fell apart when the ambulance arrived to take away the remains. In Saddam's Iraq, families had to pay for the bullets if they wanted to bury their executed relative.

I was also shown a videotaped torture session, in which the security services tested an experimental truth drug on a middle-aged Kurdish man. It didn't seem to work, and the secret police began to hit him, but the poor man couldn't stay awake. Apparently, he didn't confess to any offense, as I had the jarring experience of running into him on a Suleimania street about an hour later (possibly not purely by coincidence). The Kurds told me they had also found videotapes of rapes, which they destroyed rather than shame the victims or their families.

I heard scores of personal stories: from torture victims, from the survivors of poison gas attacks, from those who lost their homes, and from the families of the executed. At Talabani's house in Shaqlawa, I met Taimor Abdul, a fifteen-year-old boy from Qulojeo, a village near Kifri in the southernmost part of the Kurdish-controlled region. When he was twelve, tanks came to his village. He told me what happened next.

Iraqi Army vehicles took us to Gzawha near Dukan Dam. They separated the men from the women and children. I stayed with the women. No food was given to the men and so the women would throw some of our bread over the barbed wire to them. We saw the men being beaten, and then one day they were stripped to their underwear and taken away in Zil trucks. We never saw them again. A month later, the women and children were put on buses headed toward the Saudi Arabian border. I was on a bus with my mother, three sisters, and three aunts. We had no food and water all day. A woman and a child died on our bus.

We arrived in a place where we were given water and then blindfolded. The bus drove some more and then we got off. I took off my blindfold and saw the trenches. I was pushed into a trench and the soldiers started shooting. A bullet hit me in the armpit. I ran to a soldier. The officer became angry at the soldier and yelled "Throw him back in the hole." The firing resumed and I was shot in the back. There was a girl in the trench, Sergol from the village of Hawara Berza, who was still alive. I said we should escape, but she said she was afraid. When the shooting stopped and the soldiers started talking, we ran from the trench. But, she wouldn't continue and was taken away. I passed out and when I awoke, the soldiers had filled in the trench. I walked to a village, where an Arab family took care of me. They had a relative in Samawa who was a nurse. He got me medicine and bandages. The family's son was a soldier in Suleimania and he told my story to a friend who found my uncle. That is how I returned north.

After all that I heard and saw, I was convinced that the use of force to remove Saddam Hussein was morally justifiable. And I was also convinced the Kurds would never voluntarily agree to be part of Iraq again.

In Washington in late September, I faced the problem of how to get the documents out of Iraq, and where to put them. Senators Pell and Gore wrote Defense Secretary Richard Cheney asking the military to transport the documents to the United States. Cheney quickly agreed, but it took many months—and several trips to the Pentagon—to work out the logistics. Gore, who was also an overseer at his alma mater, Harvard, got the university to agree to take the documents, at least so he thought. I later got a sheepish call from the university's general counsel asking to be let out of the agreement for fear that housing them might make Widener Library a terrorist target.

Throughout the Cold War, the National Archives had kept, in total secrecy, the archives of the pre-1939 Polish Republic and, for seventy years, the records of the czarist Russian legation to Washington. These seemed worthy precedents. The archives staff explained that they were obliged by law to keep the legislative files of congressional committees. All I had to do was declare the Kurdish documents legislative files of the Foreign Relations Committee.

In April 1992, I spent two weeks in Kurdistan arranging for the documents to be transported to Zakho, where the U.S. military would pick them up. ABC *Nightline* sent a four-man team, led by correspondent Mark Litke, to record the process and to tell the story of Saddam's atrocities.

At the Shaqlawa secret police headquarters, the documents were still in the offices where the Kurds had found them. I was shown a notebook with a floral cover. It looked like something a teenage girl would carry to school, but inside, written in a careful hand, were recorded the names, birth dates, and home villages of those executed in surrounding villages during the Anfal campaign. Many of the dead were children. As the *Nightline* crew filmed, the Kurds packed the documents into boxes. At Mowat, in the high mountains on the Iranian border, the documents were stored in grain bags and ammunition crates in a leaky school building. I was glad we were getting them out since the elements posed more of a risk in this remote location than the Iraqis did. At the end of April, I personally delivered the first boxes of documents to the U.S. military in Zakho. Two weeks later, I was at Andrews Air Force Base outside Washington when an Air Force C-5 cargo plane landed carrying 847 boxes weighing fourteen tons. I declared them legislative files of the Foreign Relations Committee and the National Archives hauled them away to a specially built room in their facility in Suitland, Maryland.

The story of the documents caught the attention of Randy Fishbein, who worked for Senator Daniel K. Inouye, a Hawaii Democrat who chaired the Defense Appropriations subcommittee. At Fishbein's urging, Inouye earmarked $1 million to have the documents analyzed and catalogued. A twenty-five-man team of reservists and civilian contractors spent more than a year making brief summaries of the documents, rating each for importance, and scanning them. Eventually, the PUK received a box containing several hundred compact disks with scanned versions of all the documents.

Middle East Watch (MEW) was one of the few human rights organizations concerned with the fate of the Kurds, and they had previously done an excellent report on Iraqi human rights violations. They seemed to fit Talabani's desire to have a sympathetic researcher, and I had complete confidence in Holly Burkhalter, the Washington representative of MEW's parent organization, Human Rights Watch. In May 1992, I wrote a letter authorizing MEW to do research on the documents, and over the next two years, MEW produced the authoritative account of the Anfal, combining the documents with interviews and the forensic reports on their excavations of mass graves. Middle East Watch concluded that Iraq had committed genocide against the Kurds. Unfortunately, no government was willing to bring a genocide case against Iraq in the International Court of Justice.

• • •

By the middle of 1991, the world's attention had shifted away from Iraq. At the end of June, Slovenia and Croatia declared their independence from Yugoslavia. Fighting broke out briefly in Slovenia and more intensely in Croatia. In December, Senator Pell asked me to prepare a report on the war in the former Yugoslavia. While in Belgrade, I watched CNN reporting from Minsk, where the leaders of Russia, Belarus, and Ukraine agreed to dissolve the Soviet Union. Events in Russia and the former Yugoslavia dominated President George H. W. Bush's last year in office. They continued as the top priorities for President Clinton, with developments in the Balkans leading to the deployment of an American-led NATO force to Bosnia in 1995, and a war with Serbia over Kosovo in 1999.

In 1993, the war in the former Yugoslavia became my priority as well. President Clinton appointed me the first U.S. ambassador to Croatia, an assignment I held for nearly five years through war and a tenuous peace. After a short stint in Washington, I was seconded to the United Nations Transitional Administration in East Timor in 2000. I managed the political and constitutional component of the territory's transition to independence, working closely with the U.N. administrator, Sergio Vieira de Mello.

Before heading to my assignment in Croatia, I had made one final trip to Kurdistan in April 1993 to say farewell to Kurdish friends and to introduce George Pickart, my successor on the Middle East portfolio at the Foreign Relations Committee. We met with Massoud Barzani, the president of the Kurdistan Democratic Party, who agreed to transfer the documents in the KDP's possession to the Foreign Relations Committee as well. Under George's careful supervision that transfer took place some months later. I did not personally return to the Iraq issue until after September 11, 2001.

Iraq was a second-tier issue in the 1990s. The Clinton Administration pursued a containment policy aimed at keeping Iraq from threatening its neighbors or restarting its WMD programs. Maintaining the tough U.N. sanctions originally imposed in 1990 was the principal means for "keeping Saddam in his box." Periodically, the United States bombed targets in Iraq, notably when Saddam sent agents to try to kill former President Bush in Kuwait in 1993, after Saddam's forces entered the Kurdish city of Erbil in 1996, and when Saddam expelled U.N. weapons inspectors in 1998. President Clinton continued the northern no-fly zone for the Kurds, and extended the southern no-fly zone to the 33rd parallel, or just south of Baghdad. The southern no-fly zone, which had been set up by President Bush in 1992 under the name Operation Southern Watch, was largely symbolic in effect since the Iraqi Army and Republican Guards controlled the south and did not need to fly aircraft to repress the Shiites.

President George H. W. Bush authorized a CIA program in late 1991 to provide "covert assistance" to the Iraqi opposition. The program was not very secret. Part of the effort was to build a unified Iraqi opposition, and I attended a CIA-funded meeting of Iraqi opposition politicians at a hotel on the outskirts of Vienna in 1992. The Clinton Administration continued this program, which involved producing some very expensive videos in London and subsidies for the Iraqi National Congress (INC), a London-based umbrella organization of opposition parties put together by Iraqi exile leader Ahmad Chalabi. The CIA also ran an operation in northern Iraq that led the Iraqi opposition to believe, wrongly, that the Clinton Administration would support an armed attack from the Kurdish enclave on the Iraqi-held cities of Mosul and Kirkuk. In 1998, Congress passed the Iraq Liberation Act, which made regime change official U.S. policy and overtly funded the Iraqi opposition, including the Iraqi National Congress.

The Clinton Administration's Iraq policy was criticized by those who felt the continuation of sanctions imposed too steep a price on Iraq's children, while others felt more should be done to remove the regime. In retrospect, however, the Clinton Administration containment policy served the United States well. Saddam Hussein did not threaten U.S. interests and did not develop weapons of mass destruction. The United States continued to protect the Kurds and a major focus on human rights in Iraq helped prevent a return to the same level of mass killings that took place in the 1980s and early 1990s.

Life, however, was grim for most Iraqis. Sanctions helped destroy the middle class. Iraqis were isolated from the rest of the world, mostly unable to travel and missing out on the technological innovations of the times, including cell phones and the Internet.* Dissent generally meant death. In the south, Saddam drained the marshes, causing vast ecological damage, and destroyed the millennia-old way of life of the Marsh Arabs. Forty thousand Marsh Arabs perished, and the destruction of their unique culture is generally considered Saddam's second genocide.

For the United States, however, the containment policy accomplished its goals at a relatively low cost both financially and in terms of military resources.

---

* Kurdistan was an exception. The Kurds smuggled into Iraq the servers for an Internet system. Using British and Belgium exchanges, they also set up a cell phone network that continues to be separate from those in the rest of Iraq.

CHAPTER 5

Arrogance and Ignorance

On January 29, 2002, President George W. Bush addressed a joint session of Congress. In the aftermath of September 11, the president was riding high in the polls and the esteem of his countrymen and this was very much in evidence as he basked in the prolonged applause from both sides of the aisle. To the Congress and the American people, the president outlined a national strategy for the post–September 11 world:

> Our second goal is to prevent regimes that sponsor terror from threatening America or our friends and allies with weapons of mass destruction. Some of these regimes have been pretty quiet since September the 11th. But we know their true nature. North Korea is a regime arming with missiles and weapons of mass destruction, while starving its citizens.
>
> Iran aggressively pursues these weapons and exports terror, while an unelected few repress the Iranian people's hope for freedom.
>
> Iraq continues to flaunt its hostility toward America and to support terror. The Iraqi regime has plotted to develop anthrax, and nerve gas, and nuclear weapons for over a decade. This is a regime that has already used poison gas to murder thousands of its own citizens—leaving the bodies of mothers huddled over their dead children. This is a regime that agreed to international

inspections—then kicked out the inspectors. This is a regime that has something to hide from the civilized world. States like these, and their terrorist allies, constitute an axis of evil, arming to threaten the peace of the world.

The name-calling was then followed by a warning:

> [A]ll nations should know: America will do what is necessary to ensure our nation's security . . . We'll be deliberate, yet time is not on our side. I will not wait on events, while dangers gather. I will not stand by, as peril draws closer and closer. The United States of America will not permit the world's most dangerous regimes to threaten us with the world's most destructive weapons.

The "Axis of Evil" phrase caught the public imagination.* David Frum, a Canadian working in the White House speechwriting office, let it be known that he had come up with this clever phrase. Apparently, he had inserted the phrase into the speech without it having been seen, much less cleared, by Secretary of State Colin Powell or anyone else professionally responsible for U.S. foreign policy. This

---

* The phrase reflected poorly on its author's knowledge of geometry and history. An axis is a straight line between two points. North Korea, Iran, and Iraq could not form an axis. The historical analogy was also false. The World War II Axis (technically speaking, just Germany and Italy, hence the Berlin-Rome Axis) was an *alliance*. Iran and Iraq were bitter enemies in 2002, and have only formed a Baghdad-Tehran axis thanks to George W. Bush, whose actions made possible the January 2005 democratic elections that brought Iran's allies to power in Baghdad. North Korea is not an ally of either country, although it may have sold missile and nuclear technology to Iran. In an influential article, "Dictatorships and Double Standards," published in *Commentary* in November 1979, Jeane Kirkpatrick, then a prominent neoconservative intellectual and later Reagan's Ambassador to the U.N., denounced foreign policy actions that made the U.S. administration feel good, but which did no good. The "Axis of Evil" phrase was a classic feel-good pronouncement that served no useful national security purpose.

ad hoc approach to national security has been characteristic of the Bush White House, which oddly has had a reputation for being disciplined.

National security strategy is most likely to be successful when there are clear goals, when objectives are prioritized taking into account the risks and resources required for a particular course of action, and when there is careful planning. The Bush speech, the process by which it was produced, and the actions that followed underscore the absence of coherent strategy that has characterized the U.S. intervention in Iraq.

President Bush did articulate a goal in the Axis of Evil speech, namely that the United States would keep the most dangerous nations from acquiring weapons of mass destruction. But, even here, the objective was dangerously imprecise. All WMD are not equally harmful. For all the horrors associated with chemical and biological weapons, they do not compare in lethality or destructiveness with nuclear weapons. A more precise statement of a top U.S. goal would be to keep nuclear weapons out of the hands of states that might use them or give them to terrorists.

Bush's imprecision contributed to a decision to focus U.S. military and diplomatic resources on Iraq, which was by far the least dangerous of three "Axis of Evil" states. At the time he made his speech, Iraq had been under comprehensive U.N. sanctions for more than eleven years. While Saddam had expelled international inspectors in 1998, the United States could have a high degree of confidence in January 2002 that Iraq did not have a significant nuclear program. Since Iraq had actually produced large quantities of chemical weapons in the 1980s, and since it had not cooperated with the inspectors, the United States could reasonably infer that Iraq did still possess previously manufactured chemical weapons, but there was no intelligence to indicate that Iraq had resumed large-scale production of new chemical weapons. The evidence on biological weapons was much murkier, but these materials are extremely difficult to use effectively in warfare. Thus, based on what the United States knew or could assume in 2002, the maximum possible threat from Iraq was from previously produced chemical weapons and, more remotely, an experimental quantity of biological weapons.

By contrast, both Iran and North Korea had active nuclear programs. The U.S. focus on Iraq only made strategic sense if it would have an exemplary effect on these two more dangerous proliferators. In fact, the U.S. preoccupation with Iraq has clearly emboldened, and not deterred, North Korea and Iran.

In 2002, North Korea was a party to the Nuclear Non-Proliferation Treaty (NPT) with a stockpile of plutonium that was under International Atomic Energy Agency (the U.N.'s nuclear watchdog) safeguards. In 1994, North Korea had made an agreement with the United States, South Korea, Russia, China, and Japan to freeze all nuclear activities in exchange for shipments of fuel oil and the construction of two light water nuclear power plants, which are at low risk for diversion to a weapons program. In 2002, the Bush Administration accused North Korea of violating this agreement by establishing a covert program to enrich uranium. If North Korea was building a uranium enrichment facility, it was not yet operational and it would have been some years before North Korea acquired significant fissile material through the enrichment route. In short, if North Korea was cheating on the 1994 agreement, it was doing so slowly. Without having a fallback plan, the Bush Administration provoked a crisis by cutting off the supply of fuel oil under the 1994 agreement. North Korea retaliated by becoming the first country to withdraw from the NPT, which it did on December 31, 2002. It apparently then made six to eight nuclear weapons from the plutonium that had previously been under IAEA safeguards.

North Korea is a brutal dictatorship with an erratic leader and a track record of selling dangerous technology to the highest bidder. Busy with Iraq, the Bush Administration has done little more than name-calling in its response to North Korea. This has been demonstrably ineffective and very likely counterproductive. North Korea's major advance as a nuclear power is one direct consequence of a U.S. strategy that focused on Iraq.

Iran illustrates even better Bush's inability to think strategically.

Having decided to invade Iraq, a strategist would have considered the situation of Iran. Given that Iran funded (and in the case of SCIRI, created) Iraq's main Shiite parties, and considering that the southern half of Iraq is Shiite, it was foreseeable that Iran would have considerable influence in a post-Saddam Iraq. Even if Iran were a future target, a strategist might have wanted to minimize Iran's opposition to American efforts in Iraq, at least until he had consolidated his position in Iraq and was prepared to move against Iran.

Iran had more reasons to want Saddam gone than George W. Bush did. Saddam had attacked Iran, causing more than 500,000 dead in the Iran-Iraq War. Saddam had actually used chemical weapons on the Iranians, and Iran—not the United States—was the more likely target of any revived Iraqi WMD program. Iran's fellow Shiites would be the beneficiaries of democracy in Iraq, and Iran might well have cooperated with the United States in ensuring a quick military victory followed by a quick exit. Indeed, prior to the Axis of Evil speech, Iran was cooperating with the United States in Afghanistan, sharing intelligence on al-Qaeda, preventing fugitive al-Qaeda members from escaping through Iran, and giving the U.S. military permission to conduct search-and-rescue missions on Iranian territory for any American pilot downed in the Afghanistan war. The United States and Iran had a common foe in al-Qaeda and the Taliban, both of which have waged war on the Shiites, whom they consider to be apostates.* After the Axis of Evil speech, the Iranians ended their cooperation with the U.S. on Afghanistan, depriving the U.S. military of intelligence and assistance that could enable it to fight better the war on terror.

In the Axis of Evil speech, Bush not only offended the Iranians but also signaled that Iran might be America's next target after a successful campaign in Iraq. This gave the Iranians every incentive to make sure the United States did not succeed in Iraq. The president never under-

---

* On August 8, 1998, Taliban militia invaded the Iranian consulate in the northern Afghan city of Mazar-i-Sharif and murdered eight Iranian diplomats and a journalist. The Taliban also brutally repressed Afghanistan's Shiites in Herat, not far from the Iranian border.

stood how much influence Iran had in Iraq, or perhaps he didn't think it was important. Today, Iranian allies control much of Iraq's American-funded security forces and are a major factor in the country's civil war.

For eighteen years, Iran has had a secret program to acquire nuclear weapons technology; in this Iran has been helped by Pakistan, a supposed U.S. ally. Under international pressure, Iran had agreed to intrusive IAEA inspections and to suspend uranium enrichment activities that would give it the fissile material for a bomb. At the beginning of 2006, Iran's radical new president, Mahmoud Ahmadinejad, ended the intrusive IAEA inspections and announced that Iran would resume uranium enrichment. Iran's leaders felt confident that the United States would not act against them, and the American presence in Iraq is the major reason. As Akbar Alami, an Iranian parliamentarian, observed to the *New York Times* in January 2006, "America is extremely vulnerable right now. If the U.S. takes any unwise action [to punish Iran for pursuing its nuclear program] certainly the U.S. and other countries will share the harm."

Alami's comment was a reference to Iran's ability to ignite a Shiite uprising against the U.S. military in southern Iraq and Baghdad. Iran supported the now-dominant Shiite political parties in Iraq, and arms and funds their military wings. This includes SCIRI's 12,000-man militia, known as the Badr Organization, and Moqtada al-Sadr's Mahdi Army.* As the nuclear crisis escalated between the United States and Iran, al-Sadr went to Tehran, where he underscored his support for the Iranians, saying, "If neighboring Islamic countries, including Iran, become the target of attacks, we will support them. The Mahdi Army is beyond the Iraqi Army. It was established to defend Islam."

By sending U.S. forces into Iraq, President Bush has, in effect, made them hostage to Iran and its Iraqi Shiite allies. As a result, the Adminis-

---

* SCIRI's military wing was originally known as the Badr Corps. After the Coalition occupation authorities banned militias in 2003, the Badr Corps changed its name but not its function.

tration has no good military options to halt Iran's drive for nuclear weapons.

Looking back, the Iraq War has greatly increased the nuclear threat to the United States from two "rogue" states, North Korea and Iran. Bush has stated that "hindsight is not a strategy." The problem, however, is not the lack of foresight back in 2002 but rather the absence of a strategy for halting the proliferation of nuclear weapons to the world's most dangerous actors. This strategic failure was the outcome of a disorganized policy-making process where ideology counted for more than analysis and where a speechwriter had more influence than the secretary of state.

Although Iraq was the least dangerous member of the Axis of Evil, there were reasons to be concerned about Iraq's WMD programs, and in particular about the regime's ambitions. As a condition for the armistice that ended the first Gulf War, Iraq agreed to dismantle its WMD and ballistic missile programs and to accept a rigorous regime of U.N. inspections that required it to disclose fully all details about these weapons programs. From the start, Iraq tried to evade its obligations. It obstructed U.N. inspectors' access to suspect locations, and only reluctantly provided even partial documentation of its programs. Only after Saddam Hussein's son-in-law Hussein Kamel, who had been in charge of Iraq's WMD programs, defected to Jordan in 1995 did Iraq make a more comprehensive accounting of its activities. Then, in 1998, Saddam Hussein expelled the U.N. inspectors.

Even without inspections, sanctions and international monitoring of its imports would have made it difficult for Iraq to restart a nuclear program or to resume full-scale manufacture of chemical weapons, but it was also reasonable to presume that this was Saddam Hussein's intent. In audiotapes of Iraqi government meetings captured after the war, Saddam is heard to say he would eventually resume these programs, emphasizing that Iraq still had its previously acquired knowledge.

In 2002, the Bush Administration forced Iraq to accept renewed U.N. inspections under conditions in which the inspectors had greater access than in the 1990s. In what may be the best speech of his presidency, Bush made a well-argued, and well-received, case to the United Nations on September 12, 2002, that Iraq was in violation of its legal obligations under previous U.N. Security Council resolutions. U.S. troop deployments to the Persian Gulf region and media leaks about war plans sent a message to Saddam and to the other members of the Security Council that the United States was serious about taking military action to disarm Iraq. The congressional vote authorizing war underscored U.S. resolve.*

In part because it hoped to avoid unilateral U.S. action, the Security Council unanimously passed a resolution warning Iraq to comply with its obligations or face the consequences. Persuaded that the United States was serious this time, Saddam agreed to readmit the inspectors and to give them full access, including to Saddam's palaces.†

At this stage, Iraq was effectively prevented from manufacturing nuclear and chemical weapons, or significant quantities of biological weapons. To manufacture nuclear weapons, Iraq needed large industrial facilities and specialized equipment that could not possibly escape detection under a regime of intrusive inspections. Nor could Iraq conceal the factories required for the production of chemical weapons or secure laboratories needed to produce significant quantities of biological weapons safely. By using mobile laboratories, Iraq might have been able to produce small quantities of biological agents. Doing so, how-

---

* The congressional resolution authorized military action to compel Iraq to comply with its disarmament obligations. It was perfectly reasonable for a member of Congress to vote in favor of this resolution in order to strengthen the president's hand in making a credible threat to Iraq. Obviously, a senator or representative voting for the resolution had to accept responsibility for war if Iraq was not in compliance, but the vote was not a mandate to go to war in the event Iraq was in compliance.

† Saddam had palaces all over Iraq. Although he rarely visited most of them, the staff at each palace prepared a meal each day in case he showed up. Some of the palaces, associated buildings, and grounds covered hundreds of acres, which is why inspectors insisted on visiting them. Iraq had objected to inspections of presidential sites, citing sovereignty grounds.

ever, would have risked detection and attack for very little military gain. At lesser risk of detection, Iraq could have hidden chemical weapons that it had previously produced.

As long as U.N. inspections continued, the *maximum* possible WMD threat from Iraq consisted of some aging chemical weapons and small quantities of biological agents. Chemical weapons are horrific when used on defenseless villagers but only a minimal threat to U.S. troops equipped with protective gear. Biological agents are difficult to weaponize, dangerous to handle, and of limited value, especially in small quantities. In short, as long as Iraq was subject to intrusive inspections, it was not a serious WMD threat.

By January 2003, the Bush Administration had eliminated any serious threat from Iraqi WMD. It had the strong support of the United Nations and international community for its tough nonproliferation policy and was coming off a major success in coercive diplomacy with regard to Iraq. A strategist might then have used this international support and the credibility that came from a demonstrated willingness to use force to face down North Korea, which had just announced its withdrawal from the NPT. Bush, however, did not think strategically about WMD. He had already decided on war with Iraq and therefore let North Korea proceed with the manufacture of nuclear weapons.

Even without the benefit of hindsight and the knowledge that Iraq had no WMD, there was no strategic logic in devoting massive military and financial resources to a war over Iraq's WMD programs. In a moment of candor, Deputy Defense Secretary Paul Wolfowitz told *Vanity Fair* in May 2003 that there had been other reasons for the war.

> The truth is that for reasons that have a lot to do with the U.S. government bureaucracy we settled on the one issue that everyone could agree on which was weapons of mass destruction as the core reason, but . . . there have always been three fundamental concerns. One is weapons of mass destruction, the second is sup-

port for terrorism, the third is the criminal treatment of the Iraqi people.*

President Bush has cited the war on terror and the spread of freedom as important U.S. goals in Iraq, although the latter received greater emphasis only after no WMD were found in Iraq. Looking at the world as it was on the eve of the war in March 2003, did either of these objectives justify a war?

On September 11, 2001, Iranians watching a soccer game stood for a minute of silent tribute to the victims of the attacks in New York and Washington earlier that day. From Baghdad, Iraqi television gloated, "It is a black day in the history of America which is tasting the bitter defeat of its crimes."

In spite of Baghdad's pleasure in the attacks, Saddam Hussein had no connection to its perpetrators. Ideologically, Saddam Hussein and al-Qaeda were far apart. Saddam's Ba'ath Party was nationalist and secular, with the goal of unifying the Arab nation without regard to religion. (Its founder, Michel Aflaq, was a Syrian Christian.) Osama bin Laden seeks a universal Islamic state that transcends national and ethnic boundaries. Sunni fundamentalists, like al-Qaeda, reviled Saddam Hussein's regime as corrupt while Saddam considered the fundamentalists a threat and treated them with corresponding brutality.

Nor was an alliance of convenience between Saddam and al-Qaeda at all likely, in spite of their shared hatred of the United States. If he were to assist al-Qaeda, Saddam would be putting his fate into the hands of Osama bin Laden. Anytime al-Qaeda wanted to destroy Saddam, it could leak the connection to the Americans, who would, of

* Wolfowitz claimed *Vanity Fair* misconstrued his remarks in their story. This quote comes from a transcript of the Wolfowitz interview with *Vanity Fair* that was posted on the Department of Defense Web site.

course, come after Iraq. Saddam made many miscalculations in his thirty-five-year career, but he was canny enough not to give such power to a man and organization bent on the eradication of everything he stood for. Even the politicized U.S. intelligence process never produced a shred of evidence linking Iraq to al-Qaeda.

Logic and facts did not stop the Bush Administration from looking for connections. Vice President Cheney promoted a theory that Ramzi Yousef, the mastermind of the 1993 World Trade Center bombing, was really an Iraqi doppelgänger who had assumed Yousef's identity. The Administration circulated as authentic a raw intelligence report, apparently from an alcoholic and discredited agent, that had the September 11 mastermind, Mohammed Atta, meeting with an Iraqi embassy official in Prague in 2000. (There is no evidence that Atta went to Prague.) Not satisfied with the conclusions of the intelligence professionals at the CIA and his own Defense Intelligence Agency, Secretary Rumsfeld set up the Office of Special Plans, staffed by ideologically vetted political appointees and reporting to Under Secretary for Policy Douglas Feith, with the mission of finding the link between Saddam and al-Qaeda that the intelligence professionals had supposedly missed.

President Bush simply asserted that Iraq was integral to the war on terror. He had no basis for his claim before the war, but he turned out to be prematurely correct. As a result of the American invasion, Sunni fundamentalist terrorists have flooded into Iraq. The Sunni Arab center of Iraq has become what Afghanistan was during the Taliban—an inaccessible region dominated by shadowy figures that now host foreign terrorists linked to al-Qaeda. By staging spectacular attacks, the terrorists have given al-Qaeda new strength and have helped generate thousands of new recruits. The foreign terrorists have done real damage to the prospect for a successful outcome in Iraq. In 2003, they blew up the United Nations headquarters in Baghdad, killing Sergio Vieira de Mello, the U.N. representative in Iraq and a diplomat so accomplished that he was at the top of everyone's list to be the next U.N. secretary-general,* and driving the United Nations out of Iraq. This deprived the inexperienced, and sometimes amateurish, American occupation authorities of a wealth of relevant expertise and experience.

From the 2003 killing of Shiite cleric Bakr al-Hakim to the destruction of the Askariya shrine in 2006, foreign terrorists have helped spark civil war. By creating a climate of fear, they have cost the United States billions in additional security costs beyond what was budgeted for reconstruction, and greatly diminished the effectiveness of these expenditures. If the Americans withdraw while Iraq is still unstable, al-Qaeda can not only claim victory but will have, in Iraq's Sunni heartland, a secure territorial base to replace the one lost in Afghanistan in 2001.

In fairness to the Bush Administration, not all of this was foreseeable before the war. What was clear, however, was that Iraq was not a factor in the war on terror. It was predictable, and predicted, that the war would result in the collapse of Iraqi institutions, and that, unless the U.S. provided security, the result would be chaos. Chaos, as the Administration knew well, is the swamp in which terrorists breed. But the Administration made no plans to provide security in post-Saddam Iraq.

Democracy provided the third rationale for war. By itself, a democratic Iraq was a desirable objective but hardly one that could justify a major war. The war's architects assumed that democracy in Iraq

---

* I had worked closely with Sergio Vieira de Mello in Croatia where he headed Civil Affairs for the UNPROFOR Mission and I was the U.S. ambassador. In 1999, he asked me to join him in East Timor where he headed the United Nations Transitional Administration for the territory, arguably the most successful effort at "nation building" since the postwar occupations of Germany and Japan. Many factors made East Timor a success, including its small size, a relatively unified local leadership, and a large infusion of resources relative to the size of the country. Although he had an expansive grant of authority from the UN Security Council, Vieira de Mello deferred to the East Timorese on key decisions about the future of their country and used persuasion, rather than an arrogant assertion of authority, to accomplish hs goals. He went to Iraq at the personal request of President Bush but did not feel the American occupation authorities made good use of his skills. He was weeks from returning to his position as UN High Commissioner for Human Rights when he was murdered.

would produce a domino effect that would bring down authoritarian regimes in Syria, Iran, Saudi Arabia, and Egypt. If a democratic Iraq were to trigger a democratic revolution in the Middle East, this could justify the sacrifice and expense entailed in the Iraq War. A democratic Arab world might become an ally in the war on terror rather than a principal breeding ground for terrorists. A democratic Iran might be persuaded to give up its nuclear program, but even if it didn't, a pro-Western nuclear Iran would pose much less of a security threat than nuclear weapons in the hands of anti-American clerics. Finally, in a pro-Western democratic Middle East, one could imagine—and many of the war's architects did imagine—a comprehensive peace between Israel and the Arab countries.

For the Iraq War to fit into a larger Middle East democracy strategy, three conditions would have had to be met in sequence: first, Iraq would have to democratize successfully; second, democracy in Iraq would have to trigger democratic change in other Middle Eastern countries; and third, democratic governments in the Middle East would have to behave in a way that is more in the U.S. interest than their autocratic predecessors were. The Bush Administration simply assumed that each of the steps would occur. It did no planning that might have increased the chances of a successful democratic transition in Iraq, nor did it examine the underlying conditions in Iraq to see if it was even possible to build the united democratic state that other Middle East countries would wish to emulate. Because all Administration thinking about Iraq was based on the most optimistic scenarios, the Administration never considered the possible impact of failure in Iraq. How would other Arab countries view American-led democracy-building in Iraq that resulted in sectarian civil war, the secession of part of the country, and a de facto Iranian takeover of much of the rest?

Even if Iraq had become the pro-Western democracy that the Administration desired, there was no empirical basis for believing it would have had a positive spillover effect. Of course, this was an untestable proposition. What one can say is that elections held in the Middle East since the Iraq War have not produced the results hoped for by the Bush Administration. In Iran, voters replaced moderate reformist President Mohammad Khatami in 2005 with archconservative Mahmoud Ahmadinejad, who has publicly doubted that the Holocaust took place, advocated Israel's destruction, and pushed forward aggressively with Iran's nuclear program. In Palestine, parliamentary elections produced an upset victory for the radical Islamic movement Hamas, which denies the right of Israel to exist and is responsible for suicide bombings and assassinations in Israel itself.

A year after the Axis of Evil speech, President Bush met with three Iraqi Americans: the author Kanan Makiya; Hatem Mukhlis, a doctor; and Rend Rahim, who later became postwar Iraq's first representative to the United States. As the three described what they thought would be the political situation after Saddam's fall, they talked about Sunnis and Shiites. It became apparent to them that the president was unfamiliar with these terms. The three spent part of the meeting explaining that there are two major sects in Islam.*

So two months before he ordered U.S. troops into the country, the president of the United States did not appear to know about the division among Iraqis that has defined the country's history and politics. He would not have understood why non-Arab Iran might gain a foothold in post-Saddam Iraq. He could not have anticipated U.S. troops being caught in the middle of a civil war between two religious sects that he did not know existed.

I recount this anecdote not to illustrate the president's ignorance, but because it underscores how little the American leadership thought before the war about the nature of Iraqi society and the problems the United States would face after it overthrew Saddam Hussein. Even in 2006, with civil war well under way in Iraq, the president and his top advisors speak of an Iraqi people, as if there were a single people akin to the French or even the American people.

For this, I fault a culture of arrogance that pervaded the Bush Administration. From the president and the vice president down through

---

* I heard this story directly from two participants in the meeting.

the war's neoconservative architects in the Pentagon, there was a belief that Iraq was a blank slate on which the United States could impose its vision of a pluralistic democratic society. The arrogance came in the form of a belief that this could be accomplished with minimal effort and planning by the United States and that it was not important to know something about Iraq. Indeed, in the staffing of postwar governance in Iraq, the Administration placed a premium on those who had ideologically correct views of the kind of conservative (in an American sense) democracy that the U.S. wanted for Iraq; they excluded foreign service officers who knew the country and the Arab world.

For duping the Bush Administration into believing that the takeover of Iraq would be easy, many fault Ahmad Chalabi. Chalabi, it is alleged, persuaded Cheney and the Pentagon neoconservatives that American troops would be greeted with flowers. Defectors brought in by his State Department–funded Iraqi National Congress provided information about Iraq's WMD programs that turned out to be false. It was Chalabi who conveniently neglected to mention to his enthralled American officials Iraq's bitter ethnic and religious divisions, and other problems that might follow from an invasion. It was Chalabi who let the neoconservatives believe that Iraq's oil revenues would make the country's reconstruction self-financing, and that democratic Iraq would move quickly to establish diplomatic relations with Israel.

Ahmad Chalabi was born to an affluent Shiite family in Baghdad in 1945. He grew up in a colonial-style bungalow with thick walls and an Olympic-size swimming pool situated among several acres of date palms. In 1958, when Iraqi Army officers overthrew the monarchy, the Chalabi family left Baghdad and Ahmad did not return for another forty-five years. After taking a degree in mathematics at the Massachusetts Institute of Technology and earning a Ph.D. at the University of Chicago, he taught at the American University in Beirut and then turned his hand to business and banking. He made a lot of money. In the 1980s, Chalabi headed the Petra Bank in Jordan, and when it collapsed he was charged with fraud by the Jordanian authorities and sentenced in absentia to a lengthy jail term.

I met Chalabi in 1986 through Judith Kipper, a Brookings Institution scholar and a highly regarded Middle East expert. I was impressed with his intellect, his prodigious memory, and his commitment to the overthrow of Saddam Hussein, which was not a popular cause at the time. I never knew enough to form a view on the Petra Bank allegations, but I found plausible Chalabi's explanation that Saddam Hussein, then a close ally of Jordan's King Hussein, was behind the prosecution.

In the 1980s, Chalabi figured out that the road to Baghdad went through Washington. He made it his mission to make friends within the American foreign policy community, and I count myself as one of his friends. Some of the people he befriended—Paul Wolfowitz, former Reagan Administration official Richard Perle, congressional staffer I. Lewis "Scooter" Libby, Dick Cheney—would go on to have prominent roles in the second Bush Administration. Chalabi did not make the common mistake of cultivating only the big names then in power. He understood that some of the most important players—especially for the long term—were congressional staff, an out of office foreign policy specialist, and a beat reporter.

Chalabi worked to unite an Iraqi opposition that included the Iranian-based Shiite religious parties, the rival Kurdish nationalist parties, Syrian-based Ba'athist dissidents, Sunni fundamentalists, several royal pretenders, and the Iraqi Communist Party. In spite of this diversity and many personal and family feuds among the various leaders, Chalabi was able to bring a large part of the opposition together on a common anti-Saddam program. Unlike many other Arabs, he recognized the importance of the Kurds to the opposition, controlling as they did territory and armed forces. In 1992, at an opposition congress held in the hilltop Kurdish town of Salahaddin, Chalabi got Arab Iraqis to support the Kurdish demand for federalism. Although lampooned as a "Mayfair revolutionary,"* he spent several years in Iraqi Kurdistan in the early 1990s trying to foment an uprising against Saddam Hussein. Even his Iraqi critics praise his personal courage.

Chalabi presented Saddam Hussein in the worst possible light (not hard to do) and made an Iraqi regime-change scenario sound rosy. He

---

* For the upscale London neighborhood where he has an apartment.

understood that many journalists are less cautious about the facts when they can get a scoop. He figured out who took shortcuts and fed them tidbits that were, to put it kindly, less than fully substantiated. He promoted rolling regime change, arguing that if the United States enlarged the northern safe area—and created a southern safe area—this would have a domino effect leading to Saddam's collapse. As war approached in 2003, Chalabi was insisting to the Americans that their troops would be greeted as liberators.

Chalabi was not entirely wrong. Some Iraqis did cheer the American troops as they moved toward the capital (I was given flowers in Baghdad five days after Saddam's fall). Chalabi never supported an American occupation of Iraq, which he correctly thought would generate increasing resistance. He thought power should quickly be turned over to an Iraqi interim government, and he pushed unsuccessfully for the Pentagon to train an Iraqi exile (and Kurdish) army that would fight alongside the Americans. He wanted a major role in an interim Iraqi government, but that does not mean his ideas were wrong.

Ahmad Chalabi's role in the events leading to the American invasion of Iraq cannot, in my view, be overstated. If it were not for him, the United States military likely would not be in Iraq today. This does not make him a con man, as his critics allege. Through a twenty-year cultivation of America's foreign policy elite, Chalabi made a convincing case for a democratic Iraq and Arab democracy. He certainly spun his information and analysis in a manner maximally favorable to the case for war. On some matters, he may have lied.

Ahmad Chalabi owed no duty to the United States. He was an *Iraqi* seeking the liberation of his country. He did not have an army, and so he needed to persuade the U.S. to lend him one. As he told the *Sunday Telegraph* a year after the war: "We are heroes in error. As far as we're concerned, we've been entirely successful. The tyrant Saddam is gone and the Americans are in Baghdad. What was said before [the war] is not important."

Thousands of exiles have come to Washington seeking U.S. support for their causes back home. Rarely do they get more than coffee and sympathy. Chalabi got the U.S. military and hundreds of billions of dollars in U.S. expenditures on building a new Iraq. Any fault lies not with Chalabi but with the U.S. government officials who uncritically accepted what he was saying.

Vice President Cheney was one. As he told NBC's Tim Russert on the eve of the war: "I have talked with a lot of Iraqis in the last several months myself, had them to the White House . . . The read we get on the people of Iraq is there is no question but they want to get rid of Saddam Hussein and they will welcome us as liberators." As Cheney's comments suggest, Chalabi was not the only Iraqi political figure to spin the Americans. As war approached, the Kurdish party leaders and the Shiite clerics also put forward a political line that they thought the Bush Administration wanted to hear. In meetings in the White House and State Department, the Kurds joined Arab Iraqi opposition leaders in stressing their commitment to a unified and democratic Iraq. They made much the same point to the print media and in countless appearances on outlets like CNN and BBC. But their true feelings were not hard to discern if one listened. The Bush Administration's favorite Iraqi was not Ahmad Chalabi but Barham Salih, a British-educated Kurdish leader who served for a decade as the PUK's representative in Washington before returning to Suleimania to be one of Kurdistan's two prime ministers.* In the lead-up to the war, Barham appeared regularly on American television offering extravagant praise for President Bush and his effort to bring freedom to the Iraqi people. To the BBC, he described his Iraqiness this way: "As long as we Kurds are *condemned* to live in Iraq, I want to be a full citizen of my country." It was hardly a compellingly patriotic statement from the man the Bush Administration chose to be Iraq's deputy prime minister in 2004.

With regard to Iraq's Shiites, the war's architects assumed to be true

---

* The KDP and PUK controlled separate areas within Kurdistan, a legacy of an intra-Kurdish civil war fought in the mid-1990s. Each part had its own cabinet and prime minister but both governments used the same name, the Kurdistan Regional Government. By 2003, the two KRGs cooperated closely. In May 2006, they combined.

what they wished were true. Because Iraq was home to Najaf and Karbala, Shiite Islam's two holiest places, liberated Iraq would replace Iran
as the center of the Shiite world. Iraq's Shiites would be pro-Western
and democratic and this would be of enormous strategic importance
since it would undermine the clerical regime in Iran.

Deputy Defense Secretary Wolfowitz articulated this view shortly
after the fall of Baghdad:

> We've understood very clearly that Iraq, especially the Shia popu-
> lation of Iraq, is both a source of danger and opportunity to the
> Iranians. I think it's more danger than it is opportunity. But the
> danger itself is incentive for them to try to intervene because
> the last thing they want to see, which I think is a real possibility, is
> an independent source of authority for the Shia religion emerg-
> ing in a country that is democratic and pro-Western . . . There's
> going to be a huge struggle for the soul of Iraqi Shiism, there's no
> question about it.

The evidence to the contrary was substantial. Iran had supported
all Iraq's major Shiite parties for more than two decades. These parties
had an avowed political agenda of creating an Islamic state, as reflected
in the name of the largest, the Supreme Council for the Islamic Revolution in Iraq. Iran had supported the Shiites in 1991 while the first
Bush Administration was passively complicit in the murders of tens of
thousands. And it was improbable that Iraq's 14 million Shiites emerg-
ing from centuries of brutal repression were somehow going to challenge an increasingly confident Iranian Shiite state of 68 million. The
relationship between mentor and mentored was clear but the Administration did not wish to be bothered with inconvenient facts.

The extent to which wishful thinking substituted for knowledge
can be seen in the testimony Under Secretary of Defense for Policy
Douglas Feith gave to the House International Relations Committee
on May 15, 2003. He told the committee, "Some Iranian influence
groups have called for a theocracy on the Tehran model. But it appears
that popular support for clerical rule is narrow, even among the Shia

population. The Shiite tradition does not favor clerical rule—the Khomeini'ites in Iran were innovators in this regard ... The Iranian model's appeal in Iraq is further reduced by the cultural divide between Persians and Arabs."

But when pressed by Democratic Congressman William Delahunt of Massachusetts as to whether there was data "to support your thesis," Feith became vague. "I do not have off the top of my head whether there's polling data on that." There was no data to support Feith's proposition because it wasn't true. When elections were held in Iraq in 2005, Iraq's Shiites voted overwhelmingly—by margins in excess of 80 percent—for pro-Iranian religious parties that would like to create an Islamic state in Iraq. In Iraq's Shiite southern governorates, a theocracy already exists.

The Bush Administration's most catastrophic assumption about postwar Iraq was that it would be easy. Not only would U.S. forces be welcomed as liberators but, once Saddam and his top lieutenants fled, Iraqi bureaucrats and police would show up for work the next day, reporting to their new American masters. Security would not be a problem and there would be no need for U.S. troops to assume police duties. Iraq's oil would pay for the country's administration and reconstruction so the postwar would not be a drain on the U.S. treasury.

Contrary views were not just rejected, they were banned. General Tommy Franks, the Central Command combatant commander, who had overall responsibility for fighting the Iraq War, was barred by Pentagon higher-ups from consulting his predecessor, General Anthony Zinni. Zinni had done substantial planning for the post-combat operations in Iraq, the so-called Phase IV Operations. Zinni's plan, which included having U.S. troops provide security, was cast aside as too pessimistic, presumably because it would require more troops than Rumsfeld wanted to send. When Army Chief of Staff General Eric Shinseki told the Senate Armed Services Committee that he thought it would take several hundred thousand troops to occupy Iraq (by which he meant 300,000 to 400,000), Wolfowitz delivered a very public rebuke, asserting that Shinseki was "wildly off the mark," and that he could not imagine it taking more troops to occupy Iraq than it took to conquer it.

The Administration prepared so little for postwar Iraq that it had no idea of what it didn't know. On February 11, 2003, Feith, the man responsible for postwar planning in the Pentagon, promised a skeptical Senate Foreign Relations Committee that everything was under control: "I do want to assure the committee that when we talk about all of the key functions that are going to need to be performed in postwar Iraq, we have thought about them across the range from worst case to very good case." In fact, the Bush Administration did not consider the most likely postwar scenario: that all authority would vanish with the regime. In July 2003, Wolfowitz admitted to Reuters that the Pentagon had not anticipated the collapse of order in Baghdad following Saddam's fall. He should not have been surprised. This is exactly what happened in 1991 in the parts of Iraq where the regime lost control during the uprising.

In January 2003, the Migration Policy Institute in Washington asked me to write a paper on possible postwar scenarios, which it published as part of its policy briefs series. In it, I predicted:

[A] rapid collapse is much more likely than prolonged resistance. Based on the experience of 1991, however, I see chaos as more likely than an orderly surrender.

[In this case there would be] a quick end to Iraqi military resistance. However, neither the Iraqi Army (nor any other institution) has the ability or the will to maintain order. Shiite uprisings take place in Basra, Najaf, Karbala, Nasiriyah, and other southern cities. In Baghdad, Shiites rebel and loot the city. Thousands die and hundreds of thousands are made homeless. There are also uprisings in the north, which in Mosul also involves conflict among Arabs, Turkoman, Christians, and Kurds. In the north, Kurds "spontaneously" return to Kirkuk, and Arab settlers flee. Coalition forces move into Iraqi cities but in many places have no local authorities with whom they can work. Unwilling to take over police functions, the coalition can not quickly re-establish law and order.

I shared these views with the Pentagon planners, and I was not the only one. A stream of experts made much the same point, to no avail. Events unfolded pretty much as predicted.

Although I was an employee of the Department of Defense as a professor at the National War College, my views did not fit with the Pentagon neoconservatives' rosy assumptions about a unified Iraq and therefore I was only occasionally consulted.* Mostly, the Pentagon was interested in having me talk about the evils of Saddam Hussein's regime, including the gassing of the Kurds. (The Administration was more interested in making the political case for the war than they were in what would happen afterward.) But through these interactions as well as feedback from my Kurdish friends, I gained some insights into the planning process (if it could be called that), particularly as it related to the north. It did not inspire confidence.

In July 2002, I made a covert visit to Kurdistan to see the Kurdish leaders and make an assessment of the situation. By now, the Kurds thought war was likely and were actively preparing for it. General Babkir Zebari, a peshmerga since 1961, showed me the new recruits being drilled at a Kurdish training camp in Zawita, a village in the mountains near Turkey. The peshmerga were disciplined and highly motivated and knew the terrain. I was not impressed with their heavy weapons, a mélange of tanks, howitzers, and mortars captured from Iraq eleven years before. But if they were supplied with heavy weapons and had U.S. air support, I thought the peshmerga could be a potent ally against Saddam's armies. There were more than 100,000 peshmerga.

The Kurdish leaders worried that Saddam might retaliate for an American attack by using chemical weapons against them. They asked me to convey a request to the Pentagon leaders for gas masks, protective clothing, and atropine, an antidote for nerve gases. While in Kurdistan, I measured the runways and aprons of four of the five airstrips there.

I went to the Pentagon to describe what I had found and to discuss war-related issues. I raised four concerns: (1) the danger that Saddam

---

* No doubt my service in the Clinton Administration was also considered disqualifying.

might respond to an American invasion by using chemical weapons on Kurdish cities, (2) the risk of a Kurdish-Turkish war if the Pentagon proceeded with its plan to permit Turkish troops into northern Iraq, (3) minimizing postwar ethnic conflict in Kirkuk by putting in place a formula to speedily resolve Kurdish claims to property that was given to Arab settlers under Saddam's Arabization program, and (4) the likelihood of a total breakdown in law and order after the regime's collapse.

I passed on the request of Kurdistan's leaders for gas masks, protective gear, and medicines. With an invasion to remove Saddam from power likely to result in his death, he would have no reason not to use the chemical weapons we all presumed he still had. Iraq had no delivery systems capable of reaching the United States or Israel—his preferred targets—and chemical weapons were more an inconvenience than a threat to the well-equipped U.S. troops. This made Kurdish cities—the main ones within easy range of Iraqi artillery—the most plausible targets. My interlocutors at the Pentagon listened politely but did nothing. In October, the CIA flew Massoud Barzani and Jalal Talabani to the United States for a series of secret meetings, and they made the request for protective equipment directly to Secretary Rumsfeld and other senior officials.

In the end, the Administration said they would provide Barzani one thousand gas masks to protect the Kurdish leaders, their families, and bodyguards. Barzani refused the offer. Fortunately, Iraq did not have chemical weapons. If it had, the negligence that characterized all phases of the Iraq operation—aside from the actual military campaign itself—could have cost tens of thousands of additional lives.

Pentagon war plans involved a two-front campaign. The main American force would move north from Kuwait, skirting the southern Iraqi cities and pushing on to Baghdad. At the same time, the Army's 4th Infantry Division would move south from Turkey toward the capital. Turkey's government reluctantly agreed to the plan but demanded as a quid pro quo that Turkish troops be allowed to enter northern Iraq, ostensibly to stop refugees from fleeing all the way to Turkey. Turkey's demands obviously had nothing to do with refugees, since the territory in question was already under Kurdish control, and it was unthinkable that the Iraqi Army would counterattack north against the U.S. Army. Turkey wanted to be in northern Iraq so as to force the Kurds back under Baghdad's control in the postwar settlement. The Bush Administration was quite happy to accommodate its NATO ally in return for the 4th Infantry Division's transit rights.

The problem, as I explained at the Pentagon, was that the Kurds were not going to play dead while Turkey destroyed their freedom. They certainly were not fooled by Turkey's newfound concern for refugees. Barzani, whose peshmerga controlled the part of Kurdistan adjacent to Turkey, told me explicitly that his forces would fight an invading Turkish force.

In February 2003, Bush's Special Envoy Zalmay Khalilzad summoned Kurdish leaders to Ankara, and told them that, in spite of their objections, the United States agreed to Turkish troops in Iraqi Kurdistan. Khalilzad brushed off the angry protests. In the single-minded pursuit of their war plan, the Pentagon neoconservatives were willing to risk a war between their two allies, Turkey and the Kurds. Fortunately, the Turkish Parliament failed, by four votes, to allow U.S. troops to cross the country.

Kirkuk, I feared, was an ethnic time bomb that would explode once Saddam fell. Kirkuk city and the surrounding governorate are home to Kurds, Turcomans, Sunni Arabs, Shiite Arabs, Assyrians, and Chaldeans. For decades Kurds have claimed Kirkuk as part of Kurdistan—Kurdistan's 1992 constitution makes the city the region's capital—but Iraqi governments have refused to include Kirkuk in any Kurdish autonomous region, and for one main reason—oil. Kirkuk sits atop one of the world's largest oil fields, a field that first started producing oil in 1934 and still has more than ten billion barrels of recoverable reserves. In the 1980s, Saddam decided to make Kirkuk an Arab region by expelling Kurds and settling Arabs, mostly Shiites from southern Iraq, in their homes. After the Kurdish safe area was created in 1991, Saddam accelerated the pace of expulsions, sending Kurds from Kirkuk across the Green Line that separated government-controlled territory from Kurdish-controlled land. On the eve of war, tens of thousands of Kurds lived in tents and other makeshift housing just on the other side of the

Green Line from their previous homes. With Saddam's fall, I was concerned that angry Kurds would sweep back into the city, seize their old homes, and take revenge on the Arab settlers. Violence in Kirkuk could escalate even beyond Iraq's borders. Turkey, in its role as the self-appointed guardian of Kirkuk's Turcomans, might seize on ethnic violence in Kirkuk as the pretext to send in troops to block Kurdish ambitions.

Following my July 2002 trip to Kurdistan, I suggested to Wolfowitz that the U.S. establish a Kirkuk Property Commission to settle quickly those claims to confiscated Kurdish property. If displaced Kurds knew they could recover their homes legally, they might be persuaded not to take back their property by force.

For this idea to work, the commission needed to be in place, and publicized, at the time Kirkuk fell. This was the single piece of advice that I offered that the Pentagon seemed to accept. In December 2002, Bill Luti, who was deputy to Feith, pulled me aside after a meeting I had with Wolfowitz. They liked my idea, he said, and were setting up a Property Commission. Eighteen months later, the Property Commission had not begun its work.

Other aspects of the Pentagon's planning for Kirkuk were alarmingly vague. The week military operations began, I attended a small meeting with several Administration officials responsible for Kirkuk. I asked how they planned to maintain order—and prevent reverse ethnic cleansing by the Kurds—when the city fell. "We will rely on the local police," was the reply. I asked: "Are the local police Arabs, Kurds, or mixed?" None of the Administration officials knew. I was amazed since the facts about Kirkuk were not hard to discover and since the United States would in a matter of weeks be responsible for the city. Najmaldin Karim, the Kurdish-American neurosurgeon, was also at the meeting. He was from Kirkuk originally and explained that Kirkuk's police force was entirely Arab and had participated in the expulsion of the city's Kurds.

Not surprisingly, Kirkuk's police disappeared when American and Kurdish forces moved into the city on April 10. Unnoticed by the Americans and most of the media, Kurds did expel Arabs from some of the villages near the city. It could have been much worse. The Kurdish political parties took effective control of the city and used their influence, and peshmerga, to restrain the returnees.

The Bush Administration's failure to take postwar planning seriously was reflected in its casual—almost lackadaisical—approach to the staffing of the U.S. occupation administration that would follow Saddam's overthrow. Although the Administration had been planning the war for more than a year, Defense Secretary Rumsfeld, to whom Bush had assigned responsibility for postwar Iraq in preference to Colin Powell's State Department, only established an office for postwar administration on January 20, 2003. Called the Office for Reconstruction and Humanitarian Assistance (ORHA), it was tasked *both* with the humanitarian consequences of the war and the postwar administration of Iraq. Rumsfeld chose retired Army Lieutenant General Jay Garner to lead it. For a few months in the summer of 1991, Garner had run Operation Provide Comfort, the humanitarian relief effort for the Iraqi Kurds, and this made him a minor hero in Kurdistan. He had no other Middle East experience and no background in post-conflict nation-building. He did, however, have good connections with the neoconservatives whose views on Iraq he was thought to share.

Garner had less than two months to assemble an entire postwar administration. At the same time, he was distracted from this task by the necessity of preparing for a range of possible humanitarian disasters, and to assemble a staff for that purpose as well.

Given the importance of Iraq to Bush's presidency, one might have expected the Administration to have made a priority of finding Garner the best possible staff. But in fact the most qualified government professionals were specifically excluded from ORHA. According to Ambassador Tim Carney, who came out of retirement to serve briefly in ORHA, the State Department's professional Arabists "weren't welcome because they didn't think Iraq could be democratic." In a Pentagon of Pollyannas, a professional's understanding of the problems of Iraq was emphatically not wanted.

The State Department was not asked, nor did it offer, to break assignments of its most experienced foreign service officers to serve in Iraq. Garner had to recruit from the pool of retired foreign service officers (some quite elderly) or those without current diplomatic responsibilities. There were, to be sure, talented people in this group, but it was no way to staff an undertaking that would reshape the Middle East and define America's role in the world for a long time to come.

Conducted in haste, the recruitment process made little effort to match people with needed skills. In February 2003, Allen Keiswetter, a foreign service officer who was a colleague on the faculty of the National War College, got a call. Would he be interested in serving as Iraq's economy minister in the occupation administration?* He asked to think about it over the weekend. When he called back, he was told the Economy Ministry was filled, but would he be interested in another ministry? Taking measure of the operation at hand, he declined.

Around the same time, Robin Raphel, a former ambassador to Tunisia who was vice president of the National Defense University, was recruited to be Iraq's minister of trade, a position that put her in charge of food rations on which each Iraqi depended. Raphel, a career foreign service officer with no specific Iraq experience, had, by her own admission, no particular skills that qualified her for the administrative task she was to undertake. But at least she was a successful diplomat who had served as ambassador to an Arab country. Barbara Bodine, a controversial former ambassador to Yemen† who had served in Iraq and Kuwait, was pulled off a prolonged sabbatical at the University of California at Santa Barbara. Only after the invasion of Iraq was under way did the Bush Administration recruit Walter Slocombe, the under secretary for policy in Clinton's Defense Department, to supervise Iraq's military. (This was the single case of bipartisanship in an otherwise politically partisan occupation.) Less than a month after being selected and with no other Iraq experience, Slocombe helped dissolve the Iraqi military, a decision with profound consequences.

* Technically, the Americans were called "advisors" to their respective ministries. But since there were initially no ministers or other senior officials left, the advisors were the de facto ministers, and considered themselves as such.

† Bodine had tangled with the FBI team investigating the attack on the USS *Cole* in Aden in 2000.

For other positions, Garner pulled in his fellow retired officers—some simply looking for a bit of excitement to break a life of fishing and golf—or was stuck with political appointees long on ideological commitment and short on credentials. Aside from Ambassador Bodine, Garner's top administrators were a group stunningly short on Iraq experience.

Noah Feldman, a New York University law professor who advised Garner on constitutional issues in the occupation's early days, describes flying to Iraq in May 2003 with his fellow recruits.

> Pausing to take in the moment, I glanced around at my new colleagues. Those who were awake were reading intently. When I saw what they were reading, though, a chill crept over me, too. No one seemed to need a refresher on Iraq or the Gulf Region. Without exception, they were reading new books on the American occupation and reconstruction of Germany and Japan.

Germany and Japan are, of course, the gold standard of American-led nation-building. The victorious Americans led multiyear occupations that transformed two militaristic dictatorships into economically booming and highly stable democracies that transformed Europe and the Far East. The United States occupied Germany and Japan following years of war that the Germans and Japanese had started and in which they had been clearly and crushingly defeated. The United States had millions of troops in the European and Pacific theaters, and had planned the occupations for years. And, most important, Germany and Japan were real nations, ethnically and culturally homogeneous. Aside from some apt parallels between the Nazis and the Ba'ath Party, the American experience following World War II had almost no applicability to Iraq. But it did fit with the grand ambitions of the Bush Administration.

Larry Diamond, a fellow at the Hoover Institute, served with the Coalition Provisional Authority (CPA), the successor to ORHA. Like Feldman, he was struck by the ignorance of the Americans and by their indifference to it. In *Squandered Victory,* his account of his brief stint

with CPA, Diamond relates an encounter between an Iraqi and one occupation official.

> "You must have thoroughly studied the history of the
> British occupation of Iraq," the Iraqi said to the self-confident
> American.
> "Yes, I did," the latter replied.
> "I thought so," said the Iraqi, "because you seem determined
> to repeat every one of their mistakes."

The United States has paid a steep price for the Administration's
failure to plan for the postwar. The early mistakes, as we shall see, set
back the prospects for success and contributed to the present quagmire. Amazingly, the Administration learned little from those early
mistakes. The staffing of CPA was even less planned and less professional than that of ORHA. And, in spite of all experience to the contrary, the Americans in Iraq and in Washington continued to embrace
all the preconceptions they had before the war began.

The most durable preconception was that there was a single Iraq. In
August 2004, Condoleezza Rice, then the national security advisor,
spoke at Washington's United States Institute of Peace in what was
billed as a major address. Not long before, I had published an article titled "How to Get Out of Iraq," which had attracted a certain amount of
attention in policy circles as an alternative strategy for Iraq, and I was
invited to hear Rice in the expectation I would ask a question.

Alas, the speech was so banal that I couldn't think of a question.
Then Qubad Talabani, Jalal Talabani's son and the PUK representative
in Washington, raised his hand. Explaining that he was speaking on
behalf of the Kurdish people, he thanked Rice for "a leading role in liberating our country" and then asked why Kurdistan was being short-
changed in the allocation of U.S. reconstruction assistance, noting
"this is sending the wrong message to your allies in Iraq . . . the Kurds
[who] are spearheading the democratic movement in Iraq."

Rice replied that she couldn't discuss the specifics of aid going to the north, but then offered the following assessment:

> But what has been impressive to me so far is that Iraqis—whether Kurds or Shia or Sunni or the many other ethnic groups in Iraq— have demonstrated that they really want to live as one in a unified Iraq. And I think particularly the Kurds have shown a propensity to want to bridge differences that were historic differences in many ways that were fueled by Saddam Hussein and his regime.

Was this her understanding of interethnic relations in Iraq nearly sixteen months after the United States took over the country? I asked her how she reconciled this supposed Kurdish commitment to Iraq with the fact that 1.7 million Kurds—80 percent of Kurdistan's adults—had recently signed a petition asking for a vote on independence.

Rice noted, "Such referenda on independence have taken place in lots of places, including, for instance, Canada to our north." She added, "And so what I have found interesting and I think important is the degree to which the leaders of the Shia and Kurdish and Sunni communities have continually expressed their desire to have a unified Iraq."

I knew every Kurdish leader that Rice had met with, and I knew not one wanted a unified Iraq. It was not as if the ground truth in Kurdistan was hard to discover. Even a casual visitor to Erbil, Kurdistan's capital, notices the Kurdistan flag that flies everywhere, and that the Iraqi flag does not fly at all. (It is banned.) Crossing from Turkey into Kurdistan, the visitor's papers are processed by officials of the Kurdistan Regional Government, and the Iraqi visa requirement does not apply. Kurdistan has its own army and does not allow the new Iraqi Army on its territory. Nor do the Kurds hide their views of Iraq. They hate the country and are not shy about saying so. Understanding this does not require sophisticated analysis. All Rice needed to do was imagine how an American would feel about a country that had gassed you, destroyed your home, and executed hundreds of thousands of your kinsmen—and which you never wanted to be a part of in the first place.

Modern Iraq was built on an unpromising foundation. The Kurds did not want to be part of it at all, while Arabs were divided between the minority but dominant Sunnis, and the majority Shiites. There are, of course, successful multiethnic and multireligious states, including the United States. They work best when the ethnic communities are all mixed together, as in the United States or, as in India, where no one community dominates the state. In Iraq, each of the three main constituent communities—Kurds, Sunni Arabs, and Shiites—had a geographic space that was historically associated, more or less, with the three Ottoman valiyets from which Iraq was created.*

Iraq was one of four multiethnic and/or multireligious states that were assembled at the end of the First World War. The others tried to resolve the nationality problem by giving each group a territory where its language and culture would be dominant. They also included some elements of power sharing at the center. Iraq's dominant Sunni Arabs neither respected the others' desire to run their own affairs nor were prepared to share power.

Between the two world wars, power sharing between Czechs and Slovaks made democratic Czechoslovakia the success story in Eastern Europe. After 1948, Josip Broz Tito's elaborate construct of six republics and two autonomous regions not only held Yugoslavia together, but enabled the country to resist Stalin and thrive as a pro-Western communist state. Tito's Yugoslavia even developed a "Yugoslav" identity among some of its constituent peoples (the Serbs and Bosnian Muslims) and it survived a full decade after its founder's demise on May 4, 1980. The third multiethnic European state to emerge from World War I was the fifteen-republic Soviet Union, a state that endured the loss of some 20 million people in World War II and then competed with the United States for global domination for nearly a half century.

At least for a time, Czechoslovakia, Yugoslavia, and (less clearly) the Soviet Union were viable multinational states. Democracy, when it

* The major exceptions were the Shiite holy cities of Najaf and Karbala that were part of the Sunni Baghdad valiyet and Arab Mosul in the Kurdish Mosul valiyet.

came to Eastern Europe in 1989, destroyed Yugoslavia (1991), the Soviet Union (1991), and Czechoslovakia (1993). In each case, nationalism overcame loyalty to the larger entity.

The Bush Administration assumed that Iraq—the least successful
of these post–World War I states—was exempt from the forces that in
the end destroyed its European counterparts. It was an absurd proposition. Perhaps the architects of the Iraq policy believed that if they
talked in terms of an Iraqi people they would help create one.

Where the realities of Iraq conflicted with the Administration's
hopes, the facts were ignored. Charles Freeman, who served as President George H. W. Bush's ambassador to Saudi Arabia, put it this way:
"We invaded not Iraq but the Iraq of our dreams, a country that didn't
exist, that we didn't understand. And it is therefore not surprising that
we knocked the kaleidoscope into a new pattern that we find surprising. The ignorant are always surprised."

CHAPTER 6

Aftermath

I hope I am not responsible for Armageddon." Brian Ross from ABC News and I were talking to a Marine lieutenant in front of Baghdad's Central Public Health Laboratory. The day before, on April 16, 2003, the lieutenant and his platoon had watched as looters ransacked the building. They took vials containing black fever, polio, HIV, and cholera. These were not biological weapons, but so-called "dual use" items. They could be used to manufacture biological weapons, but they had legitimate uses for medical research. While the Security Council prohibited Iraq from possessing biological weapons and other WMD, it was allowed to keep some dual-use items. Since these could be diverted to weapons programs, they were subject to frequent U.N. inspection. Inspectors had visited the building before being expelled in 1998, and again in December 2002.

While the inspectors found no evidence that the biological samples at the laboratory had been diverted to a weapons program, the Bush Administration was deeply suspicious. On February 5, 2003, Secretary of State Colin Powell warned the United Nations Security Council about the grave danger posed by Iraqi research into biological agents: "But Iraq's research efforts did not stop there. Saddam Hussein has investigated dozens of biological agents causing diseases such as gas gangrene, plague, typhus, tetanus, cholera, camelpox and hemorrhagic fever, and he also has the wherewithal to develop smallpox."

This research, which was deemed a reason for war, took place at the Public Health Laboratory, as both the United Nations and the United

After Iraq attacked their villages with poison gas at the end of August 1988, 60,000 Kurds fled to Turkey. I interviewed them two weeks later in the high mountains of southeast Turkey.

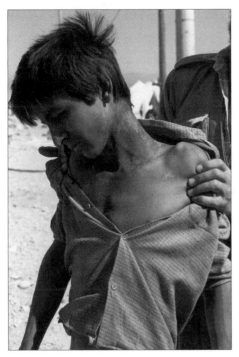

Bashir Shemseddin from Vermil village had burns characteristic of mustard gas.

During the 1991 Kurdish uprising, I attended a meeting on March 30 with Jalal Talabani (fourth from left) and local leaders in Dahuk.

The joy at liberation was premature when this photo was taken in Zakho on March 30. When the Iraqi Army attacked the next day, Mohid (right) got me safely across the Tigris to Syria.

On March 30, Kurdish leader Sami Abdul Rahman was back in Dahuk for the first time since the 1960s. He died in the suicide bombing of the KDP offices in Erbil on February 1, 2004.

When the uprising collapsed on March 31, 1991, Kurds fled to the mountains for safety. The lucky ones got a ride.

Families rested in mountain meadows on March 31. For the children, it was still an adventure.

By the end of April, dysentery and exposure had taken their toll on the refugees camped on the steep mountainsides at the Turkish border. These men are digging the grave of a child relative.

Stuffed into grain bags in a destroyed school near the Iranian border are some of the 14 tons of captured Iraqi secret police documents that Jalal Talabani entrusted to my care.

A woman holds pictures of her sons who were taken by Saddam's regime along with 5,000 other men and boys from the Barzani tribe. In 2005, Kurds found the graves containing some of them.

A peshmerga holds up a girl's garments in the raping room of the Suleimania secret police headquarters.

Taimor Abdul, then twelve years old, was the sole survivor of the 1988 mass execution of hundreds of women and children, including his mother and three sisters. He told me his story in September 1991.

In Halabja in 1991, a peshmerga showed me where a Kurdish man was found dead with a swaddled infant in his arms after the March 16, 1988, chemical weapons attack on the city. The photograph of the man and child alerted the world to Iraq's use of poison gas on the Kurds.

Near Halabja's cemetery, a peshmerga uncovers the skulls of two children who died in the gas attacks.

Ten days after Baghdad fell in April 2003, a looter took an office chair from Iraq's unguarded Foreign Ministry. The soot is from fires set by looters.

A man throws his shoes at a giant portrait of Saddam in Baghdad a few days after U.S. troops ousted the dictator.

With his foot on the just-toppled statue of Saddam at Iraq's Trade Ministry, this ex-soldier shows me his partially amputated ear. Ear amputation was the usual punishment for desertion.

I saw Ahmad Chalabi at the Baghdad Hunt Club the day he returned to his native city for the first time in thirty-five years.

Ayad Allawi (second from left), later to become Iraq's first post-Saddam Prime Minister, met me at his commandeered headquarters in Baghdad in April 2003.

In April 2005, Jalal Talabani (left) became the first-ever democratically elected Iraqi head of state. In June 2005, Massoud Barzani (right) became the first President of Kurdistan. It was an amazing turn of events for two friends whose cause had once seemed hopeless.

In April 2003, I joined Shiites on a pilgrimage to Karbala. They wanted me to know they were Iraq's majority and intended to rule.

The day Saddam's rule collapsed in the south in April 2003, local people broke down the dams that had dried out Iraq's marshes. When I visited ten months later, the reeds were coming back and so were some Marsh Arabs.

These children, celebrating Saddam's overthrow atop a destroyed Iraqi tank near Kirkuk, will probably be the first generation of Kurds to reach adulthood in their own country.

States intelligence community knew. Still, the Bush Administration had no plans to keep deadly materials out of the wrong hands. The looters entered the laboratory one full week after American troops took over Baghdad. The Marines had watched the looting from a hospital next door. The lieutenant explained, "Nobody told me what was there."

That night, I observed in my diary, "Obviously this was a major screw-up, of which there have been too many. How could a campaign be so poorly planned in its final phase? 1991 redux."

Tuwaitha is a sprawling complex south of Baghdad where Iraq once did its research into nuclear power and nuclear weapons. After the first Gulf War, the International Atomic Energy Agency (IAEA) supervised the destruction of some of the nuclear-related materials at Tuwaitha while making a careful inventory of other materials that were then secured with IAEA seals. Among the IAEA-monitored materials at the complex were barrels containing "yellowcake," unprocessed uranium that, when enriched, is the fissile material for a nuclear bomb. Tuwaitha and its contents were well known to American intelligence. But, in case U.S. officials failed to appreciate the potential dangers at Tuwaitha, IAEA Director General Mohamed ElBaradei personally told American diplomats in Vienna on April 10, 2003, of the "need to secure the nuclear material stored at Tuwaitha."

When U.S. troops arrived at Tuwaitha, the yellowcake was in a locked warehouse that had been secured by the IAEA before the inspectors left at the start of the war. While U.S. troops were actually at Tuwaitha, looters broke into the warehouse. They took the barrels and apparently dumped the yellowcake. Almost two tons went missing. In his 2003 State of the Union address, President Bush said Iraq's efforts to acquire yellowcake from Niger were so dangerous that they justified a war, even though the intelligence about Iraq's Niger connection was transparently fraudulent. Yet his Administration did not consider Iraq's actual stockpile of yellowcake important enough to justify ordering U.S. troops at the location to protect it.

In early April, U.S. troops had arrived at al-Qaqaa, a large facility thirty miles south of Baghdad. The bunkers at the complex contained

194 metric tons of High Melting Point Explosive (HMX) and 141 metric tons of Rapid Detonation Explosive (RDX). High explosives, like RDX and HMX, are used to implode a uranium or plutonium sphere and thus trigger a chain reaction leading to a nuclear explosion. "Fat Boy," the plutonium bomb dropped on Nagasaki in 1945, used one ton of high explosives. While Iraq acquired RDX and HMX for its nuclear program in the 1980s, the explosives are also used for construction and other civilian purposes. Rather than destroy these stockpiles, the IAEA monitored them in the 1990s. After Iraq agreed to resume inspections in 2002, ElBaradei ordered his inspectors back to al-Qaqaa, and reported to the Security Council in January 2003 on the stockpiles' status. Immediately after Saddam's fall, the IAEA expressed its concern about the physical security of the explosives to U.S. diplomats at its Vienna headquarters.

In spite of these warnings, U.S. troops left the al-Qaqaa bunkers unguarded. In the months that followed, looters removed the RDX, the HMX, and 5.8 metric tons of PETN, a third explosive. This was no small operation. Removing so much material would have required at least forty ten-ton trucks.

High-precision machine tools are another dual-use item essential to the manufacture of nuclear weapons.* After the U.S. takeover of Iraq, this machinery disappeared from locations the Bush Administration failed to secure. In October 2004, the IAEA reported "widespread and apparently systematic dismantlement that has taken place at sites previously relevant to Iraq's nuclear program." Using heavy machinery, organized gangs took apart, according to the IAEA, "entire buildings that housed high-precision equipment."

In some cases, the looters probably did not know what they were taking. Those who raided the Tuwaitha warehouse wanted the barrels to store rainwater. Those who attacked the Central Public Health Lab-

---

* High explosives are dual-use because they can also be used in construction projects. For this reason, the U.N. inspectors did not insist that the high explosives or precision machinery be destroyed, but rather that they be monitored to ensure no illegal diversion took place.

oratory also probably did not know what they had taken. Since the sites were left unguarded, however, it is impossible to have complete confidence that dangerous materials did not end up in the hands of those with sinister motives.

The looting of high-precision machinery from sites related to Iraq's defunct nuclear program and the removal of RDX and HMX from al-Qaqaa were well organized and took place over many months. There is no hard evidence as to what happened to these materials. Insurgents, peshmerga, and Shiite militias were collecting weapons and explosives from unguarded military depots all over Iraq for months after Saddam fell. Iranian agents were in southern and central Iraq after the war. Iran would have had a keen interest in acquiring high-precision machinery for its nuclear program, and the looted Iraqi equipment would have been particularly attractive since it could not be traced. Iran would have had access to al-Qaqaa, which is located in a part of Iraq controlled by its allies. Sunni insurgents, presumably linked to Saddam's regime and therefore knowledgeable about the facility, might also have taken the explosives, since they are an ideal weapon for terrorism. Less than a pound of RDX brought down Pan Am Flight 103 over Lockerbie, Scotland, in 1988.

In February 2003, Brian Ross, the head of ABC's investigative team, interviewed me in the library of the National War College about Saddam's sadistic eldest son, Uday, a serial rapist who ran Iraq's Olympic Committee. While the camera crew set up, I told Brian and his producer, Rhonda Schwartz, about the eighteen tons of Iraqi documents the Kurds had captured in 1991. As incriminating as they were, they were the files of the provincial offices of Saddam's security services. Presumably much more could be found in Baghdad when it fell. Brian decided the investigative team should go to Baghdad as soon as possible after the regime's fall. He and Rhonda asked me to come as an ABC News consultant. As my trip was more than a bit unorthodox for a professor at the National War College (and therefore an employee of the Defense Department), I checked it with Wolfowitz, who thought, as did I, that it was important to focus attention on the horrors of the ousted regime.*

Just before midnight on April 13, 2003, we left our Amman, Jordan, hotel in a convoy of SUVs for the Iraq border with the plan of crossing at first light. The border complex was vast on both sides—thousands of parking spaces and hundreds of inspection bays—and totally deserted. Just inside Iraq, American soldiers glanced at our press credentials and we then proceeded across Iraq's western desert toward Baghdad. The drive was probably the most dangerous part of the trip. The Jordanian drivers whom ABC had hired earned one thousand dollars per trip— more than a typical month's salary—and they wanted to make as many as possible. The routine was to leave Baghdad in the early morning, arrive in Amman around 11 P.M., and almost immediately turn back for Baghdad. The drivers slept only every other night, and in Baghdad, which was not always restful. As he sped across Iraq's western desert at 140 kilometers an hour, the driver of my SUV kept slapping his face to stay awake.

Outside Fallujah, we stopped. A car had gone off the road, and two bodies lay next to it. U.S. Army Black Hawks hovered overhead. I feared an ambush. (The coalition had not yet taken over Fallujah.) The journalists in our convoy responded as journalists do when faced with danger: they got out their cameras and filmed. It was a blown tire, not fighting, that took the lives of two Argentine journalists we had seen earlier that morning at the Jordanian border. Within a few months, insurgents would make the Jordan highway far too dangerous for foreigners to attempt at all.

Except for the looters and a few American troops, no one was on the streets in Baghdad when we arrived. As we drove into the city, we passed looters pushing furniture along the side of the road and, in one instance, watched as a man struggled to load a Xerox copier onto a city bus. Everywhere smoke poured out of government buildings, shopping malls, and banks. A few government offices, such as the Defense

---

* I did not speak directly to Wolfowitz on this, but communicated through one of his assistants.

Ministry and a telecommunications center, were still smoldering after being hit by American bombs, but most of the fires were set by looters after the American takeover.

We headed to the Sheraton, the hotel I had stayed in in 1984. Like Baghdad, the Sheraton was much the worse for wear. Only one of the lobby's glass elevators worked, intermittently. The hotel restaurant had no food, so we made arrangements with a local kebab shop for lamb, french fries, and salad, a daily fare that did not vary. The pool, where stewardesses had bathed topless in 1984, was a mixture of garbage and green slime. I had the impression that my room had not been cleaned in the intervening nineteen years.

In the first week after Saddam fell, Baghdad was chaotic but not dangerous. In the city of five million, all authority had vanished. There was no government, no army, and no police. At night, Baghdad was dark, except for the glow of the fires, the occasional car headlight, and the few buildings whose proprietors had had the foresight to get generators. American troops, stationed at traffic circles and overpasses, seemed swallowed up by the size of the city for which they were now responsible.

The day after I arrived, I went to Firdos Square to look at the fallen Saddam statue. A man had his small grandson pick some flowers for me. Near a street market, I photographed young men as they threw shoes at a gigantic portrait of Saddam Hussein, hitting it with the sole of the shoe being the ultimate gesture of disrespect. In front of the Trade Ministry, a man ground his foot into the ear of a toppled Saddam statue. Grinning, he pointed to his own ear, which was missing the top half. Saddam's regime routinely punished army deserters by amputating an ear.

In those early days, there was no sign of anger at the Americans, even from the war's victims. Brian Ross and I went to Mansour, a fashionable, predominantly Sunni Arab residential district of Baghdad, where the U.S. Air Force had destroyed on April 7 three houses with earth-burrowing bombs based on an intelligence report that Saddam was hiding in bunkers underneath. Eighteen people died in the attack, including children, and the blasts had terrified the neighbors. The houses had been built in the 1950s, and there was no more recent construction work to indicate anything had been constructed underneath. We filmed without encountering any anger or feeling any threat. Several neighbors invited us into their houses.

There were poignant scenes, reminders of the evils of the ousted regime. In our search for documents, we went first to the headquarters of Iraq's military intelligence, one of a very few buildings secured by the American military. Middle-aged Iraqi men beseeched the Americans—sitting far above them in their sixty-ton tanks—to be let in. One man showed me his photograph posing with his two brothers. They had been arrested two decades earlier. He had been released, one brother had been executed, and the third condemned to death but the family never heard if the sentence had been carried out. They now hoped to find out. Another man was looking for a brother he had not seen since 1981 when, at age 20, the brother had made the mistake of talking too freely to a Yemeni guest worker, who had reported him. I was struck by the contrast in the appearance of the men before me and the youthful faces in the often faded photographs of the missing, who were usually an older brother or cousin. Some of the men believed their relatives were still in underground prisons on the compound, and were frantic for the Americans to start looking for the hidden cells. If they waited too long, the relative might starve. In fact, most of the missing had not been heard from since a 1981 purge.

At the Iraqi Olympic Committee, until a few days earlier the personal fiefdom of Uday Hussein, I talked to a one-legged man from a poor Shiite neighborhood who was supervising friends and family as they loaded windows and scrap metal salvaged from the partially burnt building onto two donkey carts. He told me he had lost his leg "to the first Bush" when he was a soldier participating in the attack on the Saudi town of Khafji in February 1991. He blamed Saddam for not helping him. One of his companions pointed out the basement cells where Uday imprisoned and tortured athletes who failed to perform to his expectations.

Clearly many Baghdad residents were glad that Saddam was gone. Regardless of how they felt about having the Americans be the ones to topple the regime, most Iraqis now hoped the traumas of the previous twenty-five years were over. Thanks to the looting, there was a growing sense that this might not be true. On the evening of April 15, I wrote in my diary: "As I look over Baghdad I fear the U.S. will be in for a very rough time. There is no real sense of liberation in this dark, empty, frightened city. If that is the case today, what will it be like in 3 months?"

Our ABC team had no difficulty finding documents. At Uday Hussein's house on the banks of the Tigris, Bob Bauer, a retired CIA agent who was also an ABC News consultant, found the personnel records of the Saddam Fedayeen, the guerrilla force that had carried out deadly ambushes against American troops advancing on Baghdad. It later became a pillar of the insurgency. We also found Uday's medical files, which contained correspondence with a British specialist about the medical consequences of alcohol liver disease.

Across Firdos Square from the Sheraton, we found a principal Iraqi center for wiretaps and other electronic eavesdropping. Behind a set of doors and a false wall, we discovered a staircase and rooms stuffed with transcripts of conversations, including intercepts of U.N. and foreign embassies' communications. The Iraqi intelligence services even spied on each other and there were tapes of their conversations. Brian played some of the tapes on the air and Bob read translated excerpts from the transcripts.

Squatters told us they had been told to burn the papers by a nocturnal Iraqi visitor, who they presumed was from Saddam's intelligence services. I called Wolfowitz's office in the hope he could arrange protection for the transcripts. I also offered to turn over the Saddam Fedayeen files. Nothing happened. Even though the Sheraton was surrounded by U.S. troops, the deputy secretary of defense's office could not arrange a pickup of the Fedayeen documents. One would have thought it might be useful to have the names and home addresses of people already attacking U.S. troops. Of course, they did not protect the transcripts.

The most disgraceful episode of looting took place at the Iraq National Museum. On April 11—two days after Saddam's regime collapsed and the United States became legally responsible for Baghdad— looters attacked the museum. The museum housed artifacts going back to the beginning of human civilization and included the remnants of such fabled civilizations as Babylon, Ur, Sumer, and Assyria. Without doubt, it was one of the most important archaeological collections in the world, conserving not just the heritage of Iraq but of all mankind. American archaeologists knew the museum was at risk in a war, and they had repeatedly urged the Pentagon to protect it. Just before the war, Lamia Gailani, an archaeologist on the museum's staff, went to the U.S. State Department to warn that looting was a certainty. The State Department sent the Pentagon a list of fifty sites that should be protected in Baghdad, and the museum was number two on the list (at the top of the list were the paper records of Saddam's regime, the very materials I saw scattered in government ministries and intelligence headquarters). No protection was provided to the museum.

As the looters attacked, the museum staff begged for help from Marines at a nearby traffic circle. Although they were just one hundred yards away, they refused to help.* While the staff had packed away many display items, some of the most valuable objects were either too large or too fragile to move. Thirty-eight of the museum's most important pieces were stolen, and others were smashed. The looters broke into the storage rooms in the basement, and stole thousands of items including more than five thousand cylinder seals, which are the record of some of the world's earliest writing. To the intense embarrassment of the Bush Administration, the media jumped on the museum story.

I arrived at the museum on the morning of April 15, the day the Marines were finally deployed to protect the building. The museum's director, a stout Assyrian named Dony George, took me around. Statues and ancient vases lay in shards on the floor: storage cases were turned upside down. A spectacular statue from Hatra of a seated woman in Hellenistic style was missing its head. The museum library and many of its records were destroyed. Without documentation, an ancient tablet goes from being critical to understanding mankind's

---

* Obviously it was not their fault. They had no orders to safeguard Iraqi property and could have gotten into deep trouble had they moved from their position without authorization, especially if they then had to use force at the museum.

distant past to being a lump of clay with some scratches on it, George explained. He was devastated by the loss of the cylinder seals, but also of thousands of objects from more recent excavations that had not been catalogued.

Rumsfeld made matters worse when he belittled the loss as a bit of "untidiness" and then complained about television repeatedly running the same video of a man taking a vase. (Rumsfeld made so many injudicious statements about Iraq that I came to wonder why he felt it necessary for the secretary of defense to have a daily press conference, something none of his predecessors did.)

The Administration later tried to downplay what happened. Wolfowitz later told the Senate Foreign Relations Committee that all but thirty-eight of the stolen objects had been recovered, a deceit that omitted thousands of smashed artifacts and objects stolen from the storerooms, including the cylinder seal collection. He also failed to mention that those thirty-eight items included some of the museum's greatest treasures.

Looters burned the Iraq National Library, which held ancient manuscripts, an edition of every book published in Iraq, and every newspaper printed in Baghdad since the mid-nineteenth century. In effect, the looters erased the documentary record of Iraq's recent history. Iraq's Museum of Fine Arts lost most of its collection.

By not protecting Iraq's museums and National Library, the Administration failed in its legal duty as an occupying power to safeguard the country's cultural heritage. This was a consequence of an Administration too arrogant to listen to experts, so at war with its own State Department as to ignore its professional guidance, and ignorant or indifferent to international law. It is no excuse to say that Iraqis did the looting. The looting was the inevitable consequence of the breakdown of law and order that followed the regime's collapse.

Over the three weeks I was in Iraq, I went unchallenged into many important Iraqi buildings and facilities. These included the Foreign Ministry, the Trade Ministry, the former Royal Palace, the Iraqi Olympic Committee headquarters, Mosul University, Uday Hussein's house, prisons, arms depots, and intelligence facilities. Looters were at work in every building I visited but not once did I have any sense of danger. On the contrary, they were friendly, and several asked me to take their pictures as they carted off public property. At the Foreign Ministry, they helped the ABC investigative team collect documents and floppy disks, at times using original treaties from the underground vaults for torches. (I rescued several treaties, including one signed by Nehru and another by Tito, and left them with Barham Salih in Kurdistan.)

Many of the sites I visited had obvious intelligence value, and there were many more American troops in Baghdad than ABC journalists. Yet neither the Pentagon nor the CIA seems to have made any effort to mine these sites for intelligence. As part of its case for war, the Bush Administration alleged that Iraq was covertly acquiring materials for weapons of mass destruction (like the yellowcake from Niger) while Vice President Cheney insisted Saddam's embassies were in contact with al-Qaeda. The Foreign Ministry would have been a logical place to find documents relating to Iraq's foreign intelligence activities and to procurement of forbidden materials. But looters were the only people I saw prying open foreign ministry safes. They were visibly disappointed to find the safes held documents and not money.

Eventually, the new Iraqi authorities did find important documents in the Foreign Ministry. These included records of those who received bribes from Iraq under the scandal-ridden U.N. Oil-for-Food program and a list of foreign jihadists who had come to Iraq before the war. One wonders how much more information would have been recovered if the building had been secured.

What I saw was incompetence. The American servicemen and women who took Baghdad were professionals—disciplined, courteous, task-oriented. Unfortunately, their political masters were so focused on making the case for the war, so keen to vanquish their political foes at home, so certain that Iraqis would embrace American-style democracy, and so blinded by their ideology that they failed to plan even for the most obvious tasks following military victory.

The U.S. occupation never recovered from the early chaos. As a practical matter, the looting of government ministries and power stations meant it was impossible to restore essential services for months and in some cases for more than a year. As Iraqis sat in their homes—idle because their workplaces had been destroyed or there was no power to run their factories—they blamed the occupier.

The Bush Administration has said its failure to restore law and order in Baghdad was because the military campaign went much more quickly than foreseen. Even if more troops had been sent to Iraq, as recommended by General Shinseki, it would not have mattered, the argument goes, because the speed of operations meant only a small force was available to enter Baghdad. This argument is dishonest.

Even with the troops available in Baghdad on April 9, the United States could have protected the archaeological museum, the National Library, and twenty of the most important ministries. The United States protected nothing because the secretary of defense and his top aides never thought protecting public property—or maintaining public order—in Iraq was important. The president never thought about it at all.

Rumsfeld did think the Oil Ministry was important, and as I passed it on April 15, I saw an American tank and a handful of troops stationed in its walled compound. Nearby, the Ministry of Irrigation burned, destroying the plans and blueprints for Iraq's dams, barrages, pumping stations, and thousands of kilometers of canals. The implications were obvious. Oil was a priority, but the water on which millions of Iraqis depended was not. Many Iraqis had the same thought.

Iraqis had two views of the looting. They saw a United States that was either too incompetent to keep order or so evil as to desire the country's physical destruction. Either view made resistance a logical response. It is not exaggerating to say that the United States may have lost the war on the very day it took Baghdad, April 9, 2003.

On my return to Washington in May, I spent an hour at the Pentagon briefing Paul Wolfowitz on what I had seen in Iraq. My account of the looting of government ministries and of sites with dangerous materials visibly upset Wolfowitz. I hoped his anger was directed at the planning failures I was describing but I realized he was angry with me for being critical. After that meeting neither Wolfowitz nor his staff returned my phone calls and I had no further contact with the Pentagon. I left the U.S. government five months later.

CHAPTER 7

Can't Provide Anything

Although he was supposed to be Iraq's postwar ruler, Jay Garner remained in Kuwait until April 21, twelve days after American troops took over Baghdad. General Tommy Franks refused him clearance and Garner had not insisted. By the time he arrived, Baghdad was chaotic, his authority in Iraq sapped, and his credibility diminished with his Washington masters.

On April 22, Garner and some members of his team flew to Dukan, a Kurdistan resort on an artificial lake on the Lesser Zab River, to meet with Jalal Talabani and Massoud Barzani. Garner wanted the Kurdish leaders to help form an interim Iraqi government that would assume responsibility for the country in a matter of weeks. The nucleus for such a government existed. In December 2002, the Iraqi opposition had met at the Metropol Hilton in London to discuss Iraq's future. The opposition parties had chosen a seven-man Iraqi Leadership Council (ILC) to speak for them. It was made up of the two Kurdish leaders, Talabani and Barzani; leaders from the two leading Shiite religious parties, Abdul Aziz al-Hakim of SCIRI and Ibrahim Jaafari of Dawa; secular Arab leaders Ahmad Chalabi of the Iraqi National Congress and Ayad Allawi of the Iraqi National Accord; and Naseer Chaderchi, a Sunni Arab lawyer who headed the secular National Democratic Party. The ILC represented well Iraq's Shiites and Kurds but not the Sunni Arabs who were mostly opposed to regime change. (Chaderchi had no significant support.)

At that London conference in 2002, the intention was to form an alternative Iraqi government that could take over quickly after the regime fell. (Although described in the press as a government-in-exile, it was not so technically since it would be based initially in Kurdistan.) Following instructions from the State Department, the president's special envoy to the Iraqi opposition, Zalmay Khalilzad, had strongly opposed the formation of an alternative government. In light of that, Chalabi pushed the opposition leaders to agree on principles and modalities for a government. Khalilzad thwarted that effort as well.

So, as Garner set out to form a government, in April 2003, he was faced with the consequences of the earlier State Department opposition to an interim government. Even though the Iraqi political parties had come together to oppose Saddam, they were not united. The Shiites wanted an Islamic state, the Kurds wanted to preserve the de facto independence of Kurdistan, and the Arab secularists wanted a strong central government that they would dominate. Agreeing on a common program and allocating positions in a government would take time. And, as Chalabi had well understood in London, this was more easily accomplished when regime change was a theoretical prospect than when the parties were dividing up the spoils in Baghdad.

On April 23, the day after the Dukan meeting, Garner and his team helicoptered to Erbil for a lunch with Barzani, which I attended. Post-conflict environments are rife with rumor and misunderstanding, making communication and public information essential. Handling these functions for Garner was Margaret Tutwiler, an assistant secretary of state for public affairs in the first Bush Administration and, since 2001, U.S. ambassador to Morocco. She had never heard of the Anfal and undiplomatically said so in front of her hosts, who knew that the Anfal had taken place when she was the State Department's chief spokesperson. Garner left retired Major General Bruce Moore to take charge of the north. Talabani hosted a dinner the next night for Moore, who spent part of the evening bad-mouthing Tutwiler and Barbara Bodine, the hard-charging diplomat responsible for the Baghdad region. Moore was incredulous when I suggested that the Kurds were not going to give up the peshmerga. "But that's not what Talabani told Garner," he replied. I could see Garner's mission was in deep trouble.

At the Baghdad Convention Center on April 28, Garner hosted some three hundred fifty Iraqis to discuss a future government. A poorly prepared conclave did not make much sense but he had to accommodate those in the Administration who were insisting on involving nonexile Iraqis. Garner conducted the meeting without any agenda as he tried to engage very disparate communities with no experience in political dialogue. The meeting broke down in chaos. Talabani and Barzani made their triumphant entry into Baghdad that same day—I drove in the convoy from Kurdistan with them—but it was too late to influence the process.

On May 5, Garner announced he would form the nucleus of an interim Iraqi government within ten days. The Pentagon, for whom Garner worked, wanted to turn power over to the Iraqis as quickly as possible. This would mean forming a coalition of Kurds and the former exiles who led the Shiite religious parties with strong representation from secular Shiite exiles like Chalabi and Allawi.* Unfortunately for Garner, though the Pentagon's position was clear, the Administration had not decided whether it wanted an interim government. Some factions in the Administration wanted a "more inclusive" Iraqi government. The State Department was keen to give the major role to non-Ba'athist Iraqi leaders from within the country. But State could not identify many such insiders since, of course, the brutality of Saddam's regime had prevented the emergence of non-Ba'athist leaders except those in exile or in Kurdistan. Forming a more inclusive government inevitably would mean a longer and more robust occupation government.

Among the foreign policy professionals, there was a desire to broaden international participation in the postwar governance of Iraq, and to bring in the United Nations, both because of its expertise and because it provided legitimacy. A more ideologically charged faction within the Administration desired an American-led remake of Iraq on the model of postwar Germany and Japan. In their view, the new Iraq

* This is the governing coalition that emerged from Iraq's January 2005 election, which the Sunni Arab minority boycotted.

should have a free-market economy, a flat tax, privatized industry, a privatized oil sector, a new educational system, a NATO-style military, and a nonethnic, nonsectarian democratic government. Intoxicated by the rapid military victory over Saddam, and oblivious to the disaster already taking place on the ground, Rumsfeld and many of the all-important neoconservatives were moving to adopt this ambitious agenda.

Although the debate on Iraq's future had been raging for months within the Administration and in the newspapers, the issue of how Iraq would be governed had not gone to the president for a decision. As a consequence, the rival factions within the Administration pursued diametrically opposed policies. Either a rapid turnover to selected Iraqis *or* a robust occupation would have been a plausible strategy but *both* were not. In an administration with a less casual approach to national security, the president would have decided the basic questions of Iraq's postwar governance before the war. Bush, however, never decided the matter.

At the end of April, Rumsfeld told Garner that his services were no longer required. John Sawers, the British ambassador to Egypt who was in Baghdad as the eyes and ears of British Prime Minister Tony Blair, cabled Downing Street about the change: "Garner's outfit, ORHA, is an unbelievable mess. No leadership, no strategy, no coordination, no structure, and inaccessible to ordinary Iraqis. . . . Garner and his top team of 60-year-old retired Generals are well-meaning but out of their depth." The British used professionals in Iraq and saw the occupation disaster much sooner than the ideologues in the Pentagon and the White House. Blair, uniquely, was a foreigner that the Bush Administration could not afford to ignore.

To replace Garner, Rumsfeld contacted L. Paul Bremer III, known as Jerry, to ask if he was interested in being Iraq's postwar administrator. Although the Administration asserted that the change from Garner to a permanent administrator was always part of a plan, Bremer says in his memoir, *My Year in Iraq,* that he had just two weeks from when he was asked to take the job until he arrived in Baghdad. With the transition from Garner to Bremer, ORHA was dissolved and the Coalition Provisional Authority was established in its place.

In some ways, Bremer was an ideal choice for the Bush Administration. He had the skills of a career foreign service officer, which he had been, but also solid Republican credentials. As a foreign service officer, he had served as special assistant to Secretary of State Henry Kissinger, ambassador at large for counterterrorism in the Reagan Administration, and ambassador to the Netherlands. In 1989 he left government to be managing partner of Kissinger's consulting firm, Kissinger Associates. Bursting with self-confidence, Bremer proudly described himself to a reporter as a "bedrock Republican" with strong conservative values.

Bremer had never been to Iraq, did not speak Arabic, had never served in a post-conflict society, and had no experience in nation-building. And he had less than two weeks to "read into" his new assignment, a process of oral and written briefings that normally lasts several months even for a routine ambassadorial assignment such as the Netherlands. For a full year before the war, the State Department had spent millions of dollars working with Iraqi exiles and experts to prepare a fifteen-volume blueprint for how Iraq might be governed after the war. The Administration was so disorganized and so faction-ridden that the Defense Department (for which Bremer would work and which handled his briefings) did not tell him that this State Department study existed. He would learn of it in the press sometime after arriving in Baghdad.

At the same time as he was trying to learn about Iraq, Bremer recruited his senior staff. They included several retired ambassadors who had worked with him in the State Department fifteen years before, a high-powered Republican Washington lobbyist, and a career foreign service officer with expertise on administrative matters. Aside from retired Ambassador Hume Horan, they did not have area expertise, or relevant language skills.

On May 7, Bremer had lunch with President Bush, followed by a meeting that was joined by Powell, Rumsfeld, Rice, and White House Chief of Staff Andrew Card. In Bremer's account, there was a wide-ranging discussion of the issues of postwar governance, but neither the president nor his team took any decision about the future of the country. Instead, Bremer asked for, and obtained, the authority to exercise "all executive, legislative, and judicial functions" in Iraq.

Although President Bush had decided on war with Iraq not long after September 11, he never addressed the big issues of how postwar Iraq would be governed. Would the United States run a prolonged occupation as it had done in Germany and Japan? Would there be a provisional government and how would it be chosen? Would there be elections? When? How would Iraq's constitution be written and what would be in it? What was the U.S. position on federalism for the Kurds, or the Shiite desire for an Islamic state? What would be done about the Iraqi military and the Ba'ath Party? Those issues, the subject of ferocious internal battles within the Administration, would now be settled by a man who had been working on Iraq for all of two weeks.

Bremer arrived in Baghdad on May 12, 2003. On May 16, he informed the Iraqi Leadership Council that there would be no interim government and no early handover of power. This came exactly eleven days after Jay Garner—speaking for the United States—had announced that the core of an interim government would be in place by May 15. The same day, Bremer issued Coalition Provisional Authority Order Number 1. It banned persons serving in the top four levels of the Ba'ath Party from holding government employment, now and in the future. On May 23, Bremer signed CPA Order Number 2. It dissolved Iraq's army, its air force, its navy, its secret police, its intelligence services, the Republican Guards, the Ba'ath Party militia, and the Ministry of Defense.

For eighty years, Sunni Arabs were the guardians of Iraqi unity, keeping the country together by force. The American invasion ended Sunni Arab rule. Now, in a few strokes of a pen, Bremer completed Iraq's revolution by destroying the pillars on which Sunni Arabs had relied to rule Iraq—the military, the security services, and the Ba'ath Party.

Although he did not know it, Bremer had sealed Iraq's fate as a unitary nation. All the king's horses and all the king's men could not put Humpty Dumpty back together again. This did not stop Bremer from spending the next fourteen months trying to do just that.

• • •

So, Bremer's grand entry represented a 180-degree turn in strategy from Garner's. Garner planned to turn power over to Iraqis; Bremer made clear he was in charge, "putting down the hammer," as he described his very first meeting with the Iraqi leaders. Garner's team had been working with top civil servants in an effort to get the government functioning; Bremer fired most of them for being Ba'athists. The U.S. military had begun to engage Iraqi generals about recalling Iraqi Army units to handle security and reconstruction duties. Bremer dissolved the Iraqi Army.

The Ba'ath Party had elements of Hitler's Nazi Party and Stalin's Communist Party. Around the leader, Saddam Hussein, it promoted a cult of personality that Stalin would have recognized, and possibly envied. Ba'ath Party members were encouraged to inform on other Iraqis, and in particular to root out fellow members who might be unreliable. Those who were denounced faced brutal interrogations, torture, and execution. The Ba'ath Party had its youth wing, the Saddam Cubs, and it promoted the idea of a master race, the Arabs (but in reality Sunni Arabs), at the expense of Iraq's Kurds and other non-Arabs. Iraq's Shiites and Kurds would not accept that those who had held high positions by toadying to Saddam Hussein and his racist party could continue to run the country's bureaucracy. On the other hand, Bremer's decree was draconian since it also excluded from public service doctors, teachers, and other professionals who had joined the party—and advanced in it—primarily in order to do their jobs (although many respected professionals did not join the party and still had careers). A more gradual process of removing top bureaucrats from their positions would have been more prudent.

As Bremer argues, the Iraqi Army had already disappeared when he issued his decree dissolving it. I traveled all around Iraq in April 2003, and I saw almost no Iraqi soldiers in uniforms and certainly no organized units. Conscripts and officers both had shed their uniforms and gone home as looters ravaged bases and barracks, stealing all available equipment. In the north, the peshmerga were busy collecting tanks and howitzers that had belonged to Iraqi divisions in Mosul, Kirkuk, and Diyala. North of Baghdad in late April, I stopped at the base of the Mujahedin-e Khalq (MEK), an Iranian opposition militia that had been supported by Saddam Hussein. While American troops watched, and our ABC News crew filmed, the Mujahedin-e Khalq drove a tank transporter into their base with a newly acquired Iraqi tank. Although the MEK was on the State Department's list of terrorist organizations, its commanders seemed to have warm relations with the American military; the latter did nothing to stop them from scavenging Saddam's arsenal.* In southern Iraq, Shiite militias and the Iranians were free to collect Iraq's heavy weapons, although it is not clear how many made it across the border into Iran.

Given all that had happened, it would not have been easy to recall the Iraqi Army, which Garner and the U.S. military had contemplated doing. Even if the soldiers could be found, they would have had no equipment, no weapons, and no barracks. In any event, making use of these units in reconstruction or security was far beyond the capability of the CPA and the U.S. military in May 2003. This would have required forethought, planning, and resources, all of which the war's architects failed to provide.†

Most important, Saddam Hussein's Iraqi Army was a Sunni Arab

---

* It is not clear whether U.S. military cooperation with this terrorist organization was due to ignorance and poor planning (failing to have a contingency for the MEK and not briefing U.S. forces about their terrorist character) or a policy decision by the Pentagon neoconservatives to work with the MEK because it carried out military operations against Iran. In an administration as undisciplined as Bush's, it is quite believable that Pentagon activists would pursue their agenda, especially since many of them believed the MEK were Iranian freedom fighters, and not terrorists. During the war, the U.S. military dropped several bombs on the MEK barracks but at a time of day they were likely to be empty. Saddam supported the MEK for twenty years, and they repaid his loyalty in 1991 by helping suppress the Kurdish uprising. Their presence poses a quandary for the new Iraqi government, dominated by pro-Iranian Shiites and Kurds with long memories.

† It made little sense to use a Sunni Arab–dominated army as a security force when Sunni Arabs were the main threat to security in Iraq.

army, not a national one. Although Sunni Arabs are 20 percent of Iraq's population, they were never less than half the officer corps. The higher the rank, the greater was the percentage of Sunni Arabs. By 2003, there were few officers with a rank higher than captain who were not Sunni Arabs. They dominated the elite units, such as the Republican Guards and Special Republican Guards, on which the regime relied for its survival. For the most part, Shiites served as conscripted enlisted men, and had been cannon fodder in Iraq's wars against Iran and the United States. Iraq's Kurds, effectively independent since 1991, had their own army, the peshmerga, and considered the Iraqi Army the enemy.

So neither the Kurds nor the Shiites saw Saddam's Iraqi Army as a national institution. They experienced the army, and the security services, as oppressors and mass killers. The Iraqi Army and Air Force murdered over 180,000 Kurds in the Anfal, including by dropping chemical weapons on Kurdish villages. The army and Republican Guards slaughtered Shiites by the thousands in 1991. Neither community would have accepted bringing back a Sunni Arab army. The Kurds and Shiites make up 80 percent of Iraq's population.

While it would have been unwise to recall the Iraqi Army, it was unnecessary to dissolve it formally since it had already disappeared. Bremer's decree was, as his book makes clear, another way to assert his authority in Iraq from the start. To Sunni Arabs—including former officers who had no intention of returning to military service—it was a gratuitous humiliation. The Sunni Arab officers and enlisted men not only knew the locations of the arsenals the Americans left unguarded, but they also knew how to use the weapons. It made no sense to add to America's many enemies in Iraq, but this is precisely what Bremer did.

Bremer's decision to assume all power for himself rather than transfer authority to an Iraqi government was probably the most fateful of his decisions. Every Iraqi leader, including the most pro-American, says it was Bremer's decision to keep power that changed the United States from being seen by many as liberator to being universally regarded as an occupier. If an Iraqi government had disbanded the army or banned Ba'athists from public service, the outcome might have been accepted in a way that a foreigner's decision was not. Sunni Arabs, who felt powerless in the face of American fiat, probably could have negotiated some compromise with the Shiites and Kurds. If there had been an Iraqi government, it is highly unlikely there would have been a two-month-long Shiite uprising in April 2004 (the government would have been Shiite-dominated). Moreover, needed reforms (embodied in a hundred laws enacted by Bremer during the occupation) might have been designed more relevantly as Iraqi initiatives, rather than the American-imposed reforms that, for the most part, were never implemented.

Although U.N. representative Vieira de Mello diplomatically tried to explain to Bremer that local ownership is critical to successful nation-building, Bremer and the American occupation authorities never grasped the point. They assumed that they could do a better job running Iraq than the highly educated Iraqis who had spent much of their lives struggling against the Saddam Hussein regime. Having been abroad for decades, the Iraqi Arab politicians may not have been fully in touch with the realities of their country as it emerged from thirty-five years of dictatorship.* But all of them had been following events in Iraq closely, almost all had close relatives who had lived through the Saddam years, and all had been raised in the knowledge of Iraq's history, culture, politics, and religions. Even if they were out of touch, they knew much more about Iraq than a man who had been in the country for four days. And they certainly knew more about Iraq than an American president who two months before he ordered troops into the country didn't know that Islam was divided between Shiites and Sunnis.

After telling the Iraqi Leadership Council on May 16 that he would not form a government, Bremer then asked them to propose an enlargement of their council to make it "more representative." When they didn't do so, Bremer was angry, privately belittling the Iraqi politicians as incompetent and self-serving. In fact, the ILC thought of itself as representative, and with the notable omission of the Sunni Arabs who had

---

* Bremer describes Talabani and Barzani as exiles in his book, but they had been running Iraqi Kurdistan for twelve years with a mandate that came from the only free elections ever held in the country.

mostly supported the old order, it was representative. Its members had been chosen by the most democratic means available—the Iraqi opposition conference in London. In the January 2005 elections, parties headed by ILC members would win 90 percent of the vote, a figure that was somewhat inflated due to the fact that Sunni Arabs boycotted those elections. Yet in the December 2005 elections, Sunni Arabs fully participated and the ILC leaders still ended up with 75 percent of the vote.

Understandably, the ILC leaders did not want to dilute their power. When they declined to propose an enlargement of the council, Bremer did it for them. He constituted an Iraqi Governing Council in July 2003, adding eighteen names to the original ILC seven. Collectively, Bremer's eighteen names would win about 3 percent of the vote in January 2005 and even fewer votes in December 2005.*

In spite of calling his creation the Iraqi Governing Council (GC), Bremer was unwilling to devolve any of his powers to it. In July 2003, he came up with the idea that the GC should demand that the CPA do things it was already planning to do. This, in Bremer's mind, would demonstrate the effectiveness of the GC to the Iraqi people. His staff came up with a list of "early wins" that included having the GC demand the occupation authorities restore electric generation to prewar levels by October 2003 and find ways to deal with unemployment. Wrote Bremer: "Since we had these plans already in hand, this would be a win-win operation, in which the GC would get the public credit when it made a demand of the CPA and when we responded."

Not surprisingly, the Iraqi Governing Council did not make any such demand. They had wanted an Iraqi government that would have the authority to restore electricity and no doubt found Bremer's pro-

---

* Some of the eighteen ran on party tickets headed by ILC members in the elections. In the January elections, some of Bremer's designees failed to win the one-third of 1 percent required to get a single seat. In the December elections, they, along with other weak performers, joined party lists headed by ILC members. The 3 percent figure refers to those who stood on party lists other than for parties headed by ILC members. Bremer's strongest criticism of the ILC is that it did not represent properly the Sunni Arab minority. He appointed Sunni Arabs to the Governing Council but not one of them had significant electoral support among their fellow Sunni Arabs.

posal demeaning and slightly bizarre. Bremer was treating Iraq's most experienced politicians as if they were a high school student council.*
After a while, the top leaders stopped attending the GC, sending deputies instead. The CPA proved unable to restore electricity or address the unemployment problem.

After Bremer arrived, the professionals Garner had assembled were encouraged to leave or were marginalized. Rumsfeld fired Barbara Bodine, the former ambassador to Yemen who had served in Iraq in the 1980s, as soon as she got a working phone in Baghdad. Tim Carney, a retired U.S. ambassador to Sudan who had led reconstruction efforts in Cambodia and Haiti, departed with a blistering attack in the *Washington Post* on the Administration's lack of preparations. Robin Raphel, the former ambassador to Tunisia, soldiered on as de facto trade minister, before returning in disgust to the State Department. As she noted in an interview for an oral history project, "It was obvious to me that we could not run a country we did not understand. We were not prepared." Ryan Crocker, who had served as ambassador to several Middle Eastern countries and worked for years on Iraq, left to take up a teaching position at the National War College. Ambassador Bill Eagleton, a former head of the U.S. Interests Section in Baghdad in the 1980s, and a recognized expert on the Kurds, left Iraq for a medical procedure and Bremer denied him clearance to return.

In place of these professionals, the White House sent out loyal Republicans. It mattered not at all to the Pentagon that so many civilians it sent to Iraq had no relevant professional qualification, no experience in post-conflict situations, and no knowledge of Iraq. But it mattered greatly in Iraq.

Jerry Bremer had an ambitious agenda. In a June 20, 2003, op-ed piece in the *Wall Street Journal,* he outlined his economic goals.

> [T]he private sector must be encouraged to rapidly allocate resources to their most productive uses. In other transition

---

* Or, perhaps as even less mature. In an e-mail that Bremer sent his wife about the episode, and later published, he compared GC deliberations to "tee-ball with players who couldn't hit the ball teed up for them."

economies, the switch from value-destroying public enterprises to value-creating private ones has been accomplished by stimulating the growth of small and medium-sized private enterprises, which are best able to create jobs quickly. This encouragement takes place by reducing the subsidies to state-owned firms and establishing a clear and transparent commercial code (as well as honest judges to enforce it). More generally, a well-established system of property rights must be established in order for the economy to grow.

In short, privatization was the key to rebuilding a democratic, stable, and prosperous Iraq. Tom Foley, a top Bush fundraiser with no experience in handling economic transitions (and no knowledge of Iraq), was put in charge of privatizing Iraq's industry. He lasted a few months and was replaced by Michael Fleischer, a brother of Bush's first press secretary. After explaining that he had got the job in Iraq through his brother Ari, Fleischer told the *Chicago Tribune*, without any apparent irony, that the Americans were going to teach the Iraqis a new way of doing business. "The only paradigm they know is cronyism."

No privatization took place. But it is just as well that Fleischer and Foley were in charge. International law prohibits an occupying power from selling off the assets of the occupied state, although it doesn't appear that anyone in CPA was aware of this.

The job of reopening the Iraqi stock exchange—an important adjunct to a privatization program—was given to a twenty-four-year-old political operative. Bremer committed to reopening the exchange for securities trading by the end of 2003, but with greater transparency than existed in Saddam's Iraq. In fact, the new Iraq Stock Exchange (ISX) would open just four days before CPA went out of business. In its only day of trading under American auspices, June 24, 2004, fifty-one shares in six companies were traded for a value of several hundred dollars. To achieve this, U.S. taxpayers spent several million dollars on salaries, security, and building renovations. The ISX has since gone on to become one of the Middle East's smallest stock exchanges, on a par with the tiny exchange of the Palestinian Authority.

The Administration's insistence on using Iraq jobs to reward political cronies had consequences in less ideologically sensitive, but substantively more important, fields. Andy Zajac of the *Chicago Tribune* described how, in April 2003, the Bush Administration replaced the ORHA's principal health official, Dr. Frederick Burkle, a medical doctor with close working relationships with humanitarian organizations and long experience in conflict zones, with James Haveman, who was a political crony of Michigan's former Republican governor and did not have a medical degree. In contrast to Burkle, who for several months had been planning the restoration of Iraq's health care system and who was ready to put a program into action as soon as Baghdad fell, Haveman did not arrive in Iraq until June 7, 2003. Although he had never worked in a post-conflict environment, Haveman strongly denied that he lacked international experience, apparently considering his travel to twenty-six foreign countries (as he told the *Tribune*) the relevant qualification. According to the *Tribune,* Haveman did not include Iraq's private health care system in his planning, even though it serves half the country's needs. He also wasted huge amounts of money by refusing to collect data on the existing clinics.

Perhaps the most astounding story about the CPA appeared in the *Washington Post* on May 23, 2004. Titled "In Iraq, the Job Opportunity of a Lifetime; Managing a $13 Billion Budget With No Experience," it described the experiences of six young people who ended up in Iraq. Out of the blue, the six received e-mails from the Defense Department asking if they wanted to serve with the CPA in Iraq. None had ever expressed interest in going to Iraq and none had relevant experience. They were hired without interviews or security clearances. They were supposed to take relatively low-level positions in the CPA budget office, but because the CPA did not recruit qualified senior people, they ended up responsible for spending Iraq's budget. They knew next to nothing about federal procurement rules and budgeting, so they spent extremely slowly.

In an economy with 50 percent unemployment, the failure to spend money contributed to the frustration of jobless Iraqis, and undoubtedly produced recruits for the insurgency. According to the *Post,* the group, which included the daughter of a prominent conservative activist, could not figure out how they had been selected. Finally the young people realized that the one thing they had in common was that they had posted their résumés at the Heritage Foundation, a conservative Washington think tank. The Pentagon hired eleven people off the Heritage Foundation Web site, including those six who handled Iraq's budget.

Fred Barnes, a noted conservative commentator writing in the *Weekly Standard* in March 2004, boasted of all the right-wingers trooping to Baghdad:

> Liberals are famous for claiming the moral high ground for their causes and themselves. They like to pat themselves on the back. But at the scene of today's most prominent humanitarian project—Iraq—they are not a major presence. Conservatives are, hundreds of them. Despite the danger, they have volunteered to serve in the effort to make Iraq a free and democratic country. So many have come, in fact, that Coalition Provisional Authority administrator L. Paul Bremer had to cut off the flow. "There are more than I can possibly take," he says.
>
> It's not pay or creature comforts that attract them. They are a kind of conservative Peace Corps. They live in trailers, four to a unit, surrounded by sandbags. They eat institutional food. They work seven days a week, 12 to 14 hours a day. They spend most of their time inside the six-square-mile "green zone," the guarded headquarters of the CPA and Iraqi Governing Council. They face attacks from mortars and rockets and gunmen.
>
> They have sacrificed to come to Iraq.

Well, not exactly. CPA employees benefited from an extraordinarily generous pay system that included danger pay, hardship allowance, and other benefits.* With danger pay, overtime, and hardship al-

---

* Peace Corps volunteers receive a monthly stipend that averages around two hundred dollars and, after two years in arduous conditions, a "readjustment" allowance of six thousand dollars. The lowest-paid of the CPA American staff made thirty times what a Peace Corps volunteer earns.

lowances, young conservatives just out of college earned in the six figures. The more senior Republican recruits earned the maximum al-
lowable annual income for the federal government service in six
months or less, meaning they had to go home just when they had
begun to learn something about the country. But when congressional
Democrats asked the General Accountability Office (GAO) to investigate CPA pay scales, the Administration told GAO that CPA was an international organization not subject to congressional controls.

The provisional authority focused more attention than warranted
on symbolic issues that resonated in Republican circles in Washington
at the expense of substance. Perhaps the most amusing example was
Bremer's decree imposing a 15 percent flat tax on income earned in Iraq.
This was widely praised in Republican and antitax circles in the United
States where the flat tax has long been an elusive goal. The conservatives
never took note that no one in Iraq pays tax on his or her income.*

CPA's record on the economic issues that mattered was disastrous.
Ninety-five percent of Iraq's government revenues come from oil. Before the United States invaded Iraq, Iraq's daily oil production stood at
2.6 million barrels a day. At the start of the war, the Bush Administration committed $1.7 billion, much of it in no-bid contracts to compa-
nies such as Halliburton, to boost Iraq's oil production. By May 2004,
CPA's last full month, daily oil production was just 1.9 million barrels.
By December 2005, it was down to 1.1 million barrels a day. Iraq's oil
facilities were the one part of the country's infrastructure that the military secured, leaving it relatively undamaged in the war and in the
looting that followed. However, the failure to plan for security left
pipelines exposed to sabotage, which, along with theft, took an increasing toll on production.

---

* Income tax can be collected from central government salaries, but when public
sector salaries are the only income "taxed," such a tax has no different impact than
if the public service salary scale were reduced by 15 percent. Public service salaries
increased enormously under CPA, probably not something its conservatives
would want to boast about. The flat tax did not apply in Kurdistan, because the
Kurdistan Government did not—and does not—permit Baghdad any tax power
in the region, aside from customs duties.

Reliable electricity is essential to any modern economy. Before the war, Baghdad had close to twenty-four-hour electricity. In April and May 2003, the city was mostly without electricity, halting most economic activity and making daily life miserable with temperatures as high as 120 degrees. Fifteen months later, when the CPA handed over authority, Baghdad residents and businesses endured sixteen hours of outages in an average day. In spite of $7.7 billion being allocated to Iraq's power infrastructure, Iraq's electricity output after a year of American occupation was below the level Saddam Hussein's government provided.

As anyone who has worked in post-conflict situations knows, it is critical that people see an improvement in their lives quickly. Post-conflict economies have high levels of unemployment. Reconstruction projects not only repair damage but put people to work. And these must start fast. In November 2003, President Bush signed an $18.4 billion appropriation for reconstruction in Iraq. By the end of June 2004, CPA had spent about $500 million. In his memoir of his time in Iraq, Bremer blames his superiors in Washington for not putting a priority on expediting approvals for expenditures, although clearly responsibility also lies with CPA's professionally incompetent staffing. As one CPA failure followed another, Iraqis began to say its initials stood for "Can't Provide Anything."

Bremer also administered billions in Iraqi funds, including money from the sale of Iraq's oil. The CPA's inspector general Stuart Bowen issued a report saying that $8.8 billion of the Iraqi funds were spent, or otherwise disappeared, without proper accounting. Bremer has replied that normal accounting practices cannot be expected in wartime. But some of what the inspector general found went beyond the occasional lapse. Millions of dollars were kept in shrink-wrapped "bricks" of hundred-dollar bills scattered around CPA offices. In Hillah, one official stored $678,000 in an unlocked foot locker. An American soldier assigned to assist the Iraqi boxing team gambled away the funds he was given. No one could tell whether he had lost $20,000 or $60,000 since no one kept a record of how much money he had received. For money that was spent, loose or nonexistent controls seem to have been the norm. Nearly $700,000 was paid in full on a contract to rehabilitate the Hillah General Hospital, including replacing the central elevator bank. The work was not done and an elevator crash killed three people. Another contractor received $108,140 to rehabilitate Hillah's Olympic-size pool, including installing new pumps and pipes. All the contractor did was to polish the existing pumps so they would appear new.

Robert J. Stein Jr., a CPA contracting officer in Hillah, later pleaded guilty to stealing more than $2 million and to bid-rigging. He had been hired in spite of having been sentenced to eight months in federal prison for a 1996 fraud conviction. Such hires were the consequence of a personnel system that placed a premium on political loyalty but was sloppy about such routine matters as security checks.

In 2005, the U.S. government reluctantly submitted briefs in support of a whistle-blower lawsuit against Custer Battles, one of many outfits with GOP connections to win contracts in Iraq. Two former Custer Battles employees accused the company of defrauding the coalition of millions of dollars for work not performed. In 2003, Custer Battles had won a $16.8 million contract to provide security at Baghdad Airport. In spite of large cash advances, it never delivered the X-ray equipment specified in the contract. It did provide a bomb-sniffing dog and trainer, but the dog would not sniff vehicles. "I think it was a guy and his pet, to be honest with you," Colonel Richard Ballard, the inspector general for the Army in Iraq at the time, told CBS's *60 Minutes.*

The airport's director of security wrote to CPA, "Custer Battles has shown themselves to be unresponsive, uncooperative, incompetent, deceitful, manipulative and war profiteers." But instead of removing the company, CPA's financial management awarded Custer Battles new contracts. Mike Battles, the company's cofounder, was an unsuccessful Republican congressional candidate who boasted of his White House connections. British Colonel Philip Wilkinson told *60 Minutes,* "I really don't know how they got away with it. The assumption that we had was that they had to have high political top cover." In March 2006, a federal jury found Custer Battles liable for thirty-seven separate acts of fraud.

Custer Battles is just one example of CPA's contracting practices where oversight was, according to the CPA Inspector General, "relatively nonexistent." A Kurd who headed a Baghdad ministry during the occupation told me that American corruption was pervasive, something he said he never expected, having lived in Britain and having worked extensively with Americans.

Although Bremer wrote about them in his *Wall Street Journal* article, CPA never addressed Iraq's biggest structural problems: fuel and food subsidies. Due to a grossly distorted currency and plentiful supplies, Saddam's Iraq had ridiculously low gasoline prices—around 5 cents per gallon. With salaries averaging $2 to $10 per month for public servants (half of Iraq's employment), there was at least some equilibrium between the low prices and the low incomes. With Saddam's fall, the United Nations lifted sanctions on Iraq, moving it rapidly toward the world economy. The CPA greatly increased government salaries. The result was an enormous burst in demand for gasoline, but CPA did little to increase Iraq's refining capacity. To meet domestic demand, the authority imported the gasoline at world prices and then sold it at five cents a gallon. As oil prices rose, this fuel subsidy ended up costing hundreds of millions of dollars a month. And, in spite of his brave words about ending subsidies, Jerry Bremer, the self-described "bedrock Republican," was not so committed to his conservative values as to raise fuel prices. That, he understood, would be suicide.

Having dissolved Saddam's military, the CPA and the U.S. military tried to build a new one. It was an error-laden process: officers were not vetted for loyalty or skills; training was inadequate and rushed; and the process emphasized the number of Iraqi battalions created without regard to their capability. The test of these efforts came in April 2004.

On March 31, gunmen ambushed four Blackwater security guards in Fallujah. Townsmen set their vehicles ablaze, chopped up the charred corpses, and hung two torsos on an iron bridge. Appalled by the ghastly images of mutilated Americans televised around the world,

President Bush ordered the 1st Marine Expeditionary Force to retake Fallujah.

Meanwhile, on March 26, 2004, Moqtada al-Sadr had given a sermon denouncing President Bush, the United States, and Israel and praising the September 11 attacks. For many months the coalition had had an arrest warrant against al-Sadr for his direct involvement in the murder of Abdul Majid al-Khoie, a moderate Shiite cleric, on April 10, 2003, at the Imam Ali shrine in Najaf. The coalition military refused to enforce the warrant, and looked the other way as al-Sadr defied the ban on private militias, building up the Mahdi Army to a force of more than 6,000 men that ran its own prisons and administered its own brutal justice. When al-Sadr insulted America and its president, Bremer decided to take action. He ordered al-Sadr's newspaper, *Hawza,* closed for sixty days. It was a characteristic CPA action, symbolic and dissociated from the realities of Iraq. One observer compared it to attacking a tiger with a fly swatter. Bremer also acted without considering what al-Sadr would then do, and how the coalition, in turn, would respond.

Moqtada al-Sadr responded violently. The Mahdi Army took over Baghdad's Sadr City, and parts of Najaf, Karbala, Kut, Nasiriyah, and Amara. The CPA staff in southern Iraq saw what was coming and asked Bremer for more protection. Their pleas were ignored. The Mahdi Army overran several CPA compounds.

With their hands full in Fallujah and in the south, the Americans and their allies needed the help of the new Iraqi Army and police. Half the army deserted. Some Sunni Arab soldiers joined the insurgents in Fallujah, and some Shiite soldiers joined the Mahdi Army. Sunni Arabs refused to fight their fellow Sunni Arabs on behalf of a predominantly Shiite-Kurdish army and the foreign occupier. Even Shiite soldiers recruited from militias hostile to al-Sadr, like the Badr Organization, refused to join the Americans in a fight against fellow Shiites.

Many Sunni Arab policemen were already either members of the insurgency or cooperating with it. A policeman who was loyal to America's "new Iraq" in the tight-knit cities and towns of the Sunni Triangle risked assassination, but many supported the insurgency out of sympathy for its goals and not because they were intimidated into doing so.*

In the south, the Americans and British had allowed the Shiite religious parties to take over the local administration. The Shiites recruited the local police, often from their own militias. The Shiite police in the south took their guidance not from the Iraqi national authorities, but from the Shiite political leaders who were responsible for their large paychecks. (The CPA had increased public service salaries many times what they were under Saddam Hussein, which was a major reason otherwise unemployed men wanted to join the police and army.) When the local Shiite authorities didn't support the coalition against al-Sadr, the police didn't either.

At the request of the Americans, who imagined they were creating a national army, Barzani and Talabani assigned 6,000 peshmerga to the Iraqi Army. They were stood up as nine battalions, exclusively Kurdish and based in Kurdistan. These battalions were effective, loyal to their American allies, and had no qualms about fighting the Sunni Arab insurgents. But only the Americans saw them as Iraqi. The peshmerga owed their allegiance to Kurdistan, not to Iraq. More important, Sunni Arabs did not see the peshmerga as fellow Iraqis but as foreign mercenaries (most Kurdish soldiers do not speak Arabic) allied with the American enemy. As the Fallujah operation unfolded, Sunni Arabs threatened revenge against the Kurds. The American strategy of building a unified army not only failed, but sowed the seeds of civil war.

The Americans looked for operational reasons for the failure of the Iraqi Army and police in April 2004. Training was rushed and there was inadequate attention to military fundamentals. However, the basic flaw was conceptual: first, a belief that Iraqi soldiers would give their highest allegiance to the national command authority of an Iraq which, as of 2004, none of Iraq's communities felt was theirs; and, second, that Arab Iraqi soldiers would fight alongside an American occupation army against their own religious communities. Without there

* The Sunni Triangle extends from Baghdad west to the Jordanian border and from Baghdad northwest to Mosul. The third side is the Syrian border.

being an Iraqi nation, it was impossible to create a genuine national army.

The Shiite religious parties used the American insistence on disbanding militias to insert their military wings into the new Iraqi Army and the police force, especially in the south. The Americans imagined that dressing these militiamen in Iraqi Army and police uniforms would change their loyalties. It did not. Only after the Shiite religious parties took over the national government following the January 2005 elections did the Shiite soldiers and police transfer their loyalties. But since the commander of the Badr Organization, Iraq's largest Shiite militia, became the minister of interior in charge of the Iraqi police, the change was more apparent than real. The Shiite takeover of the state only served to alienate further Sunni Arabs from the army and police, making it even less likely that Sunni Arabs would loyally serve in a Shiite Iraqi police force and a Shiite Iraqi Army.

With their own state and army, the Kurds had the luxury of watching these developments from the sidelines. They made an alliance of convenience with the Shiites, and accommodated the American requests to contribute to an Iraqi military at no cost to their own military security.

With regard to the peshmerga, the CPA pursued a policy that began as bizarre and ended as farce. By April 2004, it was glaringly obvious that the peshmerga was the only indigenous military force in Iraq that was effective, reliable, and pro-American. Bremer, however, wanted it dissolved in favor of the unreliable Iraqi Army. He sent David Gompert, a RAND consultant, to negotiate the disbanding of the peshmerga. For days, Gompert met with Masrour Barzani, Massoud's razor-sharp, American-educated son who heads the Kurdistan intelligence service, and eventually reached a deal. The peshmerga would disappear. In their place, the Kurdistan Regional Government would establish three armed forces: mountain rangers, a rapid reaction force, and a counterterrorism strike force.

As Gompert waited for the helicopter to take him back to Baghdad, he observed how important it was that the Kurds, masters of Iraq's largest militia, were willing to give it up for the sake of national unity.

Some doubt may have crept into his mind as he then asked for the Kurdish translation of mountain rangers. "Peshmerga" was the reply. Had he asked, he would have discovered that "rapid reaction force" and "counterterrorism strike force" are also rendered into Kurdish as "peshmerga."

Although President Bush proclaimed America's mission was to bring the blessings of freedom to the Iraqi people, his administration was reluctant to trust them with democracy. In his testimony to the House International Relations Committee in May 2003, a month after the fall of Baghdad, Under Secretary of Defense Douglas Feith pointedly refused to say if the United States would accept the outcome of democratic elections should the Iraqis vote to have an Islamic state.

Specifically, the Administration proposed to limit the choices of the peoples of Iraq by having the country's permanent constitution written by Iraqis selected by the Americans. The hand-picked Iraqis would then be assisted by American constitutional advisors who would ensure that the constitution included Western-style human rights protections, incorporated a system of checks and balances, preserved the unity of the country, centralized control of oil, and promoted economic and social policies liked by American conservatives. The constitution would be submitted to the Iraqi peoples in a referendum. They would then be faced with the choice of either accepting the constitution and regaining sovereignty, or rejecting it and having a prolonged occupation. The scheme reflected the extraordinary ambitions of the Administration's neoconservative would-be nation-builders who wanted to leave their ideological imprint on Iraq. It was also undemocratic.

In 2003, the most influential man in Iraq turned out not to be the American viceroy, Jerry Bremer, but a frail seventy-three-year-old Shiite cleric who lived in a modest house near the shrine of Ali in Najaf. An Iranian by birth and citizenship, the Grand Ayatollah Ali al-Sistani was determined that the Bush Administration not prevent Iraq's Shiite religious leaders from creating an Islamic state if, as Sistani knew full well they would, their voters wanted one.*

Sistani adopted a straightforward position: Iraq's constitution should be written by elected Iraqis and, as a corollary, the United States should transfer power to an elected government, not an appointed one. He wanted elections held as soon as possible, but not later than 2004 and with the occupation ending immediately afterward.

Bremer came up with one strategy after another to avoid meeting Sistani's demand. As a result, the Iranian cleric became the champion of Iraqi democracy while the American administrator appeared unwilling to trust the Iraqi people. To make matters worse for the Americans, Sistani won every battle with Bremer. Bremer and the Bush Administration came across not only as undemocratic but also as weak. It was one of many public relations battles that the United States needlessly lost.

By the summer of 2003, Bremer had backed down on the issue of an appointed constitutional commission and agreed to an elected constitutional assembly, but without providing any date for the restoration of Iraqi sovereignty. In November, the White House summoned Bremer back to Washington and asked for an early transfer of power on June 30, 2004, or four months before the U.S. presidential election. Bremer then devised a complicated scheme of caucuses in each of Iraq's governorates in which CPA, the GC, the American-appointed councils in each governorate, and the American-appointed municipal councils of each governorate's five largest towns would all choose delegates who would in turn then choose an interim Iraqi National Assembly that would write an interim constitution and choose an interim government.

The system was so complicated that few Americans could explain it, and, of course, not many Iraqis understood it. Nevertheless, Sistani grasped the essential feature of the proposal: every Iraqi participating in the caucuses that would eventually choose Iraq's future government would have been chosen, at least indirectly, by the Americans. It was, as

* Sistani may have been influenced by Feith's testimony.

one Iraqi told me, election by persons selected by persons selected by Bremer. Sistani again insisted on elections and threatened to issue a fatwa, a religious decree, against the caucus system. In February 2004, Lakhdar Brahimi, the seventy-year-old former Algerian foreign minister who had just been made the United Nations special envoy for Iraq, helped devise a formula that enabled Bremer to save some face. There would be no caucuses, but Sistani also agreed there could be a short-lived interim government, chosen by the U.N., that would have a limited caretaker role from the transfer of sovereignty on June 30, 2004, until elections in December 2004 or January 2005.

As part of the transition, Bremer agreed that the Governing Council would produce a Transitional Administrative Law (TAL) by February 2004. The TAL would provide the road map to elections and the adoption of a permanent constitution and specify how Iraq would be governed in the interim. The TAL could have been brief. It needed to do no more than describe the institutions of an interim government (president, council of ministers, interim legislature), provide the government with the minimum necessary powers, and give the timetable and method for electing a constitutional assembly. A minimalist document would have left it to Iraqis to resolve the thorny issues about their future, such as the role of Islam, the distribution of power among Iraq's main communities, the status of Kurdistan, and whether Shiites could also form their own state. In the interim, the status quo—messy as it was—might continue.

The Bush Administration, however, was desperate to leave its mark on Iraq's constitution and the TAL was now its only chance. In early January 2004, Bremer and his key aides prepared a series of "principles" that they wanted as the basis of the TAL, which the CPA now began to depict as an interim constitution.

Iraq's peoples do not share a common vision of the Iraqi state nor do they have common values. Inevitably, making an Iraqi constitution would more closely resemble the negotiation of a peace treaty than the design of a blueprint for a common state. The Shiite religious parties wanted an Islamic state with many features of the Iranian model. The Kurds unanimously wanted an independent country, and, failing that, a loose federal system that gave Kurdistan as close to full independence as possible. The secular Arabs wanted a unified country with some powers devolved to provinces defined by geography and not ethnicity (basically meaning that the Kurds could not have their own region but that three Kurdish governorates could, separately, have a measure of self-government). The Sunni Arabs were not represented on the Governing Council,* but generally wanted the centralized Iraq that they had once run. While the Shiites looked to Iran as a political model and the Sunnis looked to their fellow Arabs, the Kurds looked to the West.

These divisions affected how Iraq's communities saw such issues as control of natural resources, the role of the Iraqi Army, control of international borders, the role of Islam, the rights of women, bilingualism, and whether Iraq should be considered part of the Arab world.

Bremer sought to preempt Iraq's elected constitutional assembly by resolving these questions in the TAL on American terms. He wanted a unified Iraq so he insisted the central government should control Iraq's oil and water, have a monopoly on military force, and be responsible for the country's borders. These proposals were anathema to the Kurds. The Bremer principles included protections for women and religious minorities, as well as a progressive bill of rights that effectively limited the role of Islam. This made the Shiite religious parties unhappy. The secular Arab politicians liked almost all aspects of Bremer's principles, and Bremer installed one of them, former Foreign Minister Adnan Pachachi, an elderly Sunni Arab, as the chairman of the TAL drafting committee. In reality, however, the TAL was mostly written by U.S. government lawyers and Administration political appointees, as evidenced by the text's prose and many of the constitutional constructions. One provision, so clearly made in the U.S.A., established an Iraqi Supreme Court, an innovation in Middle East jurisprudence. Like its American counterpart, it was both a court of last appeals and a constitutional court. Naturally, the court had nine justices.

---

* There were Sunni Arab members of the GC, but they had no political support among the Sunni Arab population, as became evident in the January and December 2005 elections.

The Bush Administration exercised tight control over the deliberations in the Governing Council. Although the TAL was supposed to be
a document decided by Iraqis, Bremer cleared every significant change
from the original American principles with National Security Advisor
Condoleezza Rice.

The Administration got most of what it wanted in the TAL, but not
all. Ever fearful of Sistani, Bremer accepted language making Iraq a
mildly Islamic state. Bremer dealt more brutally with the Kurds, refusing to discuss their written responses to his proposed principles and
then silencing them during the Governing Council deliberations by
threatening to sever their "special relationship" with the United States.

Bremer's heavy hand ultimately produced a Governing Council
agreement on March 8, a week after the original deadline. He cele-
brated with an elaborate signing ceremony intended to evoke compar-
isons to the 1787 Philadelphia Constitutional Convention. Twenty-five
pens were laid out on a desk used by Iraq's first king, Feisal. In turn,
each member of the Iraqi Governing Council came forward to sign a
document that the White House boasted was the most democratic
constitution in the Middle East.

It was a pyrrhic victory. Although the TAL contained an admirable
bill of rights, it never applied outside Baghdad's Green Zone. In the
south, the Shiite religious parties, now firmly in control, imposed strict
Islamic law without regard to the TAL provisions on human rights and
women. In the north, Kurdistan continued to apply its own legal and
constitutional regime. Neither the Shiites nor the Kurds gave up their
armed forces. Although bullied into accepting on paper Baghdad's
management of its natural resources and control over its borders with
Turkey and Iran, the Kurds continued to develop their own oil and to
run customs and immigration at the border crossings just as before.

The process by which the Coalition Provisional Authority produced the TAL undermined its legitimacy. It was written in secret
mostly by Americans; fewer than a hundred Iraqis saw the document
before Bremer promulgated it. There was no opportunity for public
comment or input, an omission unheard of in modern constitution
writing, and that angered many Iraqis. Also, contrary to American

hopes, the key issues they tried to settle in the TAL were decided differently in the permanent constitution. These included clauses on control of natural resources, the central government's monopoly on military power, taxation, telecommunications, the role of Islam, and the applicability of the bill of rights.

While the TAL's substantive provisions were largely ignored, Iraq's political factions supported its schedule leading to the adoption of Iraq's constitution and the election of a permanent government. The interim government was to take power on June 30, 2004. By January 30, 2005, Iraq had to hold elections for a Transitional National Assembly that would produce a constitution by August 15, with a possible six-month extension. Assuming no extension, the constitution was to be voted on by October 15. If approved by a majority of those voting (and if not rejected by two-thirds of the voters in three governorates), elections for a permanent government would be held by December 15, 2005. If the constitution were rejected nationally or by three governorates, the December 15 elections would restart the process with the election of a new constitution-drafting assembly. In the January 2005 elections, voters would also choose governorate councils and, in Kurdistan, elect a new Kurdistan National Assembly.

The TAL specified that the Transitional National Assembly would, by a two-thirds vote, elect a three-man Presidency Council, consisting of a president and two vice presidents (intended to represent each of Iraq's three main communities). The Presidency Council would then nominate the prime minister, who would choose the cabinet. The effect of this system was to require a two-thirds majority to govern, meaning the majority Shiites would need the support of at least one other group. This paved the way for the Shiite-Kurdish alliance that has governed Iraq since the January 2005 elections and which together devised the permanent constitution.

Under the deal with Sistani, U.N. envoy Brahimi was supposed to choose the caretaker interim government that would govern Iraq from the handover of sovereignty on June 30, 2004, until the government was formed following the January 2005 elections. The Administration, however, had no intention of surrendering control over Iraq's future to the United Nations. As Brahimi set out on his consultations with Iraqis in May 2004, Robert Blackwill from the National Security Council staff came to Baghdad to work with Bremer to manipulate the outcome (Blackwill's assignment was a sign that the White House was, at last, losing confidence in Bremer).

President Bush had one overriding concern. Iraq's new leaders should be publicly grateful to the United States. As he told Bremer in a May 19 meeting of the NSC, "It's important to have someone who's willing to stand up and thank the American people for their sacrifice in liberating Iraq. I don't expect us to pick a yes man. But at least I want someone who will be grateful." Actually, Bush did want a yes man, and one who would thank him. He made this point three times at the NSC meeting devoted to Iraq's new government.

Meanwhile, Brahimi settled on Hussein Shahristani, a nuclear scientist who headed Iraq's Atomic Energy Commission, as his choice for prime minister. Shahristani, a Shiite close to the main Islamic parties, was a man of unquestioned courage and integrity. He had refused to help Saddam develop a nuclear bomb, a stance for which he had been imprisoned in Abu Ghraib prison for eleven years, much of it in solitary confinement. That same integrity kept him from promising to deliver the ingratiating comments about America that Bush wanted. Carrying out the president's instructions, Bremer vetoed Shahristani.

Bremer and Blackwill also vetoed Adel Abdul Mehdi, a talented economist and moderate on matters of religion, because he was supported by SCIRI. They also refused Ibrahim Jaafari, the medical doctor who led Dawa (the "Call"), Iraq's oldest Shiite religious party. As Bremer writes, the Bush Administration did not want to turn over power to an Islamic party linked to Iran. At least, the Administration did not want to see an Islamic face on Iraq's post-Saddam government until after the American presidential elections.

The various vetoes maneuvered Brahimi into the choice the Administration had wanted in the first place: the secular Shiite Ayad Allawi. A medical doctor, Allawi had been a rising star in the Ba'ath Party when he went to London in the 1970s and turned against Saddam Hussein. One night an Iraqi agent stole into Allawi's house and tried to kill him with an axe, nearly severing one of Allawi's legs.

In 1990, Allawi helped form the Iraqi National Accord (INA), which was a rival to the Iraqi National Congress headed by his estranged relative Ahmad Chalabi. In the 1990s, Allawi convinced the CIA that his group had a network of supporters within Saddam's military and security establishment who, with support, would stage a coup. In fact, Iraqi intelligence had penetrated Allawi's network from the start. In June 1996, the Iraqi security services arrested more than one hundred military officers and others linked to the plot, executing most along with family members. A senior U.S. official told Robin Wright of the *Los Angeles Times* that it was "one of the greatest setbacks U.S. intelligence has ever suffered." The Kurds who worked with Allawi liked him, but also considered him a self-promoter prone to exaggeration.

The president of Iraq had few powers under the TAL, but the position of head of state was symbolically important. The Kurds promoted Jalal Talabani for the position. At seventy, he had been fighting successive Iraqi dictatorships for half a century. Well known internationally, quick-witted (he had a degree in law and taught himself English), Talabani was a giant of the Kurdish movement and of the Iraqi opposition. After eighty years at the margins of Iraq, the Kurds felt it was their turn to hold one of Iraq's top positions. The Kurdish peshmerga had helped liberate Iraq, and the Kurds, alone among Iraq's peoples, espoused the values the Americans said they wanted to instill in Iraq. After the Shiites, the Kurds and the Sunni Arabs were about equally numerous in Iraq's population.

Bremer, however, decided the president had to be a Sunni Arab and so informed Talabani in mid-May: "For too long they [the Sunni Arabs] have felt underrepresented in the new Iraq, Mr. Talabani." Talabani and Barzani were furious. For more than a year, the American had lectured them about the importance of being Iraqi. Now, they were being told their ethnicity disqualified them from Iraq's top jobs. Insult was added to injury when the Americans and Brahimi chose as Iraq's interim president Sheik Ghazi al-Yawar, a Sunni Arab businessman from one of the country's largest tribes who had no previous political experience. Ghazi met Bush's overriding criteria for Iraq's new leaders. According to Bremer, "the president sent word to me that he'd been favorably impressed by Ghazi's open thanks to the Coalition for overthrowing Saddam."

On May 31, Brahimi announced the appointments of Allawi and al-Yawar at a Baghdad press conference. His unhappiness with the outcome was apparent. As he explained defensively, "The Americans were governing this country, so their view was certainly taken into consideration . . . Whether Dr. Allawi was their choice, whether they maneuvered to get him, you know, in position—that, I think, you better ask them."

As the price of their support for the TAL, the Kurds had insisted that the ratification procedures for the permanent constitution protect Kurdistan from an Iraqi constitution imposed without the consent of its people. The original Kurdish proposal would have allowed the Iraqi constitution to come into effect when approved by a majority in the country but would not have applied it in Kurdistan unless approved by Kurdistan's voters. Bremer, however, saw this common-sense formulation as unacceptable ethnic favoritism. As an alternative, Bremer and Suleimania Kurdistan Prime Minister Barham Salih came up with the proposal that gave any three Iraqi governorates the option to veto the constitution by a two-thirds margin.* While Iraq's Shiites had not objected to the original Kurdistan opt-out provision, they objected to the three-governorate veto clause, in part because Sunni Arabs might also

---

* Three governorates—Dahuk, Erbil, and Suleimania—were each more than 95 percent Kurdish, making it easy for the Kurdish political parties to mobilize a no vote if necessary.

† In the October 2005 referendum, the Sunni Arabs mustered a two-thirds no vote in two governorates but could only get a 58 percent no vote in Nineveh (Mosul). In part this was because Saddam had gerrymandered Nineveh's borders to include some strategically important Kurdish areas. The Kurds overwhelmingly supported a constitution that brought them close to independence (see Chapter 9).

be able to veto the constitution.† Sistani deemed the veto clause undemocratic and said that the elected National Assembly would not have to follow the TAL.

As a matter of international law, laws made by an occupying power are not valid after the occupation ends. For the TAL legally to bind Iraq's politicians after the transfer of sovereignty, the United Nations Security Council would have to endorse it in a resolution. But neither Bremer nor his team realized this.

It was a rookie mistake. In drafting the TAL, Bremer relied on two talented young aides, one a midlevel foreign service officer and the other a twenty-four-year-old conservative who had worked in the White House. The foreign service officer was not a lawyer and the White House man was applying to law school.

The Kurds had expected the TAL would be part of a Security Council resolution confirming the end of the occupation and the restoration of Iraqi sovereignty. Sistani threatened a fatwa if the TAL were mentioned. Faced with a choice between the ayatollah and upholding its own democratic constitution, the Bush Administration chose Sistani. U.N. Security Council Resolution 1546, adopted June 8, 2004, mentioned "a federal, democratic, pluralist, and unified Iraq," but not the TAL.

For the Kurds, these developments were only a temporary setback. After the January elections, the Shiite religious parties needed Kurdish support to form a government. Talabani became Iraq's first democratically elected head of state and the Shiites committed to support the procedures of the TAL. But the entire exercise served to further harden the Kurds against the concept of a united Iraq.

On June 28, 2004, Iraq's then Deputy Prime Minister Barham Salih escorted Bremer to a West Virginia Air National Guard C-130 plane on the tarmac of the Baghdad International Airport.* As photographers snapped the picture that would appear in the next day's newspapers,

---

* With the formation of an interim government, Barham Salih gave up his position in Kurdistan to become Iraq's Deputy Prime Minister. In the government formed after the January 2005 elections, he became Planning Minister.

Bremer stood in the aircraft door and waved goodbye. The door closed, the farewell party left, and nothing happened. When the coast was clear, Bremer and his bodyguard left the C-130, ran to a nearby helicopter, flew to a different part of the airport, and then boarded a waiting jet to Jordan. If insurgents were planning to attack the C-130, he had outfoxed them.

June 30 was the scheduled date for the handover, but the White House decided to advance it by two days to outwit possible terrorists. At 10 A.M. on June 28, the CPA had scheduled a joint press conference with Bremer and Iraq's new prime minister, Ayad Allawi. When they arrived, the reporters were ushered into Allawi's office to watch as Bremer handed a letter to Iraq's chief justice formally transferring sovereignty. "I admitted," he writes, "disappointment that we had not been able to establish a secure environment." He told Allawi, "The insurgents have proven better organized and more difficult to penetrate than we had expected." There was an open line to President Bush and his team, who were then in Ankara for a NATO summit, but as Bremer, the best-protected man in Iraq, writes, "when the correspondents arrived at the former Governing Council building, our staff collected everybody's cell phones, so that they could not report the event [in] real time, or immediately after, to allow me to leave Iraq first."

What had started with neoconservative fantasies of cheering Iraqis greeting American liberators with flowers and candy, ended with a secret ceremony and a decoy plane.

CHAPTER 8

Kurdistan

C overt action should not be confused with missionary work." With these words, Henry Kissinger shrugged off the consequences of his abrupt termination of a covert operation to assist Iraq's Kurds. On March 11, 1970, Kurdish leader Mullah Mustafa Barzani and Iraqi Vice President Saddam Hussein reached a framework agreement for a semiautonomous Kurdistan.* The Shah of Iran, who had supported the Kurds in their rebellions against Baghdad, viewed the agreement with alarm since it would strengthen Iraq's Ba'athist regime and Iraq itself. Over the next few years, the Shah tried to induce Barzani to abandon the autonomy agreement and resume the Kurdish revolt. Barzani, however, did not trust the Shah, a fact of which the Shah was well aware.

So, the Shah enlisted the Americans. On May 30, 1972, President Richard Nixon and Kissinger made a twenty-two-hour visit to Tehran. In addition to giving the Shah almost unlimited access to modern U.S. weapons, Nixon and Kissinger agreed to support a covert assistance program to Iraq's Kurds, a program so secret that the American ambassador to Iran was not informed. Believing the Americans were committed to his cause, Barzani now toughened his negotiating stance with the Iraqi state, and in 1974 rejected a final offer from Saddam. The Kurdish revolt resumed.

A year later, on March 6, 1975, Saddam and the Shah conferred during an OPEC meeting in Algiers. Saddam agreed to the Shah's demand

* Mullah Mustafa Barzani was the father of Kurdistan President Massoud Barzani.

that the border between their countries be at the thalweg of the Shatt al-Arab, or the midpoint of the deepest channel. In return, the Shah agreed to turn over to Iraq 210 square miles in the central sector of the two countries' border and to end Iran's support for Barzani and his Kurdish rebels.

By this time, Nixon was gone but Henry Kissinger was now President Ford's secretary of state. Without a word of protest, he accommodated the Shah's about-face, ending the CIA's program for the Kurds. Barzani was now a refugee along with 30,000 peshmerga and family members.*

In his first visit to Kurdistan in May 2003, Ambassador L. Paul Bremer III looked at one of the many portraits of Mullah Mustafa Barzani and asked his son Massoud, "Who's that?" The Kurds were dumbfounded. Bremer was Kissinger's protégé, but he seemed not to know about the man his old boss had double-crossed. Mullah Mustafa Barzani had learned the hard way that the Kurds could not rely on American support, and it was not a lesson his son would forget. Anyone with an elementary knowledge of the history of Kurdistan or the role of the Barzani family would have known that Massoud was never going to play his assigned role in what Bremer was to call the "path to a new Iraq . . . where the majority is not Sunni, Shia, Arab, Kurd, or Turcoman but Iraqi."

Thirty million strong, the Kurds describe themselves as the world's most numerous people without a country of their own.† The Kurds

---

* Mustafa Barzani died of lung cancer in George Washington University Hospital on March 1, 1979, having lived long enough to see Kissinger lose office when Ford was defeated in 1977 and the Shah driven from power in January 1979.

† The Kurds used to say that they were the second most numerous people without their own state, after the Ukrainians. In September 1991, I was with Karim Khan, a Kurdish Agha (Agha are traditional tribal leaders), in the high mountains where Iraq, Turkey, and Iran come together. A peshmerga and I were listening to the BBC shortwave broadcast in which the Ukraine proclaimed its independence. I turned to my host to congratulate him on the Kurds' new status as the world's most numerous stateless people.

speak an Indo-European language, and are ethnically, culturally, and linguistically closest to the Persian people of Iran. By far the largest number live in Turkey, where they constitute a quarter of the population, or about 18 million. There are about 8 million Kurds in Iran, 6 million in Iraq, and smaller populations in Syria, the Caucusus, and Kazakhstan. While Kurdish culture is associated with the mountains (their favorite saying is "the Kurds have no friends but the mountains"), most Iraqi Kurds live in the cities and towns at the edge of the mountains. Iraq's Kurds are mostly Sunni,* but generally practice a more liberal version of Islam than the Arabs. Many of their rituals, including the celebration of Newroz on March 21, hearken back to their pre-Islamic Zoroastrian past.

The Kurds have suffered in all the countries where they live, but nowhere as horrifically as in Iraq. Not surprisingly, therefore, Iraq is the incubator of Kurdish nationalism, and the place where the Kurds are closest to their dream of independence.

In the aftermath of World War I, the Kurds thought they had been promised an independent state. In his 14 Points (1918), President Woodrow Wilson proclaimed national self-determination as the organizing principle of the postwar world, a promise embraced by the subjects of the collapsing empires, including the Kurds. For a brief moment the Kurds thought they had their independence. In 1920, at Sèvres near Versailles, the Allies imposed on the remains of the Ottoman Empire a treaty of capitulation. Article 64 of the Treaty of Sèvres stated:

> If within one year from the coming into force of the present
> Treaty the Kurdish peoples within the areas defined in Article 62
> [i.e., Turkey] shall address themselves to the Council of the

---

* Before Saddam came to power, there were over a million Fayli Kurds in Iraq, who lived along the Iranian border south of Kurdistan and in Baghdad. Saddam stripped the Fayli Kurds of their citizenship and many were expelled to Iran. Baghdad's Kurdish population today appears to be mostly Fayli, and in the 2005 elections they voted for the Shiite religious parties, not the Kurdistan Coalition.

League of Nations in such a manner as to show that a majority of
the population of these areas desires independence from Turkey,
and if the Council then considers that these peoples are capable
of such independence and recommends that it should be granted
to them, Turkey hereby agrees to execute such a recommenda-
tion, and to renounce all rights and title over these areas.

The same treaty assigned the Kurdish parts of Mesopotamia (now
Iraqi Kurdistan) to Britain but allowed its people to join Kurdistan if it
were created.

[N]o objection will be raised by the Principal Allied Powers to the
voluntary adhesion to such an independent Kurdish State of the
Kurds inhabiting that part of Kurdistan which has hitherto been
included in the Mosul valiyet.

For the Kurds, the Treaty of Sèvres was their holy grail, their moment in the international sun. Even today, in any discussion with
Kurdish academics on the national question—and discussion of almost any topic in Kurdistan eventually turns to the national question—
they will refer to the Treaty of Sèvres with verbatim citations of Articles
62 and 64. In Turkey, however, the Sèvres terms caused a revolution. It
led to the proclamation of the Turkish Republic and the rise to power of
Mustafa Kemal, the general who defeated the British Empire in the battle of Gallipoli and later became Turkey's great modernizer, known as
Ataturk, or the father of the Turks. Bankrupt and preoccupied with
events in war-devastated Europe, the Allies had no stomach to enforce
the terms of Sèvres. In 1923, they concluded a new treaty with Turkey in
Lausanne, Switzerland. It made no mention of an independent Kurdistan.* And just as Kurds to this day reverently talk of Sèvres, Turks fre-
quently display copies of the Treaty of Lausanne in their offices, along
with the mandatory portraits of Ataturk.

---

* The other big losers were the Greeks, who were expelled from Anatolia, and the
  Armenians, who also lost their hopes for a state.

As the Sèvres Treaty was unraveling in 1921, the British now had to decide what to do with the predominantly Kurdish valiyet of Mosul. Winston Churchill, the cabinet minister responsible for the Near East, was open to the idea of an independent Kurdistan carved out of the Mosul valiyet. He foresaw, correctly as it turned out, the myriad problems of forcing the Kurds to live in an Arab state. However, the Colonial Office professionals led by Sir Percy Cox (the British high commissioner for Mesopotamia) and his advisor Gertrude Bell argued for the inclusion of Kurdistan in Iraq, not only to enlarge the new state but to have the Sunni Kurds help the Sunni Arabs offset the numerical superiority of the Shiites.

The Kurds never reconciled to being part of Iraq, and the entire history of modern Iraq is characterized by periodic Kurdish rebellions and Iraqi repression. When Iraq gained full sovereignty in 1932, the British required it to grant autonomy to the Kurds as a condition of its admission to the League of Nations the same year. But this did not happen and the requirement disappeared in 1945 when the United Nations replaced the League.

In 1946, the Kurds in neighboring Iran proclaimed an autonomous republic in the city of Mahabad, choosing as its flag a red-white-green tricolor emblazoned with a yellow sun with twenty-one rays. Mullah Mustafa Barzani, the head of Iraqi Kurdistan's most prominent clan, went to Mahabad, where he was made commander of its armed forces. While in Mahabad, on August 16, 1946, Barzani founded the Kurdistan Democratic Party. By happy coincidence, his son Massoud was born the same day.

The Mahabad Republic was short-lived, collapsing when the Soviets—who occupied northern Iran at the end of World War II—withdrew. Barzani and his forces trekked through the mountains to the Soviet Union. Prime Minister Qazi Mohammed stayed behind, and the Shah hanged him.

Barzani returned to Iraq after the 1958 coup that overthrew the monarchy. The new republic proclaimed Kurds and Arabs equal peoples in the new Iraq, but it was a brief reconciliation. When Baghdad failed to live up to its commitments on Kurdistan autonomy, Barzani launched a new revolt in 1961. In January 1970, Mullah Mustafa's son, Massoud, received an unusual message. An Iraqi delegation had shown up at the checkpoint near Barzani's headquarters in Choman. Massoud went to meet the guests, who included several ministers, and the man who was clearly in charge: Saddam Hussein. Saddam, Massoud recalls, was friendly and practical. In a mud guesthouse he sat with Mullah Mustafa Barzani to discuss how to end the war. The elder Barzani told Saddam that no peace was possible without autonomy, and that under no circumstances would he give up the peshmerga. Saddam accepted both conditions. When Mullah Mustafa raised the question of democracy in Iraq, Saddam asked: "Why do you care what happens in the rest of Iraq? You have your autonomy in Kurdistan. What system we have in our part of Iraq is of no concern to you."

On March 11, 1970, the Iraqi government announced a limited autonomy for Kurdistan, and Mullah Mustafa ordered his peshmerga to stop fighting. The negotiations continued but the two sides could never reach agreement on whether Kirkuk would be part of the autonomous Kurdistan Region. It was at that point, in 1974, that Barzani restarted the Kurdish revolution in the belief he had American support.

After the Shah and Saddam Hussein agreed to the Algiers Accord, the Shah sent word to Barzani that he had a choice: he could surrender to Iraq or to Iran. Barzani announced the end to the Kurdish rebellion on March 23, 1975. Not all Kurds agreed. Jalal Talabani, an energetic Barzani lieutenant steeped in Marxist ideology, broke with Barzani to found the Patriotic Union of Kurdistan (PUK) in 1975. Both the KDP and the PUK carried out raids against the Iraqi regime in the late 1970s, but the Shah's refusal to allow operations from Iranian territory meant that any Kurdish military activity was small-scale. Ayatollah Khomeini, who toppled the Shah at the beginning of 1979, set his sights on overthrowing Iraq's Ba'athist regime. He resumed Iranian support for the Iraqi Kurds. In many cases, however, the KDP and PUK were as interested in fighting each other as they were in fighting the Iraqi government.

With the outbreak of the Iran-Iraq war, the KDP aligned itself with Iran. When Iran opened an offensive in the north in 1983, the PUK announced it would resist the Iranians and began negotiations with Baghdad. These negotiations broke down in 1985, and fighting between the PUK and the regime resumed. In 1987, Iraq began attacking villages in Eastern Kurdistan's Balisan Valley with chemical weapons, initiating the Anfal campaign. On March 16, 1988, Iraqi poison gas killed 5,000 civilians in Halabja. Between August 25 and 27, 1988, Iraqi airplanes and helicopters gassed forty-eight villages in Dahuk Governorate. As part of the Anfal, the Iraqi government eradicated more than four thousand Kurdish villages, relocated or deported more than one million people, and killed between 100,000 and 200,000 Kurds. In 1988, the KDP and PUK set aside their differences to form the Iraqi Kurdistan Front (with three smaller parties). Facing the full force of the Iraqi military after the August 20, 1988, end of the Iran-Iraq War and without a rural population to shelter its peshmerga, the Iraqi Kurdistan Front operated only in the most mountainous parts of Kurdistan in 1989 and 1990. Talabani and Barzani became exiles in Syria and Iran, respectively.

Iraq's invasion of Kuwait and the war that followed provided new opportunities for the Kurdish resistance. When the allied bombing of Iraq started on January 16, 1991, peshmerga inside Iraq collected intelligence on the actual damage, which was radioed to Damascus, called into a Kurdish dentist in Detroit, and then translated and faxed to me at the Senate Foreign Relations Committee. I passed it on to U.S. military intelligence, which showed little interest even though much of the Kurdish reporting about bombing damage turned out to be more accurate, and less favorable to the Air Force, than the assessments based on satellite and aerial photographs.

With Saddam's defeat in the ground war and the start of the Shiite uprising at the beginning of March, Iraq's Kurds seized the opportunity to throw off the hated Iraqi yoke. In the middle of March, the KDP and PUK leaders returned to Iraqi Kurdistan to take control of the newly liberated region. As previously told, the uprising collapsed at the end of March as the Iraqi Army moved north and the peshmerga helped evacuate the large urban population for which they had unexpectedly become responsible. At the beginning of April, the peshmerga stopped Iraqi tanks in battles at Kore north of Erbil and on Aznar Mountain east of Suleimania. This left a large swath of territory, perhaps 7,000 square miles, under Kurdish control. When the United States intervened in the northwest to establish the safe haven, it added another 3,000 square miles to the Kurdish enclave. Dahuk was the only sizable city within the enclave. Much of the rest of the Kurdish-controlled territory was empty countryside dotted with piles of stone that had once been villages.

When he set up the Kurdish safe haven, President George H. W. Bush described it as a temporary measure. Therefore, when Saddam invited Talabani and Barzani to resume negotiations on autonomy in April, they did. The dictator, Massoud Barzani thought, was very different from the practical man he had met in the mountains twenty years before. "Even his closest aides were afraid to speak in his presence," Barzani later told me. Saddam was conciliatory, but not prepared to go beyond the limited autonomy of the March 1970 agreement. Barzani gently raised the issue of the tens of thousands of Kurds who had disappeared in the preceding decade, a figure that included 5,000 members of the Barzani clan although he did not specifically mention them. "He couldn't look at me," Barzani recalls. "He said, 'Many bad things have happened. If we reach an agreement, I will release those still alive. We will also fix something for those not alive.'" At that moment, Barzani says, "I knew they were all dead."

Saddam began his negotiations with the Kurds at a time when his hold on power seemed tenuous in the immediate aftermath of the March 1991 uprisings. By summer 1991, he was more confident and less willing to compromise. As it became clear that U.S. military support would continue, the Kurds also became less flexible. In September, Saddam decided to call the Kurds' bluff. He withdrew the Iraqi military to a line that he deemed to be the boundary of Kurdistan, giving the Kurdish political parties control over the region's two major cities, Suleimania and Erbil.* He also stopped paying salaries for Kurd-ish civil servants, including teachers and police, which meant that the new Kurdish authorities were responsible for a large population but with no means to provide for them.

Saddam expected the Kurdish authorities to capitulate. Instead, teachers continued teaching and police policing, all without pay. And as the situation normalized, ordinary Kurds reveled in their new free-doms, including such simple pleasures as being able to picnic in the countryside.

In 1992, the Iraqi Kurdistan Front decided to establish a Kurdistan Regional Government and to elect a Kurdistan Assembly and Kurdi-stan president. The elections, the first-ever fully democratic vote held in Iraq, were a moving testament to the idea of democracy. In order to avoid fraud and to facilitate international monitoring, the Kurdish au-thorities set up only several hundred polling places in a Switzerland-sized territory. Kurds traveled long distances to the polls and waited up to eight hours in line to vote. Turnout exceeded 80 percent.

The outcome was as unfortunate as the balloting was extraordinary. The KDP and the PUK effectively tied in the assembly elections. Neither Massoud Barzani nor Jalal Talabani had a majority in the presidential race. Rather than pursue a divisive runoff, the parties agreed not to have a president, but to govern in a coalition cabinet with ministerial positions equally divided between the two parties. On the ground, the PUK had its base in the eastern city of Suleimania while the KDP enjoyed solid support in the Kermanji-speaking areas along the Turkish border. Erbil, the capital, remained contested territory.

The power-sharing arrangements worked tenuously, and fell apart in 1994 over disputes about sharing revenues at the KDP-controlled Khabur Bridge, where Kurdish "customs fees" on legal and smuggled trade with Turkey provided the regional authorities their only source

---

* The boundary became known as the Green Line, and is the official boundary of the Kurdistan Region as enshrined in the TAL and Iraq's permanent constitution. The Kurds administer areas beyond the Green Line where the population is largely Kurdish and claim the mixed governorate and city of Kirkuk.

of revenue. Clashes between peshmerga associated with the rival parties evolved into an intra-Kurdish civil war.

In August 1996, a PUK military offensive, abetted by the Iranians, led a desperate Massoud Barzani to ask Saddam Hussein for help. On August 31, Iraqi forces entered Erbil, ousted the PUK, installed the KDP, and left. The Clinton Administration took steps to abandon the safe area, on the grounds that Saddam had effectively retaken the territory. The U.S. evacuated some five thousand Kurds thought to be at particular risk because of their association with the United Nations, relief groups, or the U.S. military during the safe-haven period.

From the embassy in Zagreb, I called colleagues in the Administration to make the case that Barzani's action, while regrettable, did not mean the end of Kurdistan's self-rule.* I stressed that four million Kurds were at risk, not just the five thousand being evacuated, and that the U.S. should preserve the safe area. I always thought the events of 1996 gave Saddam an opportunity to eliminate a separate Kurdistan, which had become a base for opposition to his rule within Iraq. Saddam had told Barzani that the Iraqi Army would not stay in Erbil and, for whatever reason, he kept his word. By the end of 1996, the United States was back in the pattern of fully protecting Kurdistan.

In 1998, after two years of intensive diplomatic effort, the State Department brokered an end to the war between the KDP and the PUK. Each party had its own enclave, the PUK in Suleimania and the KDP in Erbil and Dahuk. Turkish peacekeepers monitored a no-man's-land between the two. Each enclave had its own prime minister and government, although both described themselves as the Kurdistan Regional Government. Over the years that followed, the two enclaves increased cooperation and eventually asked the Turkish peacekeepers to leave. At the end of 2002, the PUK members agreed to return to the Kurdistan National Assembly in Erbil, enabling it to function once again as the legislature for the entire region. In 2005, the KDP and PUK jointly supported Massoud Barzani for president of Kurdistan and in 2006 formed a single cabinet under Prime Minister Nechirvan Barzani.

* As noted, I had become Ambassador to Croatia in 1993.

In spite of their divisions, the Kurds made good use of the twelve years of freedom under U.S. and British protection. In the seventy years up to 1991 that Iraq ruled Kurdistan, the Baghdad authorities constructed one thousand schools. The two Kurdistan Governments built another two thousand schools between 1992 and 2003, recruiting and training the necessary teachers. When Saddam pulled out of Kurdistan in 1991, there was one university in the region. The Kurdistan Governments opened two new universities—in Dahuk and Suleimania. All three are of high quality. Medical instruction is in English, and Kurdistan's new doctors are qualified by the British Medical Board.

Most important, the Kurds rebuilt the four thousand villages destroyed by Saddam Hussein's army in the 1970s and 1980s. Farmers restored old water systems. Abandoned fields again sprouted wheat and barley. With funding from the United Nations under the oil-for-food program, the Kurdistan Governments embarked on an ambitious program of reforestation, planting millions of pines on hills that have been denuded for centuries. As a result, the Kurds started to change the ecology of their region. When I visited in the summer of 1987 as Saddam's effort to destroy rural Kurdistan was in full swing, I had the impression of a barren, dust-choked land. Visiting again in the summer fifteen years later, the yellow of grains waiting to be harvested had replaced the brown and gray of the earlier landscape.

As the second Iraq War loomed in 2002, many Kurds feared that Saddam's fall would mean the end of their American-protected freedom, and that the Americans might allow a more democratic Iraqi government to reduce their independence. A Kurdish shopkeeper in Suleimania told me in July 2002, "When Saddam dies, I hope he is tortured in hell for all eternity. But for now, I wish him long life."

Barzani and Talabani made a simple strategic choice. They knew they could not influence President Bush's decision on whether to go to war. But, if the United States did go to war, they decided they wanted to be firmly on the American side. In the buildup to war and in the war itself, the United States had no more enthusiastic partner. Kurdish peshmerga took more casualties than any other American ally. The severely wounded included Massoud Barzani's brother, who suffered near-fatal head injuries in a "friendly fire" incident.

However, the Americans mistook Kurdistan's devotion to the alliance as a sign that the Kurds would play their assigned role in building a new Iraq that was democratic, multiethnic, and united. It was wishful thinking, as could readily be determined by a visit to Kurdistan, or a quick review of its history.

The Iraq War produced the best possible outcome for the Kurds. The United States not only removed Saddam but also destroyed the foundations of Sunni Arab rule in Iraq, the Army, the Ba'ath Party, and the intelligence services. When Bremer applied the coup de grâce by officially dissolving these institutions, the Kurds applauded. Bremer had consolidated the independence of Kurdistan.

The war also altered the international position of Kurdistan. In February 2003, the Turkish Parliament refused permission for the American 4th Infantry Division—then circling in warships in the eastern Mediterranean—to move through Turkey to open a second front in Iraq's north. The refusal created a full-scale crisis in U.S.-Turkish relations and infuriated the Pentagon neoconservatives who had long promoted close U.S. ties with Turkey.* The Kurds made many American friends by creating the northern front that had been the assigned task of the 4th Infantry. As American forces swept north from Kuwait, peshmerga units, assisted by American Special Forces, tied down Iraqi divisions and then entered Mosul and Kirkuk as Saddam's forces collapsed.

The display of American power that swept away Saddam also had, from a Kurdish perspective, a salutary effect on two other traditional foes: Iran and Syria. As one Kurdish leader described to me:

* The Turkish government compounded American anger by suggesting the Parliament would change its vote, which it didn't. The 4th Infantry Division sailed in circles in the eastern Mediterranean before heading to Kuwait. It was still in transit when military operations actually began in Iraq.

We Kurds have always been kept at bay by four dogs—Iraq, Iran, Syria, and Turkey. The Iraq dog is dead. The Turkish dog is in the doghouse. The Iranian and Syrian dogs cower in their corners.

Two weeks after Saddam's fall, I began discussions with the Kurdish leaders on the future of Kurdistan and what they might achieve in the new Iraq constitution. I spoke to Massoud Barzani and Jalal Talabani, but their minds were, understandably, focused on forming an interim Iraqi government* and a myriad of other more immediate postwar issues. Some of my best discussions were with Kurdistan's two young prime ministers, Barham Salih in Suleimania and Nechirvan Barzani in Erbil. Nechirvan, Massoud's nephew, had been prime minister in Erbil since December 1999. He is decisive, action-oriented, and a tough negotiator. As we had more and more discussions about the future of Kurdistan and Iraq, I found him a superb strategic thinker with a very clear goal—to preserve the de facto independence of Kurdistan.

Barham Salih is an accomplished diplomat. He has a range of Washington contacts that would be the envy of any American politician and can be extraordinarily persuasive. As the PUK representative in the United States throughout the 1990s, Barham developed close ties both with the Democrats in the White House and Congress and with the neoconservatives who later came to run the Pentagon, the vice president's office, and National Security Council staff. Like Ahmad Chalabi, Barham† made the case for regime change in Iraq, but no one accused him of deception as they did Chalabi. No one—Iraqi or American—dealing with Iraq had as many friends in the media, or such consistently favorable press coverage. As prime minister of the PUK part of Kurdistan, Barham had presided over an extraordinary boom in construction, as well as major expansion in public services, of which he was justly proud.

* Bremer didn't pull the plug on this idea until May 16.

† The Bush Administration has aggressively promoted Barham Salih for influential positions in Baghdad. Unlike Chalabi, Barham was supported by all of President Bush's warring departments and agencies.

While they had secured support from the Iraqi opposition for federalism, the Kurds had yet to think through some practical issues. What powers would belong to Kurdistan and what to the central government in Baghdad? How would a Kurdistan Government be funded? Who would control the police and security forces? And there was the all-important question, Who would own the oil of Kurdistan?

I described other federal models to Nechirvan and Barham, notably Canada, where the provinces own the natural resources but the federal government taxes a share of the revenue; the United States, where states and municipalities control the police; and Bosnia, where the American-written Dayton constitution gave each federal entity its own army. Both prime ministers asked if I would be willing to provide advice as the constitutional process went forward, and I agreed to do so. On the morning of April 30, I went over constitutional issues with Nechirvan at his official residence in Erbil, pressing him as to the Kurdish agenda. As he walked me to the door, he said, "We want the maximum."

After I left Iraq in May 2003, I realized that the Kurdish leaders had a conceptual problem in planning for a federal Iraq. They were thinking in terms of devolution of power—meaning that Baghdad grants them rights. I urged that the equation be reversed. In a memo I sent Barham and Nechirvan in August, I drew a distinction between the previous autonomy proposals and federalism:

> Federalism is a "bottom up" system. The basic organizing unit of the country is the province or state. The state or province is constituted first and then delegates certain powers (of its choice) to the central government. It is different from an autonomy arrangement where the central government grants certain powers (of the central government's choice) to the local authority. In a federal system residual power lies with the federal unit (i.e. state or province); under an autonomy system it rests with the central government. The central government has no ability to revoke a federal status or power: it can revoke an autonomy arrangement.

Kurdistan, I wrote, should take the initiative by writing its own constitution before the Iraqi constitutional process began. I urged a relatively brief document with strong human rights protections (both because it is right and makes for good public relations) and which clearly defined the powers of the Kurdistan Government as against those of the government in Baghdad. Three issues—oil, police, and military—emerged as key. Kurdistan would not have meaningful self-government unless it controlled a source of revenue, which in the Iraqi context meant oil. While Kurdistan might agree to pool oil revenues with other parts of Iraq, it should, I argued, own and manage its own oil resources. With regard to police, it was not enough that the local security forces be Kurdish—Saddam had made good use of Kurdish collaborators in the 1980s—but that they be established and run by the Kurdistan Government. "You should," I wrote, "have exclusive control over police activities in the north (meaning no police or internal security forces from any other part of Iraq may operate there)."

I urged that the Kurdistan constitution explicitly guarantee Kurdistan "the power to establish, maintain, regulate, and control a Kurdistan self-defense force." I knew this went counter to the Pentagon's ambitions to build a unified Iraqi Army, but I thought that idea was both unrealistic and undesirable. The Iraqi Army was the only enemy the Kurds had ever known, and they were never going to give up the peshmerga to an Arab-dominated army supposedly reformed by the United States. Finally, I wrote, the Kurdistan constitution should make clear whose law prevails—Iraq's or Kurdistan's—in the event of a conflict: "The Constitution should state that the Constitution of Kurdistan, and laws made pursuant to the Constitution, is the supreme law of Kurdistan. Any conflict between laws of Kurdistan and the laws or Constitution of Iraq shall be decided in favor of the former." These ideas eventually became the basis of Kurdistan's proposals for an Iraqi constitution.

Every Iraqi Kurd I know wants an independent Kurdistan and I sympathize with those sentiments, not least because I know that I would not want to be part of a country that had treated me the way

Iraq treated the Kurds. My views on the future of Iraq, however, are not based on sentiment or friendship. The conventional wisdom holds that Iraq's breakup would be destabilizing and therefore should be avoided at all costs. Looking at Iraq's dismal eighty-year history, it should be apparent that it is the effort to hold Iraq together that has been destabilizing. Pursuit of a coerced unity has led to endless violence, repression, dictatorship, and genocide. I don't believe it is possible over the long run to force people living in a geographically defined area to remain part of a state against their will. Iraq's Kurds will never reconcile to being part of Iraq. Under these circumstances, I believe a managed amicable divorce is in the best interests of the peoples of Iraq, and will contribute to greater stability in the region.

By the summer of 2003, I had become a vocal critic of the Bush Administration's misconduct of the postwar situation. My views of Iraq's future were significantly at variance with U.S. policy. Unlike many other American analysts of Iraq, I would inevitably be talking about these matters with my Iraqi friends, including the Kurds. Although my position as a professor at the National War College came with guarantees of academic freedom, I did not want it suggested that I was undermining U.S. policy while on the Defense Department's payroll. So, in October 2003, I ended my twenty-four-year career with the U.S. government, and joined the Center for Arms Control and Non-Proliferation as Senior Diplomatic Fellow.

The Kurds saw the writing of Iraq's interim constitution not as an opportunity to build a new Iraq (as Bremer believed) but as a purely defensive exercise. Their goal was simple: to have a document that took the least away from them. The Kurds knew the strength of their hand: they controlled their own territory, they had their own army, and they were politically united.

The Kurdish leaders had no concern about their ability to get their way with the Arab Iraqis but were concerned about American pressure. When I returned to Kurdistan in December 2003, I tried to reassure them. The United States, I pointed out, needed the Kurds at least as much as the Kurds needed the Americans. The occupation was going poorly, and the last thing the Bush Administration wanted was trouble in the one stable and pro-American part of Iraq. I reminded Barzani and Talabani of the experience of Bosnia's wartime leader Alija Izetbegovic, who annoyed the Europeans and the Americans by turning down the many peace proposals that would have partitioned his country. Because he persevered, Bosnia survived and Izetbegovic paid no price for insisting on what he believed to be just. The Bush Administration might not like the Kurds insisting on their rights, I said, but it would respect them for doing so.

The Kurdish leaders asked me to go through the more practical aspects of how the negotiations on the interim constitution might be conducted. I explained that, if I were conducting the negotiations for the CPA, I would want to control the text. In the negotiations that led to the Dayton peace treaty (in which I participated), principal U.S. negotiator Ambassador Richard C. Holbrooke began by getting the parties to agree to general principles and then had American experts fill in the details in the way we wanted them to be. We also worked off an English language text, which gave us an advantage over Serbian/Croatian/Bosnian speaking parties.

I urged Barzani and Talabani to use negotiators rather than participate directly in the constitutional talks. Leaders rarely understand all the nuances of a text and, when they sit at the table, they are under pressure to give an immediate answer. It is usually to a party's advantage when the negotiator can explain that he needs to check any proposed agreement with an absent decisionmaker. At a minimum, this gives time for reflection, but it can also be useful in leveraging additional concessions. And, in my experience, leaders rarely make for good negotiators since their political instincts are to make people happy, and that usually means saying "yes." A good negotiator should enjoy saying "no."

On January 27, 2004, Barzani and Talabani met alone with Bremer. Bremer presented a paper of general principles on federalism: Kurdistan would be recognized as a federal unit, but it would have few powers. The central government would have responsibility for security, natural resources, the economy, and borders. The peshmerga would be disbanded or integrated into the Iraqi Army and Kurdistan's independent judiciary would disappear.

Bremer emerged from the meeting believing that the Kurds had accepted his proposals. When I went over the Bremer paper with Barzani a few days later, he was surprised by what it said and vehemently denied that there was any such agreement. I heard later that Bremer's staff was pleasantly surprised by the ease with which their boss got the Kurds to surrender most of their autonomy. This should have been a clue that there was no meeting of minds.

Massoud Barzani asked me to discuss the matter in greater detail with Sami Abdul Rahman, the KDP's chief negotiator, who had just returned to Kurdistan from medical treatment in the United States. On the morning of January 31, I gave Sami a copy of the supposed agreement, and explained its implications. Sami proposed that we discuss the matter over dinner that evening. Around 6 P.M., he sent me a note postponing the dinner to the next day, saying he had a visitor from far away.

February 1 was the Id al-Adha, a major Muslim feast marking the sacrifice of Abraham. Sami, who was deputy prime minister of the Kurdistan Regional Government, went to the KDP headquarters to receive the public. Because of the press of well-wishers, the Kurdish security forces stopped screening visitors. A suicide bomber joined the receiving line, detonating himself at its head. Nearly simultaneously, another bomber blew himself up at the PUK headquarters in Erbil. I visited the PUK building the day after the explosions. There was an enormous scorch mark where the bomber had detonated himself, and the back wall of the large reception room had collapsed on a car parked behind the building. Congealed blood formed bright red pools on the floor. I found it hard to imagine that one man could carry enough explosives to cause so much carnage.

Altogether 101 died, including three cabinet ministers in the Kurdistan Regional Government, the governor of Erbil Governorate, the deputy governor, and the mayor of Erbil city. Sami, whom I had known since the 1980s, died as did his visitor from far away: his eldest son, a London businessman with two young daughters.*

Within the tight-knit and often intermarried Kurdish political leadership, everyone lost relatives and lifelong friends. Attitudes hardened toward Iraq. A closer union with Baghdad seemed to carry the risk that Iraq's chaos would be imported into hitherto stable Kurdistan. On February 5, I accompanied Nechirvan Barzani from Erbil to Dahuk, where we made a condolence call on Sami's family and visited his grave. On the way, Nechirvan and I discussed what to do next. I said that, if there were no deal, the Kurds had to tell Bremer soon, because it was in no one's interest for Bremer to labor under a false impression. Nechirvan agreed but knew others would be nervous about offending the Americans. Nechirvan told me he would convene a Kurdistan leadership group to prepare its own proposal for Bremer and asked if I would give them some ideas.

Fortunately, it was Bremer who backed off the January 27 proposal first. After a condolence call on the Kurdish leadership on February 6, Bremer drew Massoud Barzani aside to say that he had to send "our agreement" back to the White House, and that there had been changes. The White House, he explained, wanted to eliminate all references to the Kurdistan Regional Government from the interim constitution, which would mean Iraq's federalism would be based on Saddam's eighteen governorates. This was unacceptable to the Kurds, not only because they thought of Kurdistan as one entity (in spite of having two governments), but also because Saddam's governorate boundaries did not match the territory administered by the Kurdistan Government. The White House also wanted to eliminate a provision from the January agreement making Kurdish an official language of Iraq along with Arabic.

---

* The Kurdish leaders all sacrificed their family lives to the cause of Kurdistan. As a peshmerga, Sami was separated from his family for months and years at a time. It was a small consolation that he spent his last evening with his son rather than in a constitutional discussion with me.

These changes were yet another example of ideology trumping reality and common sense. The White House was dreaming of a nonethnic
Iraq. They wanted the federal units based on "geography"—as if Iraqi
provinces should resemble U.S. states where the lines on the map define
the community. The Kurds thought of themselves primarily as Kurds,
not as residents of three Iraqi provinces with borders established by
Saddam Hussein. They were not about to give up their cherished Kurdistan. The White House commitment to making the Kurds into
nonethnic Iraqis included having Arabic as the common language. No
one in the White House seemed to realize that Arabic is also the language of an Iraqi ethnic group.

The Kurds were thrilled with the White House changes. It now
meant they could submit their own proposals.

On February 10, Nechirvan convened a meeting at the Kurdistan
National Assembly of the top leaders of the PUK and KDP. I presented
a draft of a "Kurdistan Chapter" to be included in the interim constitution.* The chapter recognized the Kurdistan Regional Government as
the official government of the territory administered by the Kurds as of
March 18, 2003—the day before the war began. Except for a few matters assigned to the federal government (notably foreign affairs), laws
passed by the Kurdistan National Assembly would be supreme within
the region. The Kurdistan Regional Government could establish an
armed force, called the Iraqi Kurdistan National Guard, under its command. The Kurdistan National Assembly would have to approve any
presence of the Iraqi military in Kurdistan and also approve any deployment of the Iraqi Kurdistan National Guard outside the region.

The Kurdistan Region would own its land, water, minerals, and oil.
Kurdistan would manage future oil fields (and keep the revenues) but

---

* The Kurdistan Regional Government was assisted by a team of constitutional
  scholars: Professor Khaled Salih from the University of Southern Denmark, Professor Brendan O'Leary from the University of Pennsylvania, and, somewhat later,
  Professor Karol E. Soltan from the University of Maryland. Their work focused on
  a range of constitutional matters that affected Kurdistan and Iraq, and included an
  impressive theoretical framework. My own discussions were on the much nar-
  rower issues described here.

the federal government in Baghdad would continue to manage all oil fields currently in commercial production. Because there were no commercial oil fields within Kurdistan as defined by the March 18, 2003, boundaries, this proposal had the effect of giving Kurdistan full control over its own oil. However, if Kirkuk became part of Kurdistan, Baghdad would still manage the gigantic Kirkuk oil field, which was already in production. The Kurds had long insisted that they were not after Kirkuk for the oil, and their proposal made this clear.

Kurdistan would receive a block grant from the federal government. The federal government could only impose taxes in Kurdistan in accordance with an agreement to be negotiated with the Kurdistan Government. The permanent constitution of Iraq would apply in Kurdistan only if it were approved by a majority of Kurdistan's voters.*

Kosrat Rasul, the veteran PUK peshmerga who had served as Kurdistan's second prime minister in 1994, wanted to clarify that deployments of the Iraqi Kurdistan National Guard outside the region should not only be approved by the Kurdistan National Assembly but should only occur at the request of the federal government in Baghdad. His amendment underscored the Kurds' reluctance to be involved in Iraq's wars. With Kosrat's change, the proposal was accepted. Speaker Rowsch Shaways forwarded it the next day, February 11, to the CPA as a submission by the Kurdistan National Assembly.

Bremer's reaction was swift. He asked to see Massoud Barzani immediately, a trip that was delayed twenty-four hours by a Baghdad dust storm that was a blizzard in Kurdistan. (As Barzani explained to him, "You see, Mr. Bremer, even our weather is different.") Once in Kurdistan, Bremer refused to discuss the Kurdistan proposal, insisting that everyone go back to the January 27 agreement. Only after an angry exchange with Nechirvan Barzani did he concede there was no such agreement.

Nonetheless, Bremer got most of what he wanted in the Transitional Administrative Law. The Kurds did not insist on official recognition for the peshmerga and they accepted language that could mean its

---

* The full text is in Appendix 1.

eventual dissolution if followed to the letter. They agreed to awkwardly phrased language that seemed to give the federal government control over water and oil resources.* Kurdistan would remain a single entity within its March 19, 2003, borders and Kurdish became an equal official language of Iraq along with Arabic. The TAL provided a partial formula to resolve the status of Kirkuk: displaced Kurds could return while Arabs who had been moved in under Saddam's Arabization program would go back to their places of origin. There would be a census but its final status was deferred to the permanent constitution.

The Kurds never implemented the provisions of the TAL they did not like. They never gave up control over their international borders with Turkey and Iran and they continued to develop their own oil resources without reference to Baghdad. Of course, they kept the peshmerga.

As Iraq moved to write its permanent constitution, Massoud Barzani† took the initiative to organize a Kurdish delegation and negotiating position that would achieve each objective outlined in their February 11 proposal, and then some. In one of its first acts after convening in June 2005, the newly elected Kurdistan National Assembly adopted a law to prohibit the Iraqi military from entering Kurdistan without the assembly's approval.‡

* The language was ambiguous on the ownership of oil and water resources, allowing both Kurdistan and the central government subsequently to claim ownership. In a late-night session, the Iraqi Governing Council agreed to language that would have given Kurdistan full control over its natural resources. While Bremer had been present, neither he nor his staff understood the import of the language. The next day, Bremer asked Barzani and Talabani to reverse the change, which, to my amazement, they did.

† Talabani had become president of Iraq and assumed the role of consensus builder in the constitutional process. It was, of course, an enormous asset to the Kurdish negotiating team to have one of their own in that position.

‡ This was done as part of the law establishing the office of president of Kurdistan, and under the guise of restricting the president's power unilaterally to permit Iraqi forces into Kurdistan.

The permanent constitution, adopted in the October 2005 referendum, recognized the Kurdistan Region as Iraq's first federal region. The constitution allows Kurdistan, and any future Iraqi regions, to have its own military, called Guards of the Region. Except for the few subjects listed as being within the exclusive jurisdiction of the federal government, the Kurdistan constitution is superior to the federal constitution within Kurdistan, and Kurdistan law prevails when there is a conflict with federal law. This means that Kurdistan's secular legal system and Western-style constitutional human rights protections will continue to apply as other parts of Iraq evolve toward theocracy.

Under the permanent constitution, Kurdistan owns and manages its land and water. As the Kurds proposed in February 2004, the regional governments have exclusive control over future oil fields (those never in commercial production) within their region. The Kurdistan Regional Government, and not Baghdad, determines the legal regime for the development of new oil fields, decides where drilling will take place, and makes investment decisions. The federal government shares control of existing oil fields with the government of the oil-producing region, meaning the Kurds will get a voice in the management of the Kirkuk oil field should Kirkuk become part of Kurdistan. This sharing represented a significant advance for the Kurds over their February 2004 proposal, which gave the federal government sole responsibility for existing commercial production.

The list of exclusive federal powers is much shorter than in the Transitional Administrative Law.* The federal government has exclusive control over foreign affairs, but Regions have offices within Iraqi embassies to handle their affairs. The federal government is responsible for defense policy, but has no control over regional guards and cannot deploy troops to a Region against its will. The federal government prints money but has no power to impose taxes unless the affected Region agrees to be taxed. The federal government regulates weights and measures, thus ensuring that a meter in Basra is the same length as one in Erbil.

---

* These are the only matters where federal law is superior to regional law.

If Bremer had left it to the Iraqis, they would have come up with an interim constitution different from the TAL. It would most likely have resembled the permanent constitution since the same Shiites and Kurds who sat on the Governing Council were the main players in the negotiations on the permanent constitution.* Had the Iraqis been allowed to strike a constitutional bargain in 2004, they would not have given the central government as much authority as the TAL provided, but the deal might have carried through to the permanent constitution. In their proposal for a Kurdistan chapter in the TAL, the Kurds would have placed their self-defense force under the ultimate control of the Baghdad Defense Ministry (subject to caveats) and would have ceded some tax powers to the federal government. Bremer rejected the idea of an Iraqi Kurdistan National Guard outright and would not consider the Kurdish tax compromise. With their ideas having been rejected in the TAL, the Kurds took a tougher line in the negotiations for a permanent constitution and won on every point. They have a Regional Guard that is not subject to Baghdad's supervision, and the central government cannot impose taxes in Kurdistan. The permanent constitution institutionalized a virtually independent Kurdistan, the very result Bremer sought to avoid.

Bremer's handling of the Kurdish question inadvertently inspired the Kurdistan independence movement to pursue its goals more aggressively. In January 2004, a coalition of Kurdistan nongovernmental organizations had founded the Referendum Movement with the goal of permitting Kurdistan to vote on its future status. In three weeks, the Referendum Movement collected 1,700,000 signatures asking for a vote on independence, an amazing number of signatures considering Kurdistan's adult population is around 2,300,000. In February 2004, the organizers came to Baghdad to present their petitions to Bremer as the paramount authority in Iraq. Neither he nor anyone senior in CPA would accept their petitions or meet with the movement's leaders.

* The Sunni Arabs on the Governing Council were either not elected to the Transitional National Assembly or came in on parties with very few seats. Since Sunni Arabs boycotted the elections for the constitution-writing assembly, they were not players in the drafting of the permanent constitution.

After showing their boxes of petitions at a press conference, the Referendum Movement's organizers returned to Kurdistan feeling angry that they had not been heard. They were even more upset when they saw how much power the TAL took from Kurdistan.

In September 2004, the Referendum Movement organizers asked me to meet with them at Erbil's brand-new Sheraton hotel.* As we sipped Turkish coffee, we discussed how other independence movements had promoted their own causes. I recalled that at least one independence movement conducted an unofficial referendum on the same day as the country's general elections, setting up informal polling places near the official ones. The Referendum Movement leaders thought this was an interesting precedent but doubted that the Kurdistan authorities would allow it. I explained that in a democracy the authorities could not prevent such expression of free speech as long as the organizers did not interfere in the official voting.

I recounted these conversations to Nechirvan Barzani and Karim Sinjari, the Kurdistan interior minister who was responsible for election security. Both had the same reaction, that this was the Referendum Movement's democratic right. When the January 2005 elections took place, there were referendum booths just outside, or actually inside, every polling place. Two million Kurds voted in the referendum and 98 percent chose independence.† The outcome put Kurdish and Iraqi Arab leaders on notice that Kurdistan's voters would reject a permanent constitution that required any significant reintegration of the Region into Iraq.

Kurdistan's desire for independence will continue to overshadow all other aspects of its relationship with Iraq. In the referendum, the Kurds vehemently affirmed their wish for separation, an outcome brought nearer by Iraq's permanent constitution.

* The hotel is not affiliated with the Sheraton chain, but Sheraton denotes quality in Iraq. Hence good hotels are often called the Sheraton.

† The ballot asked, "Should Kurdistan be part of Iraq or should it be independent?" There was an Iraqi flag next to the Iraq option and the Kurdistan flag next to the independence option.

Civil War

On April 18, 2003, I drove south from Baghdad to Karbala, which along with nearby Najaf is one of Shiite Islam's two holiest cities. In 680, the Umayyad caliph sent four thousand men to arrest Hussein ibn Ali, the grandson of the prophet. Trapped with a small band of followers in what is now Karbala, Hussein refused to surrender. His forces were defeated and Hussein's head was sent to the caliph, Yazid, in Damascus.

Shiites have mourned the martyrdom of Hussein for thirteen hundred years. On this April day, pilgrims converged on the city from all directions, walking along the side of the road, sometimes barefoot, carrying banners and portraits of Hussein. Periodically, the march stopped as men formed a circle to chant: "Hussein, Hussein, we will never forget Hussein." The devout flayed their backs with chains.

Saddam Hussein feared the religious enthusiasm of the Shiite pilgrimages, and they had been banned for twenty-nine years. A few miles from Karbala, I walked with the pilgrims. Although the American invasion had made the pilgrimage possible, I detected no gratitude. Instead, there was, amidst the religious fervor, a strong sense of entitlement. The world had changed and now for the first time in thirteen hundred years in Iraq, the Shiites would be in charge. One pilgrim gave me a harangue, expressing a sentiment I was to hear over and over again. "The Americans will learn that the Shiites are the majority," he told me.

The Sunni Arabs, or at least a sizable proportion, did not accept Iraq's new order. Even those who were glad to see Saddam gone—and there were many Sunni Arabs who hated the old regime—did not want to see Iraq turned over to the Shiites, and especially to the Shiite religious parties and their Iranian allies. Iraq's Sunni Arab insurgency began as a rearguard action against the American invaders, drew in foreign terrorists to fight the Christian invaders, but became a war against the Shiites.

As Iraq's divisions hardened, Shiites expressed their identity more and more in religious terms. In the January 2005 elections, the Shiite United Iraqi Alliance (UIA) won between 75 and 80 percent of the Shiite vote. In the December 2005 elections, the UIA list was markedly more religious with the inclusion of Moqtada al-Sadr's followers and the departure from the list of the more secular Shiites such as Ahmad Chalabi, who ran on his own Iraqi National Congress list. This more religious UIA list won over 80 percent of the Shiite vote.

As Shiites increasingly defined themselves politically by religion, they excluded Sunnis. State radio and television became more Shiite in its religious programming, with Shiite clerics dominating and by following Shiite rituals for prayer rather than the slightly different Sunni ones. Shiite religious holidays became national events. As Iraq moved from civil to Islamic law, Shiite provisions on inheritance, multiple wives, and temporary marriage started to apply, or at least to be considered.

Even Sunni Arabs who were reconciled to the loss of their dominant position found it impossible to accept that Iraq should become a Shiite state. Had Iraq's new political regime been secular or Arab in character, many Sunni Arabs might have accepted being in the religious minority. For the new order to be defined in a way that relegated Sunni Arabs to a second-class status was unacceptable to almost all.

Iran became the critical factor in the estrangement between Iraq's Shiites and Sunni Arabs. Iraq's Shiites viewed the Islamic Republic as a friend, the land of coreligionists, and a model of a powerful Shiite state. Iran had protected and nurtured Iraq's Shiite leaders for two decades. Khomeini's regime had sponsored the founding of Iraq's largest Shiite party, the Supreme Council for the Islamic Revolution in Iraq (SCIRI), in Tehran in 1982. It established, trained, and apparently still funds the

Badr Organization. Dawa's leaders found refuge and support in Iran for many years, and elements of the Iranian regime have close ties to the firebrand cleric, Moqtada al-Sadr. During most of this period, Washington spurned the Shiites, even placing its oldest political party, Dawa, on the State Department's terrorism list. Iran has good relations with secular Shiites, including Ahmad Chalabi. Iraq's most influential political figure is an Iranian, the Ayatollah Ali al-Sistani, who refused an offer of Iraqi citizenship, saying "I was born an Iranian and will die one." *

Iraq's Sunni Arabs see Iran in a diametrically opposite way than do the Shiites. Iran is the ancient enemy that now threatens to destroy Iraq's Arab identity. Many Sunni Arabs see Iraq's Shiites as a fifth column that has already given Iran the political victory that Iraq fought a brutal eight-year war to prevent. With Shiite authorities dismantling monuments to the Iran-Iraq War, and Shiite crowds holding up photographs of Khomeini at political rallies, Sunni Arabs found confirmation of their belief that Iraq's Shiites are disloyal and not real Iraqis.

There is nothing new to the lack of trust between Iraq's Shiites and Sunni Arabs. In the 1920s, Shiites saw the Sunni Arabs as collaborators with the British colonialists. When the Shiites boycotted the colonial administration, Sunni Arabs exploited the opportunity to consolidate their rule over all Iraq, a reign that lasted until 2003. In 1991, Shiites saw Sunni Arabs line up behind Saddam Hussein while Shiite rebels put their lives on the line to overthrow the tyrant.

• • •

* Wishing to believe Iraq's Shiites would oppose Iran, the Administration war planners ignored all these connections. Instead, they argued that Iraq's Shiites were Arab, as if this would genetically program them to oppose the Iranians. They also pointed out how Iraq's Shiite majority army fought loyally for Iraq in the Iran-Iraq War. However, they overlooked the fact that Shiite conscripts filled the lower ranks while Sunni Arabs dominated the upper ranks of the officer corps. Helping Iran would have been a capital offense for the conscript and his family, and most conscripts wanted to survive. Even so, there were Shiite defections to Iran during the Iran-Iraq War.

All the ingredients for civil war existed in Iraq in 2003: Sunni Arabs bitter at their ouster from positions of power and privilege, and fearful of the future; Shiites insistent that Iraq will be ruled on their terms; a Sunni belief that the Shiites are traitors bent not only on destroying the Iraq the Sunnis had built, but also on handing the country over to a bitter national enemy; a Shiite belief that many Sunni Arabs were unrepentant supporters of Saddam Hussein who would enthusiastically resume the killing of Shiites if ever again given a chance at power.

Like most civil wars, it is hard to give a precise date for when Iraq's began. August 29, 2003, is one possibility. In Najaf that day, an SUV drove the wrong way down a one-way street just as the Ayatollah Bakr al-Hakim was leaving Imam Ali mosque; it detonated. Al-Hakim, the leader of Iraq's largest Shiite party, SCIRI, was literally blown to smithereens. Ninety-four others died with him. March 2, 2004, is another possibility. Pilgrims packed into Karbala for the first Ashura, Shiite Islam's holiest day, since Saddam's fall. Near the Imam Hussein shrine, a suicide bomber exploded himself. This was followed by several other explosions. Nearly simultaneously, another suicide bomber detonated near the Kadhimiya mosque, the most sacred Shiite shrine in Baghdad. At least 180 Shiites died.

Certainly the civil war was well under way by the middle of 2004 as car bombs and gunmen claimed Shiite lives: 37 at a mosque near Hillah in June, 70 queuing for jobs in Baghdad in July, 45 pilgrims in Kufa in August, 52 army recruits on leave in October. In 2005, the attacks became more frequent and more deadly. A suicide ambulance killed eleven Shiites at a wedding party, a car bomb killed 135 Shiites waiting for medical cards in Hillah, a suicide bomber killed 50 at a Shiite funeral in Nineveh, a fuel truck exploded killing 98 Shiites in the central market in Musayib, a car bomb killed 99 at the market in Balad, and an exploding minibus killed 111 mostly Shiite day laborers near Baghdad's Kadhimiya mosque. From the riverbank home of Iraq's deputy prime minister in the Green Zone, I listened on August 17 as three bombs went off in twenty-minute intervals across the Tigris. The first bomb went off near the bus station that serves the Shiite south, the second as the rescue workers arrived, and the third near the hospital as the wounded were being brought in. Forty-three died.

The most deadly single incident of the civil war took place August 31, 2005, the anniversary of the death of the seventh Imam, Musa Kadhim. Sunni Arab insurgents fired rockets near Kadhim's shrine in Baghdad, sending frightened worshippers running for the nearby Aimma Bridge. There they ran into a much larger crowd of Shiite pilgrims coming toward the shrine. A rumor spread that a suicide bomber was on the bridge. Some 965 died in the panic as pilgrims jumped into the Tigris or were trampled to death.

In response to these attacks, Shiite clerics have publicly urged restraint. But the Shiite authorities and militias have responded covertly. Police or militiamen wearing police uniforms—and it is not usually clear which—have picked up thousands of Sunni Arabs, many of whose mutilated bodies have been dumped in vacant lots or on the sides of roads. The death squads target suspected insurgents and their supporters, including Sunni Arab clerics. Revenge is also a factor in the killings. The victims include Ba'athists, former secret police, and military officers believed to have participated in the suppression of the 1991 uprising. In 2005, there were reports that Iranian agents were working with Shiite militias to assassinate Iraqi pilots who flew missions against Iran in the Iran-Iraq War. Jalal Talabani considered these reports sufficiently credible that he offered to resettle the pilots in Kurdistan, even those who had dropped chemical bombs on the Kurds. Since the February 2006 destruction of Samarra's Askariya shrine, Shiite death squads have increasingly targeted Sunni Arabs living in Shiite or mixed neighborhoods and ordinary Sunni Arabs trying to cross police or militia checkpoints.

On November 13, 2005, American soldiers looking for a missing thirteen-year-old boy uncovered a secret prison run by Iraq's Ministry of Interior. They found 169 half-starved Sunni Arab prisoners, some showing physical marks from torture. Sunni Arabs made the secret prison a political issue in the ongoing election campaign, accusing Iraq's Interior Minister Bayan Jabr of sponsoring torture. Before becoming minister, Jabr headed the Badr Corps. As interior minister, he worked assiduously to place his Badr men in the police and other security services. Few Sunni Arabs think of the police as a national institution. Changes at the top of the ministry, as urged by the U.S. ambassador to Iraq, Zalmay Khalilzad, will not alter the perception, or reality, of a highly partisan sectarian ministry and national police. Sunni Arabs will not join Iraq's central authorities in the fight against insurgents and terrorists when they think of the authorities as terrorists.

Iraq's civil war is being fought where Iraq's three communities mix: Babil Governorate south of Baghdad, where Sunni Arabs ambush Shiites on the way from Baghdad to the holy cities; Diyala Governorate east of Baghdad, home to Shiites, Sunni Arabs, and Kurds; Nineveh, which has seen clashes between Sunni Arabs and Shiites and also between Kurds and Sunni Arabs in Mosul city; Kirkuk, a volatile mix of Sunni Arabs, Shiite Arabs, Turcomans, Kurds, and Christians; and Baghdad, a city of five million from all Iraq's diverse communities that has become the central front of the civil war.

Body counts dramatically illustrate the difference between the homogeneous areas of Iraq and the mixed areas. Dahuk Governorate in the northwest is purely Kurdish. From 2003 through 2005, three civilians and one policeman died in war-related violence, according to figures collected by the organization Iraq Body Count (IBC).* In Baghdad, the IBC counted 14,829 civilians and 453 police killed. The actual casualty figures are certainly higher, perhaps much higher. In July 2005

---

* The Iraq Body Count figures include the dead from the actual invasion—March 19, 2003, to April 9, 2003, as well as those who died in subsequent coalition actions and in civil strife. The overwhelming majority of civilian casualties in Baghdad and in Iraq as a whole took place after George W. Bush declared an end to major combat operations on May 1, 2003, in Iraqi-on-Iraqi incidents and attacks by foreign terrorists. Since the invasion came from the south, the civilian body count for the southern governorates is considerably higher than in Kurdistan, but this mostly reflects deaths in the fighting in March and April 2003, notably around Basra and Nasiriyah. Since then, killings in the south have been a result of insurgent attacks on pilgrims in Najaf and Karbala, fighting between the coalition and the Mahdi Army in April and May 2004, and selective killings of Sunni Arabs, notably in Basra. See www.iraqbodycount.net.

alone, the Baghdad morgue handled more than a thousand murder cases, a majority related to sectarian conflict. The morgue's figures do not include victims of car bombs and suicide bombs, where the cause of death is known and the relatives take the remains directly for burial.

Civil war generally takes a bigger toll on minority groups, and Iraq is no exception. Shiite militias have gone after Basra's Sunni Arabs, assassinating some of the community's leading figures, including several university professors.* In Baghdad, Shiites living in Sunni Arab neighborhoods and Sunni Arabs living in Shiite neighborhoods have been threatened, attacked, and murdered. As a result, many have moved into neighborhoods of their own sect or out of Baghdad altogether. Just in the first four months of 2006, some 100,000 Sunnis and Shiites fled neighborhoods where the other group was the majority. This sectarian cleansing has been particularly brutal for Iraqis living in mixed Shiite-Sunni marriages, which were fairly common, especially among Baghdad's more secular elite.

Iraq is mixed ethnically and religiously, but it has never been a melting pot: Kurds live in Kurdistan† and Shiites in the south. Even in mixed cities like Baghdad, Shiites, Sunni Arabs, and Kurds have tended to live in their own neighborhoods. And because of the civil war, Iraq is less mixed even than it was.

The United States has never had good intelligence on the Sunni Arab insurgency, which has greatly complicated the battle against it. Igno-

---

* Some of these appear to be revenge killings of those thought to have been too close to Saddam's regime.

† Some analysts have argued that Kurdistan could not separate from Iraq because there are a million Kurds in Baghdad. There has been no reliable census in Iraq for decades, but the January and December 2005 balloting provides an excellent proxy as Iraqis overwhelmingly voted their identity. The Kurdistan Alliance got just 1 percent of the vote in Baghdad, suggesting that the Kurdish population of the capital is actually around 50,000. Some have argued that most of Baghdad's Kurds are Fayli (Shiite) Kurds. If so, they do not identify with the Kurdish nationalist cause but with the Shiite religious parties.

rance did not stop senior officials from making broad assertions about the insurgency, mostly by underestimating its depth. The Bush Administration admits failing to anticipate it. When the insurgency began, Secretary Rumsfeld belittled the rebels as a bunch of "former regime dead-enders." President Bush baited the insurgents on July 2, 2003: "There are some who feel like—that the conditions are such that they can attack us there. My answer is, bring 'em on."

In war, it is a terrible mistake to underestimate the enemy. Having failed to plan for the contingency of an insurgency, the president never ordered measures that could, rather easily, have kept weapons and explosives out of insurgent hands. As it turned out, the insurgents did "bring 'em on," killing two thousand Americans in the two years after the president's challenge. Nor did the Administration learn from its early dismissal of the insurgency. On May 31, 2005, Vice President Cheney told CNN's Larry King the happy news: "The level of activity that we see today from a military standpoint, I think, will clearly decline. I think they're in the last throes, if you will, of the insurgency."

The insurgency began to take shape shortly after Saddam's regime fell. As the leaders of the old regime fled Baghdad—or disappeared into the population—they took with them hundreds of millions in U.S. dollars. The U.S. Army found $600 million in hundred-dollar bills in a garden shed near Uday Hussein's house in mid-April 2003.* When he was captured, Saddam had with him $750,000 in cash. It is reasonable to presume that there was a lot of cash that the U.S. never found, and that some of the old regime's money was sent out of Iraq before the war.

---

* The day before, our ABC News team filmed at Uday's house. The cameraman and soundman climbed to the roof of the garden shed for a better shot. They noticed that the shed's window and door had been filled in with cinderblocks, but thought no further about it. The next day, a U.S. Army captain ordered several enlisted men to cut some low-hanging branches that interfered with military traffic on the adjacent road. They were more curious and broke through the cinderblocks, finding the loot. Our crew was distraught when they heard the story, and perhaps not entirely because we missed an ABC News exclusive.

Another element of the Sunni Arab resistance may have developed in response to U.S. actions. On April 11, 2003, U.S. bombs hit the home of the head of the important Dulaym tribe in Ar Ramadi, killing twenty-two family members. An intelligence report had indicated that a high-ranking Iraqi official, possibly Saddam, was present. The report was false, but the United States now had a powerful local enemy. In Fallujah on April 28, 2003, American soldiers fired into a crowd of protesters, killing at least thirteen, including children. Reports indicate someone in the crowd may have fired on the Americans. If so, the returned fire is exactly what the shooter wanted. The incident helped make Fallujah insurgent territory.

The turmoil in Iraq's Sunni Arab regions provided a golden opportunity for foreign terrorists and jihadis to fight the United States. Al-Qaeda moved into Iraq, generating spinoffs, allies, and imitators. A Jordanian thug, Abu Musab al-Zarqawi, set up al-Qaeda in Mesopotamia, and claimed responsibility for some of the most spectacular bombings and gruesome killings, including the videotaped beheading of Western hostages. Like the Ba'athists, the foreign terrorists and the indigenous fundamentalists seem well funded.

As a direct consequence of not having a contingency plan for an insurgency and then prematurely claiming victory after one had begun, the Bush Administration did not make or keep Iraq's weapons depots secure. Many were left unguarded for months after the American invasion. Insurgents helped themselves to a huge supply of explosives, mortars, and artillery shells. The improvised explosive device (IED)—mostly roadside bombs—became the weapon of choice against American troops. Using high-caliber artillery shells, the insurgents developed an improvised bomb that could penetrate the heaviest American military vehicles. By the end of 2005, IEDs had killed more American troops in Iraq than gunfire or any other cause.

Iraq's Ba'athists and Sunni Arab Islamicists have the same enemies—the Americans and the Shiites—but very different goals. In other circumstances, they would be bitter enemies. The Ba'athists would like to restore the old system, or some variant of it. The Islamicists want a fundamentalist Islamic state—Taliban Afghanistan is one model—but they also see Iraq as just one part of a larger struggle over the future of the Islamic world. The Ba'ath Party is an Arab nationalist party and its roots are strongly secular.* The Islamicists consider the Ba'athists to be part of a corrupt Arab elite. Tribes, such as the Dulaym, may be motivated by revenge in the short term, but over the longer term they do not necessarily want the Ba'athists or the Islamicists. All the Sunni Arab insurgents want the Americans gone, and for fairly obvious reasons. They are foreign invaders who overthrew a system that favored the Sunni Arabs and they are Christians and Jews in a Muslim land.

Both the Ba'athist and al-Qaeda wings of the insurgency see the Shiites as the most dangerous enemy. The Ba'athist and al-Qaeda leaders know that, sooner or later, the Americans will be gone. The Shiites, on the other hand, intend to rule. Salafis, a school of Sunni fundamentalists prominent in the insurgency, consider Shiites apostates. They have declared the Shiites *takfir,* the Islamic equivalent of being excommunicated. As such, they are not Muslims, and their lives and property may be taken.† The Ba'athists see the Shiites as hostile to their version of Arab nationalism (really Sunni Arab nationalism) and as traitors for their close links to Iran and cooperation with the Americans. A Sunni-Shiite civil war serves the interests of both wings of the insurgency. For al-Qaeda, killing apostates approaches a religious duty and is a necessary step to establishing a pure and universal Islamic state.

Civil war provides a strategy that the Ba'athists may see as a plausible route for a return to power. By escalating the civil war, they can hope to undermine the Shiite-led Iraqi government and encourage the Americans to withdraw. If the Iranians intervene more openly on the side of the Shiites, the Ba'athists might hope to secure assistance—most likely covertly at first—from Arab states that would see a Ba'ath

* As noted earlier, the Ba'ath Party was founded by a Christian, Michel Aflaq.

† The extremists also assert a right to declare takfir those Muslims who drink alcohol or fail to follow all the religion's injunctions. This justifies bombings such as those that killed scores of Sunni Muslims at a wedding party in an Amman, Jordan, hotel on November 9, 2005. Mainstream Sunni theologians reject the notion that any Muslim can declare another takfir, saying these are judgments left to God.

restoration as preferable to an Iranian-dominated Shiite republic. Chaos provides an opportunity to reassemble the old Iraqi military, to stage a coup, or to negotiate new political arrangements.

The Kurds have largely been on the sidelines of Iraq's Sunni-Shiite civil war. Security is tight in Kurdistan to keep out potential terrorists. The peshmerga maintain checkpoints on Kurdistan's borders with Arab Iraq, at the entry to all Kurdistan cities and towns, and at frequent intervals on the region's main roads. Cars driven by Arabic speakers are searched with such thoroughness and frequency that most Arabs complain they are not welcome in Kurdistan, which is in fact true. This security has made it hard, but not totally impossible, for insurgents and terrorists to operate in Kurdistan. But the local population is overwhelmingly loyal to the Kurdistan Government and political parties. There are many eyes on the lookout for suspicious activity. Except for the February 1, 2004, suicide bombings, Kurdistan has been mostly free of the horrific attacks that occur almost daily in Arab Iraq.

Mosul, Iraq's third largest city, and an Arab nationalist bastion that has produced a large share of the country's army officers, is one of the places where Arabs and Kurds have clashed. The Tigris divides the city between a Sunni Arab west bank and a mostly Kurdish east bank. In setting up the governorate and city council after the war, U.S. Major General David Petraeus favored Arab residents over the Kurds. (Fairly consistently, the U.S. has slighted its friends in Iraq in a vain effort to appease its foes.) This proved no small miscalculation when the Arab police chief he had appointed and almost all the Arab police abandoned their posts—or went over to the insurgents—in November 2004, when insurgents launched well-coordinated attacks that gave them control of large parts of the city. By contrast, the Kurdish police defended their police stations. The insurgents retaliated by killing Kurdish professionals, especially doctors, who made easy targets as they commuted to hospitals on the west bank. As the Americans lost control of the city, they called in the peshmerga, worsening ethnic tensions.

North of Mosul, KDP peshmerga have been helping Kurds move

back to villages from which they were expelled by Arab Iraqi governments over the previous decades.* This alarmed Sunni Arabs, as well as some of the Christian, Shiite, and Turcoman minorities living in the affected areas, who see in these returns a stealth enlargement of Kurdistan. As a result of all these factors, Mosul city and the surrounding Nineveh Governorate are extremely tense.

Kirkuk has long been described as Iraq's ticking ethnic time bomb, and perhaps the most remarkable feature of Kirkuk in the three years since Saddam's fall is not that the city is tense but that it hasn't exploded. The Kurds have long claimed Kirkuk as part of Kurdistan. The 1992 Kurdistan constitution makes the city the capital of the Kurdistan Region, although it was under Saddam's control at the time. Massoud Barzani and Jalal Talabani have described Kirkuk as the "heart of Kurdistan" and "our Jerusalem." If it were included in Kurdistan, Kirkuk would be one of its uglier places. Years of neglect under Saddam have left it shabby. The Khasa River, which flows through the city, is little more than a sewer and the air can be foul. In the 1990s, Saddam destroyed the centuries-old houses on Kirkuk's citadel: it had been a wonderful warren of old streets and decaying buildings, some incorporating Roman columns scavenged hundreds of years ago. On seeing the city after liberation, some peshmerga were quoted as asking, "We have fought all these years for this?"

Some of Kirkuk's pollution is attributed to its greatest asset. Kirkuk sits atop one of the world's largest oil fields, a field that started producing in the 1930s and still has at least 10 billion barrels in recoverable oil.† While Iraqi regimes, including Saddam's, have been willing to

---

* Arabs, Turcomans, and Christians contest the Kurdish assertion that all the villages were once Kurdish. The area once had a much larger Assyrian and Chaldean Christian population and some of the villages the Kurds now claim were once Christian.

† There is controversy about how much recoverable oil remains. Some experts assert that the reservoir has been significantly damaged by the way it was produced under Saddam Hussein's regime, especially after sanctions were imposed in 1990.

grant the Kurds an autonomous region, no Arab Iraqi government has been willing to give the Kurds Kirkuk for fear its oil would create the economic base for an independent country. Turkey has adopted the same line, even warning in 2003 that it might intervene militarily to keep Kirkuk out of Kurdistan.

In addition to the Kurds, Kirkuk city is home to Turcomans (ethnic Turks left over from Ottoman times), Sunni Arabs, Chaldeans, and Assyrians. Before 1948, it also had a thriving Jewish population. The villages to the east and north of the city are, or were, Kurdish while Arabs occupied the Hawija plain to the west. Interspersed are Turcoman villages and towns. From the 1930s on, Iraqi governments favored Arabs and discriminated against Kurds when it came to jobs in the oil sector.* Oil brought Arabs to Kirkuk, over time altering its demographics. In the 1980s and 1990s, Saddam Hussein pursued the vigorous policy of "Arabizing" Kirkuk. Kurds were expelled, and after 1991 forcibly sent over the Green Line into rebel-held territory. Turcomans and remaining Kurds were pressured to "correct" their nationality by reregistering as Arabs.

After Saddam fell, the Kurdish political parties and peshmerga filled the vacuum in the city with quiet American support. As in Mosul, the peshmerga stopped most of the looting while the PUK and KDP took effective control of the city's administration. There was some "reverse ethnic cleansing" in the immediate aftermath of liberation. I visited several abandoned Arab villages in April 2003, with bewildered animals still wandering around, but could not tell if the departures had taken place in anticipation of the governorate's fall or if they were forced.† On the whole, however, the new Kurdish authorities

---

* In 2003, the Northern Oil Company, which managed the Kirkuk oil field, employed just forty Kurds out of a workforce of sixteen thousand. A year later, Kurdish employment was up to two hundred.

† Kirkuk was not a priority for the thousands of journalists who swarmed into Iraq in April 2003, nor did the U.S. military or civilian authorities pay any attention. As a result, the story was almost entirely ignored.

exercised considerable restraint considering the pressure from displaced Kurds for immediate action to recover property.

At the insistence of the Kurdish parties, the TAL required specific steps to facilitate the return of displaced persons, for Arab settlers to go back to their homes, and for the drawing of new governorate boundaries to undo the effects of Saddam Hussein's gerrymandering. But few of these steps were actually implemented. Nor did the CPA get its property commission functioning to address claims by those who had been expelled.

In the January 2005 elections, the Kurdish-led Kirkuk Brotherhood slate (which included Turcomans, Arabs, and Christians) won a majority in the Kirkuk Governorate Council, thanks in part to a ruling that allowed displaced persons to vote in Kirkuk even if they had not yet returned.* Iraq's new constitution requires a referendum on Kirkuk's status. The Kurdish coalition won a majority of the vote in Kirkuk in the December 2005 parliamentary elections, which indicates that Kirkuk will vote to join Kurdistan even without further returns by expelled Kurds and without reverting to the earlier (and more Kurdish) governorate boundary.

The Kirkuk issue is volatile, not only because it pits Kurds against Arabs and some Turcomans, but also because it could bring in Turkey. In 2003, the Turkish intelligence services were actively supporting one of the Turcoman groups, the Iraqi Turcoman Front (ITF), with cash and arms (at least one shipment was intercepted when U.S. forces inspected a Turkish humanitarian convoy). Since then the ITF has fallen apart and Turkey's relations with the Kurdistan Regional Government have warmed considerably. Nonetheless, Turkey opposes Kirkuk's incorporation into Kurdistan and could cause major difficulties as the referendum date approaches.

Kurdistan's people have no commitment to Iraq, and the Sunni-Shiite civil war reinforces the already strong popular opposiition to close cooperation with the rest of Iraq. Few Kurds want to risk importing the "Iraq diseases," chaos and sectarian conflict, to Kurdistan. And

---

* The same rule applied in Bosnia's first postwar elections.

many Kurds see Iraq's civil war as bringing closer the day when they can declare independence.

Kurdistan's president, Massoud Barzani, said so directly in a little noticed interview with Turkish television station NTV broadcast on November 18, 2005, just after a day of fresh bombings of Shiite mosques. "May God save us from civil war, but if others start fighting among themselves and there is an outbreak, we will have no other alternative [to independence]." As he has said in other interviews, Barzani insisted that independence was a "natural and legitimate right" for Iraqi Kurds. Given that Iraq is already in a civil war, Barzani's comments, reflecting the views of almost all Iraqi Kurds, cannot be encouraging to American hopes for a unified Iraq.

President Bush's military strategy for Iraq can be summed up by a phrase in his June 28, 2005, speech to the nation. "As the Iraqis stand up, we will stand down." There is little reason to think that this will happen soon, or ever.

In 2005, the Iraqi Army nominally had 115 battalions, or 80,000 troops. This figure, often cited by those who see the Iraq occupation as a success, corresponds only to the number of troops listed on the military payroll. When the Ministry of Defense decided to supervise the payment of salaries, a third of the payroll was returned. (In Iraq's all-cash economy, commanders receive a lump sum for the troops under their command; this acts as an incentive for them to maintain ghost soldiers on the payroll.) A top ministry official estimated that barely half the nominal army exists and that just 10 percent show up for combat.

Claims about weapons provided by the U.S. to the Iraqi Army are still more doubtful. Iraqi defense officials say the Americans have not provided them with records of who has been receiving weapons. Without such controls, soldiers sell their weapons on the open market, where some are bought by insurgents. Most weapons captured come from stocks supplied to the Iraqi Army and police. Craig Smith reported in the *New York Times* that the U.S. military is now unwilling to provide more sophisticated weapons to the Iraqi military for fear they will be used in a civil war, or against Americans.

The problems with the Iraqi Army go beyond the many opportunities for corruption. The army reflects the country's deep divisions. Of the 115 army battalions, sixty are Shiite, forty-five are Sunni Arab, and nine are Kurdish peshmerga, although they are officially described as the part of the Iraqi Army stationed in Kurdistan. There is exactly one mixed battalion (with troops contributed from the armed forces of the main political parties) and it is in Baghdad. While the officer corps is a little more heterogeneous, very few Kurds or Shiites are willing to serve as officers of Sunni Arab units fighting Sunni Arab insurgents. There are no Arab officers in the Kurdish battalions, and Kurdistan law prohibits the deployment of the Iraqi Army within Kurdistan without permission of the Kurdistan National Assembly.

Because the Sunni Arab battalions are not reliable, the Iraqi government and coalition have been using Shiite troops, and some Kurdish ones, in the fight against the insurgency. The Americans think of these troops as Iraqis, but the Sunni Arab population does not see them that way. To the Sunni Arabs, the Shiite troops are not fighting for Iraq but for a pro-Iranian Shiite-dominated political order. The Shiite troops have aggravated this feeling by scrawling religious graffiti where they bivouac, and by displaying pictures of their clerics. A strategy that entails Shiite and Kurdish troops fighting against Sunni Arab insurgents plays into the insurgents' hands by rallying the population against the new army and the authorities they represent.

Following the January 2005 elections, the Shiite list and the Kurdistan Alliance formed a coalition. In exchange for making Dawa leader Ibrahim Jaafari prime minister, the Kurdish leader Jalal Talabani became president.* The coalition divided up the key ministries with the

---

* Although the Shiite United Iraqi Alliance won a majority in the parliament, the election of the president and two vice presidents required a two-thirds vote, and the president had to nominate the prime minister.

188 Peter W. Galbraith

Shiite list taking interior, oil, and finance and the Kurds foreign affairs. A Sunni Arab, Sadoun Dulaimi, became defense minister while a Kurd, Babkir Zebari, remained chief of staff of the Iraqi Army and another Kurd, Bruska Noori Shaways, served as the ministry's top civil servant. Ahmad Chalabi and the former speaker of the Kurdistan Parliament, Rowsch Shaways, became Iraq's two deputy prime ministers. SCIRI's Adel Abdul Mehdi became the Shiite vice president and former President Ghazi al-Yawar (who refused to vacate the presidential residence) became the Sunni vice president. A Sunni Arab from California, Hajim al-Hassani, was elected speaker of the National Assembly.

For the Kurds, there was a lot of symbolism in these appointments. Not only was a Kurd Iraq's first ever democratically elected head of state, but two Kurds, Talabani and Foreign Minister Hoshyar Zebari, represented Iraq at the Arab League summits in 2005. The Kurds did not forget that the Arab League never criticized Brother Saddam Hussein for gassing them. But when it came to positions with real power, these went mostly to the Shiites, which was acceptable to the Kurds since the Baghdad government's writ did not extend to Kurdistan.

Although in coalition, the Kurds and the Shiites did not forge a common program. The two sides are too far apart with regard to their values and visions for the future. Instead, they have made a deal: the Kurds would let the Shiites run Arab Iraq in exchange for Baghdad not interfering in a de facto independent Kurdistan. For the Shiites, the deal is an acceptable price to be able to get their own way in Arab Iraq. For the Kurds, Iraq is a secondary consideration to protecting Kurdistan.

After the January 2005 elections, the Bush Administration lobbied the Kurds hard not to form a coalition with the Shiites, in the hope that Ayad Allawi, with support from the Kurds, could draw enough support from the UIA (itself a fairly broad coalition) to head a secular government. With Allawi, the Americans argued, the Kurds could build a new Iraq. The Kurds were, however, much less interested in a new Iraq than in Kurdistan. They needed to make a deal with a party that wanted its agenda as much as the Kurds wanted theirs, and that was the Shiites.

Not surprisingly, the Shiite-Kurdish coalition was not a comfortable one. Although the TAL gave most political authority to the prime minister, it was not in Talabani's nature to take a backseat. The president and prime minister clashed on matters of protocol so intensely that they could not agree who would give Iraq's speech at the United Nations General Assembly in 2005, and so both did. When Talabani made an official visit to Washington as the president of Iraq in September 2005, Jaafari ordered the Shiite ministers to boycott. This didn't faze the Kurds, who joked that the almost all-Kurdish delegation was a sign that the United States now recognized Kurdistan.

Talabani worked hard to bring Sunni Arabs into the political and constitutional process but mostly encountered hard-headedness from both Sunnis and Shiites. (In a moment of exasperation, he jokingly complained to me about "your English cousins" who had created such an unworkable country.) Long before anyone else seized on the issue, Talabani protested the Ministry of Interior's role in the disappearance and summary execution of Sunni Arabs. Kurds and some Shiites also complained about Jaafari's ineffectiveness. And, as best I could tell, they had a point. On the eve of Iraq's constitutional deadline and with many critical issues about the future of the country unresolved, Jaafari convened a cabinet meeting that spent three hours discussing tomato paste, and whether it would be included in the food rations distributed for Ramadan.

The Shiites and Kurds have never shared common ground as Iraqis. But they did find a way to accommodate each other's main interests. They had in common a shared history of oppression and of struggle against the dictatorship. In many ways, it was fortunate that Sunni Arabs boycotted the January 2005 elections. The Sunni Arabs had a political agenda opposed on almost every important point to the goals of the Kurds and of the Shiites. It is hard to see how a three-way coalition could have been formed, especially with the contentious constitutional questions still to be resolved. But the Kurds and Shiites shared, through bitter experience, a common perspective on Iraq's dark history. The Sunni Arabs could not acknowledge there had been a problem.

The TAL required Iraqis to come up with a constitution, a national compact, by August 15, 2005, just six and a half months after the elections. But it took three months for the Shiites and Kurds simply to form a government without the Sunni Arabs. In July, Defense Secretary Rumsfeld visited Baghdad with one message: the United States would not accept any postponement of the constitutional deadline, even though the TAL allowed it. Meanwhile, the Americans recruited Sunni Arabs to participate in the deliberations, even though they had not been elected to the National Assembly. The Americans were still thinking in terms of Iraqis. Official Washington was clueless as to how little the Kurds, the Shiites, and the Sunni Arabs had in common. This became apparent as the three groups debated Iraq's permanent constitution.

CHAPTER 10

The Three State Solution

Hours before the second deadline for Iraq's new constitution on August 22, 2005,* Shiite and Sunni Arab leaders met in a conference room at the Baghdad headquarters of Kurdistan's President Massoud Barzani. The Shiites wanted the constitution's preamble to mention Saddam Hussein's atrocities and the Sunni negotiators were objecting. As I sipped tea with Kurdish and Arab politicians in the next room, I could hear voices rising in anger. Then Nabeel Musawi, a Shiite parliamentarian with a long record as a human rights campaigner, came out of the meeting. "The Sunnis," he told me, "claim that Saddam only killed five farmers in the south and some Kurds." Nabeel's father had disappeared after being arrested by Saddam's security services in 1981, one of 300,000 Shiites murdered by the Ba'ath regime during its thirty-five years in power. The deadline was missed.

Three days later, President Bush telephoned Abdul Aziz al-Hakim, the Shiite cleric who leads the Supreme Council for Islamic Revolution in Iraq (SCIRI), Iraq's largest and most pro-Iranian political party, to ask for concessions on behalf of the Sunni Arab negotiators on the controversial issues of federalism and de-Ba'athification. Hakim politely thanked the president who, not being well versed in the intricacies of Iraqi politics (or even its broad outlines), was reduced to

---

* An hour before midnight on August 15, the National Assembly amended the TAL to extend the deadline one week.

pleading that his requests be taken seriously. President Bush then asked Hakim to honor women's rights. Hakim assured him they were sacred.

The president's call was pointless. Bush was asking Hakim to make concessions that the Sunni Arab negotiators themselves did not consider sufficient. Hakim's idea of women's rights is very different from what Bush wanted, but the president did not know enough to respond to the cleric. The Hakim episode revealed just how little the president and his advisors understood the divisions in Iraqi society more than three years after the invasion. Small concessions cannot paper over the differences between the victims of atrocities and those who deny that any crimes took place. There was also no small amount of hypocrisy in the president's expressions of concern about women. His diplomats had already agreed to soften key protections for women, and two days before expressing his concern to Hakim, Bush had publicly congratulated Iraq on "a democratic constitution that honors women's rights."

While the president's personal intervention into the Middle East bargaining was predictably inadequate, his ambassador to Iraq, Zalmay Khalilzad, did much to produce the constitution that emerged. Days after taking up his post in early August, Khalilzad had summoned Iraq's top leaders to the capital's Green Zone, initiating three weeks of nonstop talks that produced the Kurdish-Shiite deal that is the basis of Iraq's constitution.

At first glance, Khalilzad seemed an improbable mediator for this Iraqi constitution. An Afghan-American whose Republican links go back to the Reagan Administration, Khalilzad openly expresses the fiercely partisan sentiments that have characterized the Bush Administration's efforts in Iraq. In the buildup to the Iraq War, he was associated with the neoconservative group that plotted the war and then failed to plan for its aftermath. For seven months starting in November 2002, he acted as President Bush's envoy to the Iraqi groups that opposed Saddam Hussein. He came to Iraq after serving a two-year tour (2003–2005) as U.S. ambassador to Afghanistan, where he was widely known as "the viceroy."

Khalilzad had little time to master the complexities of Iraq's politics, and on some issues it showed. Khalilzad did not know, until I told him, that Kurdistan had voted in a January referendum for independence. While in Afghanistan, Khalilzad obviously had not had time to follow Iraq, yet no one in the State Department apparently thought the referendum was a sufficiently important detail that the man negotiating a constitution with the Kurds should know about it.

If Khalilzad arrived in Baghdad still believing in the Bush Administration's formula of a "democratic, federal, pluralist, and unified Iraq," he swiftly caught on to the reality. Shuttling from faction to faction, he approached the process of drafting a constitution not so much as an exercise in "nation-building" but rather as a negotiation of a tripartite peace treaty, which is largely what it was.*

Khalilzad faced two major obstacles: the absence of common ground among Iraq's Kurds, Shiites, and Sunni Arabs, and the incoherent U.S. policy that preceded his arrival. The Kurds saw the constitution as a threat to their continued independence, and examined every proposal from that perspective. As the majority faction, the Shiites controlled the drafting of the text—and whether through inexperience or self-serving intentions, they often simply disregarded agreements others thought had been reached. Naturally, this fed Kurdish suspicions. The Sunni Arabs objected to practically everything that was proposed, frustrating the Shiites and Kurds to the point that they stopped negotiating with them. In the end, Khalilzad had the U.S. Embassy record agreements, incorporate them into the text, and prepare drafts.

Khalilzad inherited policy decisions—made both in Washington and in Baghdad—that complicated his task. In May, Condoleezza Rice had flown to Baghdad to insist that Sunni Arabs, who had boycotted the January elections and were therefore only minimally represented in the National Assembly, be included as members of the constitution drafting committee. Such inclusiveness in constitution-making is, of

---

* I was struck by the similarities to the three-week Dayton talks ending the Bosnian war, in which I took part in 1995. In Baghdad, as at Dayton, the three factions never engaged in substantive negotiations as a group. Instead, agreements were worked out in bilateral talks between two of the factions or by American diplomats shuttling among the residences of the leaders.

course, desirable; but President Jalal Talabani warned her emphatically that the particular Sunnis selected by the United States to represent their community were not prepared for serious dialogue; nor for the most part were they representative. These warnings were ignored.

The Sunni delegation represented a variety of views, but it was dominated by former members of the Ba'ath Party. The group's spokesman and de facto leader was a former Ba'ath Party functionary, Saleh al-Mutlaq, who argued against nearly everything that was proposed, and did so in an aggressive way that offended the Kurds and Shiites and some of his fellow Sunnis. Also on his team were Saddam Hussein's former translator and several other former Ba'athist functionaries, as well as representatives of the Iraqi Islamic Party, a Sunni religious party. The leaders of the Iraqi Islamic Party ended up supporting the new constitution, but their voices were drowned out in the anti-Shiite, anti-Kurd rhetoric of the others.

By pandering to unelected former Ba'athists, the Bush Administration made them appear as more authentic representatives of the Sunni Arabs than those few Sunnis who were actually elected to the National Assembly, and who shared more the Western values that the U.S. wanted expressed in the constitution. These elected Sunni Arabs included Iraq's Vice President Ghazi al-Yawar and the speaker of the National Assembly, Hajim al-Hassani. Although they were not part of the Sunni negotiating group, both were inclined to agree to a compromise, and Hassani, a liberal who had spent years in California, objected not to the provisions on federalism or de-Ba'athification but to the inadequate protection of the rights of women.

In favoring the Ba'athists among the Sunnis over the more secular liberals, the Bush Administration continued its pattern in Iraq of trying to appease its enemies at the expense of its friends. And, as usual, the Americans got Iraqi politics wrong. Al-Mutlaq's neo-Ba'athists were noisy opponents of the constitution and, aided by the deference shown them by the Americans, helped undermine the constitution's legitimacy among Sunni Arabs in Iraq and elsewhere in the Arab world. (Among other things, al-Mutlaq's demands led to a high-profile

U.S. intervention that unnecessarily highlighted America's role in the constitutional process.) Nevertheless, when Sunni Arabs voted in December 2005, al-Mutlaq's party, the Iraqi Front for National Dialogue, won just eleven seats, earning less than 20 percent of the Sunni Arab vote. Nearly 80 percent of the Sunni Arabs voted for the Iraqi Accord Front, a coalition of Sunni Islamic parties that included the pro-constitution Iraqi Islamic Party. (Yawar and al-Hassani ran on Allawi's secular list, which got a small part of the Sunni vote.)

The second big problem Khalilzad inherited was the deadline. The TAL, as we saw, allowed just six and a half months from the January 30 elections to the August 15 deadline for the National Assembly to write a constitution. Even in a country where there was a high degree of political consensus, this would have been a tough deadline to meet. Of the twenty-eight weeks allotted to constitution writing, twelve were consumed trying to form a Shiite-Kurdish government. Then, as a result of Rice's May visit, the process had to be opened up to the recalcitrant Sunni Arabs. Although they had little influence on the final document, they greatly delayed it.

Logically, the National Assembly should have invoked a clause in the TAL allowing for a six-month extension of the drafting process. But President Bush, wanting to show progress to an increasingly uneasy American public, insisted that Iraqis needed to meet their deadlines. Although every senior Iraqi leader with whom I spoke wanted the six-month extension, none dared say so openly. As it turned out, the constitution was not done by August 15, and so the deadline was extended twice, the first time by amending the TAL to allow an extra week and, the second time, extralegally, for three days by consensus of the leaders. The effect of a short deadline was to empower those most determined to win: namely, the Kurds and Shiite clerics.

The Administration also made other mistakes, some of which bordered on the bizarre. Although it was obvious that the Administration needed the Kurds to be flexible on their core demand for a nearly independent Kurdistan, American diplomats seemed to go out of their way to offend the Kurds. For more than a decade, the KDP part of Kurdistan has banned the Iraqi flag as an Arab nationalist symbol under which Iraqi troops carried out the Anfal (in the Suleimania region, the PUK flies an out-of-date version of the Iraqi flag on a few public buildings).* Iraqi officials and U.S. diplomats have routinely attended events in Kurdistan where only the Kurdistan flag flies. Yet when the Kurdistan Government decided to host a July 4 party for the Americans, the Bush Administration showed no appreciation for the only Iraqis who wanted to so honor the United States. Instead, the embassy office in Kirkuk was instructed to snub the party unless the Kurds flew the Iraqi flag. The Kurdistan Government canceled the party. Since the Americans certainly knew the Kurds would not change their position on the flag, it is hard not to conclude there was a conscious decision to create an issue with the Kurds. Given the timing, the purpose is a mystery.

A few days after the July 4 fiasco, the U.S. Embassy's political counselor briefed the foreign press in Baghdad on various constitutional proposals, including one submitted by the Kurdistan National Assembly. In the briefing, he compared Kurdistan's leaders to carpet sellers who set a high price with the intention of settling for much less. Kurdistan's President Massoud Barzani was furious. But he also had the last laugh. Almost all of his proposals were accepted. The Americans, it appeared, were the suckers who paid the first price.

Barzani dominated the constitutional negotiations. After forging a consensus in Kurdistan among all its important political and ethnic groupings, Barzani presented to the Kurdistan National Assembly a nonnegotiable minimal set of demands: supremacy of Kurdistan law, continuation of the peshmerga, Kurdistan control of its natural resources, a referendum to settle Kirkuk, and a future right to self-

---

* The Iraqi flag is three horizontal bars of red, white, and black. The identical bars appear on the Egyptian, Syrian, and Yemeni flags. The Iraqi flag has three green stars, the Syrian two, and the Yemeni none. Saddam added "God is Great" in his own hand after the 1991 war but this is omitted from the version flown in the PUK part of Kurdistan. The tricolor is a symbol of Iraq's Arab identity and, as such, excludes the Kurds.

determination. Armed with an endorsement and having committed to bringing any constitutional deal back to the assembly, Barzani went to Baghdad with a mandate and no room to compromise. When he told the Arabs and the Americans that Kurdistan preferred no constitution to one that did not meet their demands, they had every reason to believe him.

The ruling Shiite parties had a common agenda on issues of religion and state. They wanted Iraq defined as an Islamic state; Sharia law to replace Iraq's secular civil code; the *marjah* (leading Shiite ayatollahs) to be recognized in the constitution: and a constitutional court established to review legislation for its conformity with Islam. Taken together, these provisions would resemble the main features of Iran's Islamic republic.

The Constitutional Court, as proposed by the Shiites, would include respected clerics who could overrule, for reasons of religious doctrine, decisions of the elected parliament and government. The constitutional role of the marjah is reminiscent of the status Iran accorded Khomeini. Even without giving the marjah specific powers, the constitutional recognition would certainly enhance the role in government of what was already Iraq's most powerful institution. While the Kurds and secular Arabs saw these proposals for what they were, the Bush Administration remained in denial over what was happening in Iraq, continuing to insist that Iraq's Shiites did not want to copy Iran.

On August 11, SCIRI leader Abdul Aziz al-Hakim shook up the negotiations by proposing that all nine southern Shiite governorates form a single region exercising the same powers as Kurdistan. Dubbed "Shiastan" by secular Iraqis and the Western press, the proposed super-region raised immediate concerns that SCIRI was looking to break up Iraq. In fact, by the time Hakim made his proposal, Iraq's Shiite south had already broken free from Baghdad's control. Hakim's proposal would give the south a government with recognized competencies and therefore bring structure to what was an informal system of rule by religious parties and their associated militias. A single Shiastan would be a formidable force in Iraq and in the Persian Gulf region, controlling some 80 percent of Iraq's oil, 40 percent of its people, and Shia Islam's two most holy places. Neither the Sunni Arabs nor the Americans were reassured by the fact that Hakim made his proposal—without any advance notice to those outside his party—at a large rally in Najaf where Khomeini pictures abounded.

Hakim's proposal apparently took some of the other Shiite leaders by surprise. While the established parties also supported federalism, they had advocated two or more Shiite regions. Basra's leaders had reservations about Hakim's proposal, not the least because they might have to share Basra's oil more widely. Dawa's Jaafari opposed Hakim on regional control of oil, perhaps because he was the central government's prime minister. Moqtada al-Sadr declared his opposition to all forms of federalism, but refused to participate in the constitutional process on the grounds that it was being drafted while Iraq was under occupation. A major part of al-Sadr's constituency lives in Baghdad's Sadr City, which would not have been included in Hakim's Shiastan.

Some American diplomats suggested privately that Hakim made his proposal to shock the Kurds out of going too far in their demands for a separate state. SCIRI has been extremely effective in developing a grassroots organization in all the southern Shiite provinces and controlled the governorate councils in eight of the nine. As SCIRI likely would dominate Shiastan, there was no reason to doubt the sincerity of Hakim's proposal. Still, if it was intended to intimidate the Kurds, it backfired. Shiastan strengthened Kurdistan's own position, and if it led to the breakup of Iraq, so much the better, although few Kurdish leaders would say so openly.

In the end Barzani and the Shiite leaders struck a deal. The Kurds would get what they wanted on federalism and the Shiites would get some of what they wanted on Islam, women's issues, and the role of the clergy, provided these provisions did not apply in Kurdistan. Both sides agreed to limit the exclusive powers of the federal government to a handful of issues: foreign affairs, defense policy, monetary policy, fiscal policy, assigning broadcast frequencies, postal services, managing water flows on the Tigris and Euphrates, conducting censuses, and regulating weights and measures. Other powers, including taxation,* can be exercised only with the consent of the affected region.

Superficially, the constitution makes Iraq into a relatively mild Islamic state. Islam is the official religion and "*a* basic source of legislation." The Shiite religious parties wanted Islam to be *the* basic source of legislation, and so the actual constitutional formula is something of a triumph for secularism. But the constitution then stipulates that "no law may be enacted that contradicts the established provisions of Islam." Iraq's Federal Supreme Court must review the constitutionality laws, including making sure they are not un-Islamic. The constitution further requires the court to include on its bench "experts in Islamic jurisprudence."

For Iraq's secular leaders, having Islamic scholars on a court charged with reviewing laws smacked of the Iranian system. Led by National Assembly Speaker al-Hassani, they objected strongly. The religious parties, though, had an unlikely ally, the American ambassador. In a meeting at Barzani's headquarters, Khalilzad argued to the secular Iraqis that the constitutional prohibition on laws that contradict Islam's established principles meant that religious experts had to be on the court to determine the applicable principles. This was the exact argument advanced by the Shiite religious parties, and the secularists were disheartened to hear it from Bush's representative. Khalilzad knew the Shiites could not accept a constitution that did not include some part of their proposal for religious review, and the American could not both defend Western values and meet his deadline. President Bush had already made clear his priority was the latter.

---

* A British treasury official serving as an advisor to his country's embassy nearly derailed the constitution two hours before the final deadline. He was reading an English translation being made as drafts of the Arabic text became available, and realized the federal government had no tax power. He was about to charge into a meeting of Iraq's political leaders when a quick-thinking Kurdish constitutional advisor grabbed an available Westerner—me—to explain the situation. The omission, I told him, was no mistake and he might want to consult with his ambassador before reopening an issue that could bring down Iraq's delicate compromise.

The Kurds reluctantly went along with Khalilzad because they had won almost all their points, and now wanted the constitution to go ahead. But, as the price of accepting religious scholars on the Supreme Court, they stripped it of the power to review regional laws. In any event, the Kurds had never been much impressed with American arguments for a supreme court. When their negotiators looked at the American model, they did not see an independent judiciary but a dangerously partisan institution where judges could decide a presidential election based on their personal political preferences. Under no circumstances were they going to grant comparable powers to judges in Baghdad.

After the constitution was adopted, many Westerners focused on provisions of the charter on human rights and gender without understanding that they are largely irrelevant. The human rights chapter of Iraq's constitution has been praised as among the best in the Middle East. The provisions on women have been criticized as a step backward.*

Religion, human rights, and gender are not among the exclusive powers of the federal government. Since they are not exclusive federal government powers, regional constitutions and law have primacy. This arrangement enables Kurdistan to preserve its secular status and to keep human rights protections in its constitution that are superior to those in the federal constitution (although not always followed). It also means that the Shiite region (or regions) will apply a much stricter version of Islamic law, particularly in the treatment of women, than exists in the federal constitution.

Iraq has already divided into three disparate entities. Kurdistan left Iraq in 1991, and is not coming back. Iraq's Shiite revolution and Sunni

---

* The constitution purports to replace Iraq's relatively progressive civil code with a system in which individuals choose to be governed by the rules of their religious sect or by the civil code. Since Islamic law generally favors men in personal matters like divorce or inheritance (a sister gets half the inheritance of a brother), there is an incentive for the man to choose Islamic law and the woman the civil code, if in fact she is actually allowed a choice.

Arab–initiated civil war have split Arab Iraq along sectarian lines. Iraq's constitution has two great virtues: First, it provides a structure for Iraq's Shiites and Sunni Arabs to form their own institutions of self-government that may facilitate economic development in the south and help bring an end to the chaos in the Sunni Arab center. (Kurdistan, of course, already has a functioning Regional Government and security force.) Second, the constitution provides a formula to resolve the contentious issues that could widen Iraq's civil war— territory, distribution of oil revenues, and control over the national government in Baghdad.

In the constitutional negotiations, the Sunni Arabs objected to the formation of new federal regions on the grounds it would lead to the breakup of Iraq. (Initially, they had also objected to federalism for the Kurds, but eventually even Saleh al-Mutlaq recognized this was a reality.) Since a unified Arab Iraq would be a Shiite-dominated one, Sunni Arab opposition to federalism was contrary to interest, and therefore most likely a pretext to try to wreck the whole constitutional process. With the constitution now adopted (over an almost unanimous Sunni Arab "no" vote), there is reason to hope that Sunni Arabs will see the merits of forming their own region.

It is unclear whether the Shiites will form one super-region, as proposed by Hakim, or several smaller ones. In the constitutional negotiations, Khalilzad and some of the Sunni Arabs tried unsuccessfully to limit the number of governorates that could form a region to four. Very belatedly, the Bush Administration woke up to the strategic consequences of the invasion of Iraq, but limiting the size of Shiastan is not likely to make a big difference. The Shiite regions will cooperate with each other in a Shiite confederacy. Further, from a strategic perspective, a single powerful Shiite state may over time be more likely to assert its independence of Iran than several weaker ones.

The constitution has a formula to resolve Iraq's most enduring territorial dispute: between Kurdistan and the rest of Iraq over the oil-rich province of Kirkuk. The constitution continues provisions of the TAL for the return of displaced Kurds, the repatriation of Arab settlers, and the adjustment of the borders of Kirkuk Governorate. But, unlike the TAL, it brings the Kirkuk issue to closure with a referendum to be held by the end of 2007. By themselves, these Kirkuk clauses do not ensure that the Kirkuk issue will be resolved peacefully. Sunni Arabs object strongly to losing part of what they consider to be their patrimony and want all of Iraq to vote in the Kirkuk referendum. This signals a likely Sunni Arab irredentist response to losing.

Within Kirkuk, the referendum is a zero-sum proposition. While there is no outcome that can make both sides happy, it is possible to mitigate the losers' pain. Kirkuk will need arrangements for entrenched power sharing among all its communities—Kurds, Arabs, Turcomans, and Chaldo-Assyrians—as well as a high degree of autonomy regardless of whether it ends up in Kurdistan or Arab Iraq. Optimally, the referendum's losers should notice no real change in how their city and governorate are governed regardless of the vote.

If properly and fully implemented, the Kirkuk clauses of the constitution are of enormous significance. They can resolve the issue that has been at the heart of eighty years of Kurd-Arab conflict in Iraq. The Kirkuk procedures also apply to other territories claimed by the Kurds, but not formally part of Kurdistan. Khanaqin, south of Suleimania, and Makhmur, west of Erbil, are purely Kurdish and their incorporation into Kurdistan seems generally accepted. Other groups contest the Kurdish claim to Sinjar, near the Syrian border, and to certain areas in the vicinity of Mosul. These could become major flashpoints. Thanks to their well-organized political parties, their already existing Regional Government, and the peshmerga, the Kurds now hold the upper hand in the territorial disputes with the Iraqi Arabs. They will need to be mindful of the dangers of overreaching.

Oil is power in a one-resource country like Iraq. Although the Bush Administration pushed hard for central government control over all oil, this was never going to be agreed. Massoud Barzani and Kurdistan National Assembly made clear that no constitution was better than one that gave the center all the country's revenue. Because so much oil is in the south, many Shiites also wanted regional control of oil. The constitution's "old oil, new oil" compromise, in which the federal government collects and distributes revenue from oil fields currently in production while the regions manage and benefit from new fields, ensures an equitable distribution of revenues for several decades. Only over time, as existing fields are exhausted and new fields come into production, will the balance gradually shift in favor of the regions. But, as the Kirkuk oil field—first put into production in 1934 and still with billions of barrels of recoverable reserves—demonstrates, Iraq's existing "super giants" have a long production span. While most of Iraq's existing oil production is in the north and south, all three Iraqi communities occupy land that is prospective. Baghdad itself may sit atop a potential super-giant field. As long as the constitutional provision requiring equitable distribution of existing oil revenues is followed, Sunni Arabs are decades from having to worry about being left without financial resources. However, the new arrangements are different in one important regard. Instead of Sunni Arabs apportioning Iraq's oil revenue to the north and south (while keeping most of it), Kurds and Shiites will be cutting the monthly check.

Finally, the constitution helps resolve the struggle for power and influence in Baghdad. Since 1920, Sunni Arabs have occupied Iraq's top leadership positions; they were most of the country's generals, provided most of the ambassadors, and held the best positions in the civil service. Indeed, Jalal Talabani is the first non–Sunni Arab ever to serve as Iraq's head of state. With its effective requirement for supermajorities to choose the president, the prime minister and cabinet, and judges, the constitution strongly promotes power sharing in the federal government by all three of Iraq's major constituencies. More important, it so diminishes the powers of the center that there is little for Iraq's Sunni Arabs, Kurds, and Shiites to fight over.

The constitution provides no solution to the problem of Baghdad city, a city that is 60/40 percent Shiite-Sunni (a rough estimate that excludes significant Kurdish and Christian minorities) and is the front line of Iraq's civil war. Under the constitution, Baghdad may not join any other region, but can become a region on its own. It is hard to see how this resolves the sectarian divide in what is by far the world's most dangerous capital city.

The constitution is also not a national compact. It was made by Shiites and Kurds without the Sunni Arabs. As I have said before, there was no alternative. Not only did the Sunni Arabs choose to boycott the elections for the assembly that wrote the constitution, they also had positions that were completely incompatible with those of the Kurds and Shiites. In short, what the Sunni Arabs most wanted was for the Shiites and Kurds not to have what they wanted. Under these circumstances, no common ground could be found. Still, the constitution is an Iraqi solution to an Iraqi problem. The Kurds and Shiites concluded that Iraq cannot function as a single state, and have worked out arrangements to divide it amicably. The Sunni Arabs refused to take part in this process—in part because they objected to the premise of division—but the Kurds and Shiites left space for them. The Sunni Arabs have the same rights as the Kurds and Shiites, and that is a remarkable—and even magnanimous—result considering Iraq's history.

Iraq's constitutional referendum held October 15, 2005, and the election of the Council of Representatives (the new name for the parliament) two months later on December 15 confirmed how divided Iraq is. In the October referendum, each of three purely Kurdish governorates approved the constitution with 99 percent voting yes. The yes vote in the nine southern Shiite governorates ranged from 95 to 98 percent. By contrast, the overwhelmingly Sunni Arab Salahaddin Governorate voted 81 percent against and the entirely Sunni Arab Anbar Province voted 97 percent against. The constitution was approved because the Sunni Arab majority in Nineveh Province (which includes Mosul) is only about 60 percent. Nineveh rejected the constitution with a 54 percent no vote, less than the two-thirds needed for the Sunni Arabs to defeat the constitution altogether.* In the December Council of Representatives elections, fewer than 2 percent of Iraq's Kurds voted for non-Kurdish parties while fewer than 15 percent of Iraq's Sunnis and Shiites voted for nonsectarian parties.†

* Three governorates voting against by two-thirds would defeat the constitution under the so-called Kurdish veto.

† Appendix 2 has a fuller explanation of the election results.

The constitution's many critics argue that it is a formula for the breakup of the country. Actually, it may be the last chance to hold the country together. Iraq's Kurds do not want to be part of Iraq, a country most of them hate. However, they know that pursuing formal independence is risky and therefore may settle for the indefinite continuation of their de facto independence as allowed by this constitution. Outside pressure for a more unified Iraq will only intensify the demand for independence, as Bremer's misadventure in nation-building illustrated. And no one should be under any illusions about the long term. The moment the international environment permits an independent Kurdistan, the Kurds will declare it.

The sectarian divisions between Iraq's Sunni and Shiite Arabs may not be unbridgeable. Religion has never been as important a part of Iraqi politics as it is now,* and its importance may recede over time. Iraq's professional, business, and bureaucratic elite has long been secular, and many are bewildered by the emphasis in Iraq today on whether one is Shiite or Sunni. These have never been important considerations for them, and they have a hard time comprehending its importance to a class of Iraqis that they don't know. Democracy has released passions in Iraq, including Shiite enthusiasm, that have yet to run their course (and may not).

With sectarian civil war under way, Iraq's Sunni and Shiites are moving further apart. Iraq's system of loose federalism allows each community to develop its own political and social institutions in security and without threatening the other. Thus, the Shiites can have their Iranian-style Islamic republic, but only in the Shiite parts of the country. With their own ministate, Iraq's Sunni Arab leaders will be up against the difficult task of governing rather than the easy route of opposition. A Sunni Arab government—whether neo-Ba'athist or Islamicist—will have strong incentives to crack down on the insurgents.

From an American perspective, none of this is attractive. Few Americans would have supported an invasion of a WMD-less Iraq in order to have half the country become an Iranian satellite with a theo-

---

* By contrast, nationalism is the constant and dominant fact of Kurdish politics.

cratic government. But this result is better than having a national government allied with Tehran trying to impose a Shiite theocracy on all Iraq. Based on the December election results, the Sunni Arab entity will also likely elect Islamicists but with a significant part of the population supporting the neo-Ba'athists. There is no guarantee that a Sunni Arab regional government will in fact be able to exercise effective control over its area or that it will be willing and able to take on the insurgents. However, an elected government providing for security with its own military has a better chance for creating stability in the Sunni Arab parts of Iraq than does a Shiite national army serving what Sunni Arabs see as an alien and treasonous government in Baghdad.

Iraq's three-state solution could lead to the country's dissolution. There will be no reason to mourn Iraq's passing. Iraq has brought virtually nonstop misery to the 80 percent of its people who are not Sunni Arabs and could be held together only by force. Almost certainly, Kurdistan's full independence is just a matter of time. As a moral matter, Iraq's Kurds are no less entitled to independence than are Lithuanians, Croatians, or Palestinians. And if Iraq's Shiites want to run their own affairs, or even have their own state, on what democratic principle should they be denied? If the price of a unified Iraq is another dictatorship, it is too high a price to pay.

American policy makers are reflexively committed to the unity of Iraq, as they were to the unity of the Soviet Union and Yugoslavia. The conventional response to discussions of Iraq's breakup is to say it would be destabilizing. This is a misreading of Iraq's modern history. It is the holding of Iraq together by force that has been destabilizing. This has led to big armies, repressive governments, squandered oil revenues, genocide at home, and aggression abroad. Today, America's failed effort to build a unified and democratic Iraq has spawned a ferocious insurgency and a Shiite theocracy.

In his 2000 election campaign George W. Bush spoke of the need for humility in our approach to the world. Yet we went into Iraq with the arrogant belief that we could remake the country as we wanted it to be. We failed miserably. We should do now what we should have done at the start—defer to the peoples of Iraq. They have concluded that a single country is not possible, except in name. They have incorporated what is effectively a three-state solution into a constitution over-whelmingly approved by 80 percent of the population. It is true that the Sunni Arabs did not accept the constitution, but what was the alternative? A constitution acceptable to the Sunni Arabs would have been rejected by 80 percent of the country.

The United States should now try to make Iraq's new political arrangements work, not continue a futile effort to undo them. This means helping Iraq's regions develop their own governments and security forces, including militaries. This is in our interest. As Iraq's regions become stable, U.S. and coalition forces can withdraw. And, if one or more of Iraq's peoples want out, we should facilitate an amicable divorce. Civil war is not inevitable when states break up, as the Soviet Union and Czechoslovakia showed. In Yugoslavia in the spring of 1991, the United States and Europe put all their diplomatic energy into a doomed effort to keep the country together when they should have focused on preventing the war that followed. Two hundred thousand people died in a war that might have been prevented with more realistic policies. The same mistake should not be made in Iraq, a country already in a civil war.

CHAPTER 11

How to Get
Out of Iraq

On March 19, 2006, the third anniversary of the start of the Iraq War, Defense Secretary Donald Rumsfeld wrote an article for the *Washington Post*. In it, he made the usual claims of progress: Iraq's security forces are robust and democracy is on the march. Even the bombing of the Askariya mosque in Samarra on February 22 had a silver lining, since the aftermath demonstrated that "the vast majority of Iraqis want their country to remain whole and free of ethnic conflict." * Then came a startling admission: "If we retreat now, there is *every reason to believe* Saddamists and terrorists will fill the vacuum. Turning our backs on postwar Iraq would be the modern equivalent of handing postwar Germany back to the Nazis."†

Given that the United States was still fighting in Iraq with the same number of troops that it used to invade Iraq three years before, one

---

* In support of his proposition, Rumsfeld cited the fact that the "leaders of Iraq's various political parties and religious groups condemned the violence and called for calm," and that it was "Iraqi forces—not U.S. or coalition troops—that enforced curfews and contained the violence after the attack on the Golden Shrine in Samarra." This conveniently ignores the fact that one of the leaders most vocal in calling for calm was Moqtada al-Sadr, whose Mahdi Army was responsible for much of the anti-Sunni violence that followed the Samarra attack. It also ignores the role Iraq's police and Shiite commandos had in directing some of the attacks and in the death squads that took advantage of the curfew to kill scores of Sunni Arabs.

† Emphasis added.

might have hoped for candor from the secretary of defense. Iraq's security forces are a major factor in the country's descent into civil war and the widening chasm between Iraq's ethnic and sectarian communties is far more significant than the (sometimes insincere) lip service paid to national unity by Iraq's politicians. On the other hand, the consequences of an American withdrawal are not nearly as dire as Rumsfeld asserted. There is no chance that the Ba'athists will take over the country again. Before the Administration can level with the American people, it needs to face up to the truth itself.

There is no good solution to the mess in Iraq. The country has broken up and is in the throes of civil war. The United States cannot put the country back together again and it cannot stop the civil war. If it scales back its ambitions, it can help stabilize parts of the country and contain the civil war. But the U.S. needs to do so quickly. As long as the United States remains in Iraq pursuing impossible goals, the Administration is providing neither the leadership nor resources required to meet the most serious challenges to American security, including Iran's drive for nuclear weapons and the continued threat from al-Qaeda.

At the beginning of 2006, the Administration invested heavily in diplomatic efforts aimed at forming a national unity government that included the Shiites, Kurds, Sunni Arabs, and secularists. As the largest bloc in the parliament, the UIA coalition had the right to nominate the prime minister. The Administration's preferred candidate was the SCIRI nominee, Adel Abdul Mehdi, the French-educated economist and a relative liberal (who, ironically, Bremer had vetoed for interim prime minister in 2004). Mehdi was well liked by the Kurds and generally acceptable to the Sunni Arabs in the Council of Representatives. On February 12, the UIA parliamentarians met at Abdul Aziz al-Hakim's fortified riverfront residence in Baghdad and, by 64–63 vote, chose the incumbent Prime Minister Ibrahim Jaafari for a second term over Mehdi. Moqtada al-Sadr, who sponsored thirty of the parliamentarians on the UIA list, strongly supported Jaafari, giving him sixty votes when combined with Jaafari's own thirty-member Dawa block. Al-Sadr allegedly intimidated several wavering independents on the Shiite list into supporting Jaafari, providing his margin of victory.

Although the UIA had close to an absolute majority in the parliament, the constitution provides that the three-man Presidency Council (consisting of the president and two vice presidents) must unanimously nominate the prime minister, in effect giving the Kurds and Sunni Arabs a veto over the choice.* Talabani took the lead in opposing Jaafari and was supported both by the Kurdish parliamentarians and the two Sunni Arab blocks. Khalilzad also encouraged the opposition to Jaafari whom the Administration viewed as divisive, ineffective, and too close to al-Sadr. The result was deadlock. As long as Jaafari insisted on remaining the UIA nominee, the Shiite coalition refused to reconsider the choice for fear that doing so would fracture the UIA. The impasse over the prime minister prevented the Council of Representatives from convening (except briefly) and from electing its officers and a new Presidency Council. At the beginning of April, Secretary of State Condoleezza Rice and British Foreign Secretary Jack Straw made an unannounced visit to Baghdad to pressure the parties to reach an agreement. Jaafari's supporters (and some of his foes) criticized the U.S. and Britain for interfering in an internal Iraqi matter and said the trip was counterproductive.

On April 20—more than four months after the elections—Jaafari finally quit his effort to stay in office. As part of the deal by which Jaafari withdrew, Dawa got to nominate his successor. They chose the UIA spokesman, Nuri al-Maliki, as the new candidate for prime minister. President Bush quickly embraced the choice, saying "The Iraqi people have rejected the terrorists' effort to divide them, and they have chosen the path of unity for their nation." In fact, the Bush Administration knew next to nothing about Maliki, including his first name. (U.S. diplomats had assumed that his nom de guerre, Jawad, was his real name.) The State Department, in planning the Secretary's trips to Iraq including the one two weeks before Maliki's designation, did not con-

---

* The Constitution requires a two-thirds vote to elect the Presidency Council which effectively means a two-thirds majority is necessary to form a government. Although not spelled out in the constitution, it was understood that one member of the Council would be a Kurd, another a Shiite, and the third a Sunni Arab.

sider him important enough to put on her schedule which was other-wise packed with meetings with Iraqi politicians. Like all of Dawa's principal leaders, Maliki spent much of his life in exile, but unlike Jaa-fari who lived in London and speaks English, Maliki took refuge in Iran and then Syria. He served as deputy chairman of the constitution draft-ing committee,* earning a reputation as a hardliner opposed to com-promises with the Sunni Arabs on de-Ba'athification and as an advocate of a more centralized Iraqi government than was tolerable to the Kurds or SCIRI. Maliki had no experience in government and never headed a major political movement. The Kurds considered him too sectarian for the job, and the Sunni Arabs also had misgivings, but President Bush's swift embrace and American pressure to form a government—any gov-ernment—led both groups to decide to go along with Maliki.

With the nomination of Maliki, the Council of Representatives at last met on April 22 to elect the president, the two vice presidents, and the speaker of the parliament. Talabani was re-elected as president and Adel Abdul Mehdi continued as one of the vice presidents. Since a Shi-ite was prime minister and a Kurd president, the speaker of the Coun-cil of Representatives needed to be a Sunni Arab. The Sunni Arabs initially wanted Tariq al-Hashimi, the head of the Iraqi Islamic Party, to fill the slot, but the Kurds and Shiites opposed him as too extreme. Instead, Hashimi became a vice president, where he can veto any pres-idential act including signing legislation into law (the three-man Pres-idency Council must act unanimously). For speaker, the Sunni Arabs nominated Mahmoud al-Mashhadani. In his speech to the Council of Representatives after his election, Mashhadani warned, "The unity of Iraq is an obligation for all of us. Any hand or tongue that harms this unity by wrong doing or provocation deserves to be cut off." Mah-moud Othman, a veteran Kurdish political leader and frequent spokesman for the Kurdish side, described the speech as "alarming."

Iraq's "government of national unity" is hardly that. It is made up of leaders with diametrically opposed goals. Among the very top leaders,

---

* The drafting committee was superseded by the leaders' meetings that began in Au-gust 2005 and had no role in resolving the key constitutional questions.

only Talabani and Mehdi have experience in government, including a record of being able to make the compromises necessary for Iraq's consensus-oriented decision-making procedures to work. The others are known primarily for their strong views. Iraq's government is not likely to function very well. But, even if it did, there is a more pertinent question: what will the government govern?

Not Kurdistan. The Kurdistan Regional Government insists on its constitutional authority to run its region. Baghdad ministries are not allowed even to open offices in the north.

Not the Shiite south. It is run by a patchwork of municipal and governorate officials who front for the clerics, religious parties, and militias who are the real power in the south. Without regard to the freedoms promised in Iraq's interim and permanent constitutions, the south has been ruled as an Islamic state where militias and religious police enforce religious law with varying degrees of strictness. Basra's rulers have tapped into Iraq's oil wealth, siphoning off billions of dollars' worth of oil between the last metering point near Basra city and the loading terminal in the Persian Gulf.

Not the Sunni Arab heartland. It is a battleground. The American military, assisted by Shiite troops, are at war with insurgents and foreign terrorists. Many Sunni Arabs despise both sides of this battle, but it does not mean they will accept the authority of a Shiite-led government that they see as installed by the Americans and aligned with Iran.

Not Baghdad, at least outside the Green Zone. Even before the sharp escalation of sectarian violence in February 2006, Iraq's capital was a city of armed camps. Nine-foot-high concrete walls, known as Bremer barriers, surround public buildings, hotels, and the residences of the rich and powerful. Wealthy Iraqis maintain private armies for security.

Ministers and other top government officials use their own militias for protection, or borrow peshmerga forces from the Kurds. Only the reckless would rely on the police or Iraqi Army for protection, unless those units were in fact peshmerga or militias in the guise of being Iraqi Army or police. Outside the Green Zone and the private fortresses, Baghdad's misery is compounded by an explosion of violent crime—murder, kidnapping for ransom, armed robbery, and rape—that is the consequence of the breakdown of authority.

After February 22, the killings in the world's most dangerous city became more numerous, less targeted, and crueler. In late March, fourteen corpses were dumped in Al Adil, a Sunni neighborhood that is an insurgent stronghold. According to the *Sunday Telegraph,* each man's identity card was neatly placed on his chest, and the police quickly noticed that they all had the same first name, Omar. Omar was the second Caliph, and is reviled by Shiites as an usurper. Sunnis and Shiites are now killed for wearing the wrong clothes, speaking with the wrong accent, or having the wrong name. The daily body count in Baghdad in early 2006 was averaging forty a day, with many corpses found with eyes gouged out, flesh drilled, and other marks of beastly torture.

Most of Iraq's ministries are outside the Green Zone, though many ministers live inside. Going to work involves a dangerous transit through a Green Zone checkpoint and the prospect of being stuck for hours in Baghdad's traffic jams, congestion made worse by periodic bombs and the closing of many streets for security reasons. Regardless of the size of his or her security detail, a minister stuck in traffic is a sitting duck. Most ministers rarely go to their offices, and instead spend their days visiting colleagues in the Green Zone. There is much talk at the highest levels of Iraq's government, but little government.

The situation in Iraq should be blindingly obvious to the top U.S. officials who visit. After three years of an American occupation, they cannot leave the Green Zone, stay overnight, or even move within the Green Zone without a security detail the size of a small army.* The Bush Administration may wish that Iraq were different, but wishes will not change the reality. Perhaps Administration officials can console themselves with the thought that Iraq's breakup was probably inevitable once Saddam left the scene, as eventually he would have. Iraq's Sunni-imposed forced unity was already coming apart before the invasion (Kurdistan was gone from 1991) and the U.S. merely hastened the end.

---

* After the press pointed out that no high official had spent the night in Iraq, Condoleezza Rice and Jack Straw did stay overnight in April 2006.

The United States now needs a strategy based on the reality of Iraq. Even when the United States and Great Britain had full legal authority in Iraq in 2003 and 2004, they did nothing to arrest the breakup of the country. In the south, the British and the Americans allowed the Shiite clergy and religious parties to take power and to build their Islamic states. Although proclaiming a commitment to rule of law and the rights of women (as was to be embodied in the Transitional Adminis- trative Law), they took no action to stop militias from enforcing dress codes on women, shutting down music shops and liquor stores (often murdering their Christian owners), and running their own court sys- tems. While saying that Kurdistan should rejoin Iraq, nothing was done to reduce any part of Kurdistan's autonomy. While outlawing armed forces not part of the Iraqi Army, the coalition allowed militias to pro- liferate during the occupation and made no effort to disband any of them. If the coalition could not prevent Iraq's unraveling when it was fully in charge of the country, it is illogical now to put all the emphasis on building strong national institutions, such as a single Iraqi Army and powerful central government, when U.S. influence is much diminished.

With the American people overwhelmingly viewing the war as a mistake and Bush's approval levels reaching Nixonian lows, the United States will not now engage in the kind of aggressive nation-building that it failed to do when it had more authority. In short, an indepen- dent Kurdistan, a theocratic south, militias, sectarian control of the police and army—all are facts of life in Iraq. The Administration has no intention of changing any of this. The Administration needs to be honest with itself and with the American people. Only by acknowledg- ing how little it will accomplish can the Administration chart a way out of the Iraq mess.

Eleven of Iraq's eighteen governorates are secure.* This provides the starting point for an exit strategy. Kurdistan comprises three gover-

---

* The Administration asserts that fourteen governorates are secure and four are not. Its list of insecure areas consists of the Sunni Arab governorates of Anbar, Nin- eveh, Salahaddin, plus Baghdad. But the civil war is also being fought in religiously mixed Babil and Diyala. Kirkuk (officially known as Tamin) is also unsafe.

norates in their entirety and parts of three others. The peshmerga (the Kurdistan Regional Guard) is Iraq's most capable military force and the only one that is reliably pro-American. The United States should want to strengthen its only friends in Iraq. This means providing technical assistance to help make the Kurdistan Regional Government more effective in the delivery of services such as education, policing, and health care. Already, the Administration is promoting Kurdistan to investors as the safe part of Iraq that could be the gateway to the rest of the country. This should be continued. And, while Kurdistan justifiably boasts of being the most democratic part of Iraq, political reforms are needed in a region where two main parties have dominated politics for decades. U.S.-sponsored democracy programs would find fertile ground among Kurdistan's urban elite, media, and academics.

The peshmerga's capabilities should be enhanced with training, armored vehicles, heavy weapons, and helicopters. As noted, these are America's friends, and the United States may need their assistance in future operations within Iraq.

The Kurds fought alongside the Americans to overthrow Saddam in 2003. They consistently supported U.S. policy during the CPA period and afterward. In the negotiations on Iraq's government in 2006, Khalilzad used the Kurds to push the American agenda, which included blocking Ibrahim al-Jaafari's candidacy. For their collaboration with a country most Arab Iraqis see as the enemy, the Kurds could pay a price. The U.S. has a moral debt to an ally. Arming the peshmerga is one way to discharge that debt. The U.S. could promise air support in the event of an Iraqi attack north, and it might consider keeping a small base in Kurdistan both to protect the Kurds and as insurance against a terrorist takeover in the Sunni Arab parts of the country. While there are compelling arguments against permanent bases in Arab Iraq, the Kurds want American bases in Kurdistan.

Looking ahead, a fully independent Kurdistan appears to be a matter of when, not if. The younger generation of Kurdish leaders (those in their forties and younger) have no use for Iraq and will press for full independence as soon as the situation allows. If Kurdistan's borders are settled, its secession will have a limited impact on the rest of the country. Arab Iraqi leaders have told me privately that they accept Kurdistan's right to self-determination and understand why, after all that was done to the Kurds, Kurdistan's people do not want to be part of Iraq. Some seem to prefer that Kurdistan should leave, having grown weary of Kurdistan's refusal to make any concession to a shared state. Ahmad Chalabi, the Deputy Prime Minister, has publicly said the Kurds have the right to secede. Ayad Allawi told me the same thing when I interviewed him for ABC News in Baghdad in 2003, although he said Kurdistan's separation should be negotiated and not unilateral. With settled borders, the split between Kurdistan and Arab Iraq could be more like Czechoslovakia's velvet divorce than Yugoslavia's wars.

With more Kurds living within their borders than live in Iraq, Turkey and Iran both oppose an independent Kurdistan.* Because of its size and its strategic importance to the United States as a NATO ally, Turkey has long been considered the major obstacle to Kurdish dreams for an independent state.

Turkish attitudes toward Iraqi Kurdistan have evolved significantly since 2003. Before the war, Turkey repeatedly stated its opposition to federalism in Iraq and tried, even after the war began, to get U.S. authorization to send troops into northern Iraq. More recently, however, the Turkish Government has embraced federalism in Iraq and has even toned down its public opposition to the incorporation of Kirkuk into Kurdistan. (Prior to the war, Turkey had said that a Kurdish takeover of Kirkuk was a "red line" that, if crossed, would force Turkey to intervene militarily.)

Turkey's change of position reflects the reality of Iraq. While it might reject a unilateral Kurdish decision to create a federal unit or annex Kirkuk, it has no legal basis to oppose actions that follow from a constitution lawfully adopted by the sovereign state of Iraq. In its effort to pressure the Kurds before the war, Turkey positioned itself as the champion of Iraq's Turcomans and insisted it would intervene to protect its three million kinsmen from forced incorporation into Kurdis-

---

* Syria has between 500,000 and one million Kurds and would also oppose an independent Kurdistan. It has, however, no influence on the future of Iraqi Kurdistan.

tan. In the January 2005 elections, Turcoman parties won just three seats, an indication that Iraq's Turcoman population is just a fraction of what Turkey and the Turcomans claimed.* As a result, the Turcoman issue has receded in importance.

In December 2003, Prime Minister Nechirvan Barzani and I were watching television in the government guest house in Salahaddin when news came that the European Union had given Turkey a date to start accession talks. We both agreed that this was one of the most important events in Kurdistan's history. Turkey knows that many European countries are looking for an excuse not to let it into the European Union. A Turkish military intervention in northern Iraq would derail its chances of joining the European Union and could even lead to sanctions (as did the 1974 invasion of Cyprus). The Turkish General Staff also understands that an invasion of Iraqi Kurdistan would not be a simple matter. From 1984 to 1999, the Turkish Army battled PKK (Kurdistan Workers' Party) guerrillas in southeast Turkey in a conflict that took 30,000 lives. At most, the PKK had 5,000 fighters at any one time. In northern Iraq, Turkey would face a seasoned peshmerga army of more than 100,000 operating on its terrain.

Turkey's pragmatic approach to northern Iraq is not just due to an absence of alternatives. Some Turkish strategic thinkers, including those within the so-called "deep state" comprising the military and intelligence establishments, see Iraqi Kurdistan as a potential asset. They note that the Iraqi Kurds are secular, pro-western, and non-Arab. This makes them natural allies for Turkey and a buffer to an Islamic Arab state to the south. Turkey also has growing economic interests in Iraqi Kurdistan. Turkish companies are the biggest foreign investors in the region, and Turkish oil companies have secured potentially lucrative

---

* Because Iraqis voted their ethnic and religious identities in the two elections, they are a good proxy for a census. Iraq's Turcomans are divided between Sunni and Shiites, and the Shiite Turcomans may have voted for the UIA. The Sunni Turcomans, who identify primarily according to their ethnic identity, probably are not more than 200,000, and at least some voted for the Kurdistan Alliance, which included Turcomans on its slate.

concessions from the Kurdistan Regional Government to develop new fields.

As of 2006, Turkey remains adamantly opposed to a fully independent Kurdistan. But Turks no longer see it as the threat they once did, and many recognize that it is inevitable. Shrewdly, Turkey has positioned itself to have maximum influence over an independent Kurdistan when it happens.

Iran, which has historically supported Kurdish separatists in Iraq, may be the more ferocious opponent of a fully independent Kurdistan in Iraq. Developments in Iraq have inspired Iranian Kurds to demand more rights, frightening the Tehran regime into brutal crackdowns in 2004 and 2005. Iran, however, has many fewer options to prevent the emergence of an independent Kurdistan in Iraq. The United States and its allies would not tolerate a direct military intervention. Subversion and terrorism, Iran's usual policy instruments in such circumstances, can inflict pain but cannot deter a Kurdistan determined on independence. And, in any event, Iran's primary interest in Iraq is in the Shiite south.

If the Shiite south forms a region, it can set up a government and establish a Regional Guard. The government will be theocratic, and the Guards will consist mostly of militias (probably the Badr Organization since SCIRI dominates politically eight of Iraq's nine southern governorates). Even so, an elected Regional Government with a Guard responsible to it would be preferable to the current ad hoc system of informal Islamic rule enforced by sometimes competing militias. By providing technical assistance to a southern government, the U.S. and its coalition partners may have some influence on internal developments. Even a theocratic government can provide the political and economic stability needed to permit new investments in producing the south's vast oil reserves.

A two-way split into Arab Iraq and Kurdistan is much more likely in the near future than a three-way split into Kurdistan, a Sunni state, and a Shiite state. The question is whether Iraq's Sunni and Shiite regions (assuming they are created) will eventually want to become independent. Although being Shiite is a religious identity, many Shiites talk as if it were an "ethnic" or national identity. This is not as unusual as it may sound. Tito's Yugoslavia considered the Muslims in Bosnia to be an ethnic group, not just a religious one.* Anecdotal evidence suggests that Iraq's Shiite masses may be more strongly in favor of self-government and more "Shiite nationalistic" than their leaders, except for SCIRI. In the 1920s, many Basra residents wanted their own state (akin to Kuwait), and there has been a revival of Basra separatism since 2003. It is a complicating factor, as a Basra state would not include Shiite areas such as Najaf and Karbala but would have most of Iraq's oil. Civil war, in which so many Shiites have been killed because of their identity, accelerates the development of a Shiite nationalism and may fuel demands for a separate Shiite state.

Egypt's President Hosni Mubarak probably overstated the case when he told al-Arabiya on April 9, 2006, that the Arab world's Shiites are more loyal to Iran than their own countries, but he did not totally miss the mark either. No matter how the Shiite south evolves, Iran will be the dominant power. Partition, whether into loosely confederated regions as envisioned under Iraq's constitution or into fully independent states, *may limit* Iran's influence to the southern half of Iraq.

The Bush Administration has engineered a remarkable transformation of the politics of the Middle East, giving Iran opportunities it never had in Shiite Arab lands: Iraq, Kuwait, Saudi Arabia's Eastern Province, and Bahrain.† No matter what it says, the Bush Administration has no ability, and no intention, of countering Iran's position in southern Iraq, or elsewhere in the Shiite Arab world. These are not welcome developments, but they need not be catastrophic.

---

* Thus, a Croat or Serb in Bosnia who converted to Islam would retain his or her ethnic identity. He or she would be a "Muslim Croat" or a "Muslim Serb." I once asked Bosnian Foreign Minister Haris Silajdzic whether a Muslim who converted to Catholicism would be a "Catholic Muslim." He replied that a Muslim would not convert. Because of these problems, the Bosnian government changed the name of the Muslim ethnic identity to "Bosniak" in 1993. It is possible to be a Catholic Bosniak.

† Kuwait is Sunni majority but with a significant Shiite minority. There is no reliable census data for Saudi Arabia's Eastern Province, which may have a Shiite majority. Bahrain is majority Shiite.

• • •

The United States and the world's Shiites (including the Iranians) have a common interest in defeating al-Qaeda and its kindred Sunni fundamentalist movements. Not sharing the tortured history of mutual grievances that characterize the U.S. relationship with Iran, the United States could have good relations with a southern Iraqi Shiite theocracy that, like it or not, came to power through a democratic process coalition troops made possible. In the event of confrontation with Iran, however, Iraq's Shiites would line up against the United States.

The continued presence of American and British military forces in Iraq's south can only aggravate relations with the Shiite authorities without any corresponding gain in what is a relatively secure part of Iraq. In 2005, British troops clashed on several occasions with local police and militias, with one incident where British forces attacked a police station nearly escalating out of control.* As long as the coalition remains in the south, there is a risk of more incidents. Troops should be withdrawn in a rapid but orderly fashion.

A coalition withdrawal from the south will strengthen the position of the United States and the Europeans as they try to devise a strategy to prevent Iran from acquiring nuclear weapons. With coalition troops in the south, the U.S. has no military option, and the Iranians know it. Once out of southern Iraq, the United States and Great Britain will have more negotiating power precisely because a military option—albeit still an unattractive one—will exist.

In the Sunni Arab governorates, the United States faces a dilemma. The American military presence among hostile Sunni Arabs seems to generate an endless supply of new suicide bombers and insurgent fighters. If the United States withdraws from the Sunni heartland, even more territory may fall into the hands of insurgents and terrorists. In the worst case, Iraq's Sunni heartland could become what Afghanistan

---

* The objective was to rescue two British special forces who had been arrested while working undercover in civilian clothing.

was under the Taliban: a secure base from which terrorists could plot attacks on the United States.

The pogroms that followed the destruction of the Askariya shrine served as a wake-up call to many Sunni Arabs. In a Sunni-Shiite civil war, Sunni Arabs realize, they will lose. Some of America's most vocal foes changed their position from demanding a U.S. withdrawal to asking for U.S. protection. In Fallujah, Sunni tribal leaders from the surrounding villages sent their tribesmen to join a Fallujah brigade of the Iraqi Army that the U.S. was trying to create. They seem to have concluded that it is better to have local Sunni Arabs protecting the city than to leave it to Shiite soldiers.

Sunni Arabs may come to see the formation of a region as essential for self-protection and therefore be less worried that federalism will lead to the dissolution of Iraq. If the Sunnis establish a regional guard, it could take over security responsibilities from the Americans and from the Shiite-dominated Iraqi Army. The United States could then withdraw while making clear that American forces would return only if the regional authorities allowed al-Qaeda and other anti-Western terrorists to operate freely from the region. If the Sunni Arabs do not form a region, the United States should still withdraw, and leave security duties to the Iraqi Army, which would presumably continue to use Shiite forces there.

Since the U.S. withdrawal from the Sunni heartland is necessarily conditional on the regional authorities suppressing the terrorists, the U.S. will need to keep a force nearby, ready to intervene if they fail. Kurdistan is the ideal location. It is close, the local population friendly, and it is still in Iraq. Locating an "over-the-horizon" force outside Iraq, as some have suggested, would make it politically difficult to return, to the detriment of the U.S. ability to fight terrorists.*

* Once U.S. forces were out of Iraq, there would be enormous domestic opposition within the United States to going back in. Given how it misrepresented the intelligence on Iraqi WMD before the war, the Administration would have a hard time making a convincing case for intervention even if it had good intelligence on a terrorist threat. A divided Iraqi Government might find it hard to reach agreement to allow U.S. forces to return.

Partition works as a political solution for Kurdistan, the Shiite south, and the Sunni Arab center because it formalizes what has already taken place. Partition is the reason Kurdistan is stable and the south relatively so. It is an Iraqi solution, embodied in the constitution, and not an imposed one. By contrast, the American effort to build a unified state with a nonsectarian, nonethnic police and army has not produced that result nor made much progress toward it. If the U.S. were to try seriously, it would destabilize the parts of Iraq that are today secure. The Kurds will resist violently any effort to make them more than nominally Iraqi, while the creation of mixed Sunni/Shiite units in the military and police in the context of civil war is a recipe for ineffectiveness, and possibly violence within the unit.

Accepting partition is a way to get most coalition forces out of Iraq quickly. It does not solve the problem of Baghdad. That is because there is no good solution.

No Iraqi armed force is trusted by both Baghdad's Shiites and its Sunnis. The police and the army are part of the problem. A Baghdad resident who encounters men in police uniforms may have no idea if they are bona fide police carrying out lawful duties, Shiite police commandos staging an abduction, or criminals masquerading as police. For a person with the wrong name, a police checkpoint can be deadly. The army is only somewhat better. In March 2006, the Ministry of Defense broadcast public service messages warning Baghdad residents against allowing either the police or the army to take them away, not that most people would have had a choice.

Theoretically, the United States has the power to provide some level of security in Baghdad. U.S. soldiers would have to become the city's police, manning checkpoints, confiscating weapons, arresting criminals as well as terrorists, and disarming powerful militias, including those within the police and army. It would mean a radically different mission, require many more troops, and result in many more casualties. And it may not work. U.S. troops, operating without necessary language skills and local knowledge, and rightly concerned with protecting themselves, are not a good substitute for reliable Iraqi policemen. In the current political environment in the United States, it is hard to imagine that there is any support for this role.

The alternative is to recognize that there is not much that the United States is able and willing to do to stop the bloodshed in Baghdad. Once they get started, modern civil wars develop a momentum of their own. Atrocities tend to produce new atrocities and rarely the revulsion needed to bring them to an end. Most people, of course, do not want a civil war and do not condone sectarian killing. Civil war empowers the most extreme elements, and over time, more people gravitate toward the extremists on their side. The alternative is the extremists on the other side. Advocating moderation becomes dangerous as it equates to treason toward one's own community.

In recent times, outside powers have intervened to end similar wars. Syrian troops ended Lebanon's fifteen-year civil war in 1989 and then stayed on for another fifteen years. NATO deployed to stop the war in Bosnia,* and European troops are still there eleven years later. Foreign troops have been essential to the tenuous peace that now exists in Liberia, Sierra Leone, and Congo.

There are no foreign forces that will play this role in Baghdad. The United States is unwilling. The Arab League could be asked for troops, but this would require a substantial deployment from the largest and militarily most capable Arab country, Egypt. Iraq's Shiite government may object to troops from any Sunni Arab country, and they certainly will not want troops from a country whose president sees them as disloyal agents of Iran. Iranian troops would be objectionable to Sunni Arabs in Iraq, to Iraq's Sunni neighbors, and to the United States. The Kurds have opposed any role for Turkish troops, and Turkey is, in any event, not willing to devote its army to a thankless and dangerous peacekeeping mission.

There is a danger that factions in Iraq's escalating civil war will ask for more assistance from their allies than they presently receive. It is

---

* Bosnia was not technically a civil war since Serbia and Croatia deployed forces there and directed the activities of the local Serbs and Croats, respectively.

not far-fetched to imagine Iranian troops assisting Iraq's Shiite government while troops from Sunni Arab countries assist the Sunnis. In this
way, Iraq's civil war could spill over the country's borders.

Iraq's civil war is the messy end of a country that never worked as a
voluntary union and that brought misery to most of its people most of
the time. By invading Iraq and mismanaging the aftermath, the United
States precipitated Iraq's collapse as a unified state but did not cause it.
Partition—the Iraqi solution—has produced stability in most of the
country and for this reason should be accepted. In Baghdad and other
mixed Sunni-Shiite areas, the United States can not contribute to the
solution because there is no solution, at least in the foreseeable future.
It is a tragedy, and it is unsatisfying to admit that there is little that can
be done about it. But it is so. No purpose is served by a prolonged
American presence anywhere in Arab Iraq.

The war's architects believed they could change the Middle East.
And so they did.

Special Provisions for the Kurdistan Region of Iraq

Article 1: Continuity of the Kurdistan Region

Section 1: The Kurdistan Regional Government:—The Kurdistan Region is a self-governing region, with its own laws and government. The Government of the Kurdistan Region includes the Kurdistan National Assembly, the Council of Ministers, and the Kurdistan Judiciary.

Section 2: Territory of the Kurdistan Region:—For the purposes of this Transitional Law, the Kurdistan Region consists of those territories in the governorates of Ninevah, Dohuk, Erbil, Kirkuk, Suleimania, and Diyala that were administered by the Kurdistan Regional Government on March 19, 2003, and is the territory within Iraq that is north and west of the former cease-fire line ("Green Line") as it existed on March 18, 2003.

Section 3: Continuation of Law:—Except as otherwise provided in this law, all laws in force in the Kurdistan Region as of the effective date of this Transitional Law shall continue in force. Except as related to matters within the exclusive competence of the Provisional Government of Iraq, the Kurdistan National Assembly shall enact all laws in force in the Kurdistan Region. On the territory of the Kurdistan Region, law enacted by the Kurdistan National Assembly shall be supreme.

Article 2: The Iraqi Kurdistan National Guard;
Security of the Kurdistan Region

Section 1: Establishment of Iraqi Kurdistan National Guard:—The Kurdistan National Assembly shall raise, regulate, recruit, and officer an Iraqi Kurdistan National Guard, and shall appoint its Commanding Officer. The Iraqi Kurdistan National Guard shall be a component of the Armed Forces of Iraq and under the command of the lawful civilian authorities of Iraq provided:

(1) The Iraqi Kurdistan National Guard may be deployed outside the boundaries of the Kurdistan Region only at the request of the lawful civilian authorities of the Provisional Government of Iraq and only after the Kurdistan National Assembly has authorized such a deployment, provided further that the Kurdistan National Assembly may restrict the deployment of the Iraqi Kurdistan National Guard outside the boundaries of the Kurdistan Region to a specific location and for a specified period of time;

(2) No weapons shall be removed from the possession and control of the Iraqi Kurdistan National Guard without the consent of the Kurdistan National Assembly; and

(3) The Provisional Government of Iraq is democratic and operating pursuant to all provisions of this Transitional Law.

Section 2: Transition to Iraqi Kurdistan National Guard:—Within a reasonable period of time after enactment of this Transitional Law, the Kurdistan National Assembly shall authorize the formation of the Iraqi Kurdistan National Guard. Peshmerga units shall be demobilized and all armaments (except for personal weapons) shall be transferred to the Iraqi Kurdistan National Guard.

Section 3: Recognition of Peshmerga Contribution to National Liberation:—The Kurdistan National Assembly and the Provisional Government of Iraq shall honor, through the striking of a medal or other appropriate means, the contribution the Peshmerga made to the liberation of Iraq.

Section 4: Composition of Iraqi Kurdistan National Guard:—The Iraqi Kurdistan National Guard shall be representative of all the peoples of the Kurdistan Region, including Kurds, Turcomans, Assyrians, Chaldeans, and Arabs.

Section 5: Non-deployment of other Iraqi Armed Forces to Kurdistan:—Except for the Iraqi Kurdistan National Guard established by this Article, the Armed Forces of Iraq shall not enter the territory of the Kurdistan Region without the consent of the Kurdistan National Assembly. The Kurdistan National Assembly may confine the presence of any Iraqi Armed Forces to specified places within the Kurdistan Region and may limit the numbers and duration of any presence by Iraqi Armed Forces on the territory of the Kurdistan Region.

Section 6: Protection of International Borders:—In accordance with policies determined by the Provisional Government of Iraq and decided in consultation with the Kurdistan Regional Government, the Iraqi Kurdistan National Guard shall be responsible for the protection of Iraq's international borders that are also the borders of the Kurdistan Region.

Article 3: Natural Resources in the Kurdistan Region

Section 1: Ownership of resources:—The Natural Resources located on the territory of the Kurdistan Region, including water, petroleum, and subsoil minerals, belong to the Kurdistan Region.

Section 2: Public Land:—All public land in the Kurdistan Region belongs to the Kurdistan Region.

Section 3: Water:—

(a) All water in the Kurdistan Region belongs to the Kurdistan Region. The Kurdistan Regional Government shall regulate the generation and distribution of hydro-electric power within the Kurdistan Region, the exploitation of fish and other aquatic resources, and the irrigation of cropland within the Kurdistan Region.

(b) Water flowing through the Kurdistan Region shall be managed in close coordination with the relevant ministries of the Provisional Government of Iraq so as to assure an equitable division of water between the Kurdistan Region and other parts of Iraq.

Section 4: Minerals and Petroleum:—

(a) Petroleum and minerals on or under the surface of the land of the Kurdistan Region belong to the Kurdistan Region.

(b) Except for petroleum from reservoirs in commercial production on the effective date, the Kurdistan Regional Government shall regulate the exploitation and sale of petroleum and minerals in the Kurdistan Region, and shall receive the proceeds from their sale.

(c) The exploitation of petroleum in the Kurdistan Region shall be managed in close coordination with relevant ministries of the Provisional Government of Iraq;

(d) Petroleum from reservoirs in commercial production on the effective date may be managed by the Provisional Government of Iraq for the benefit of all the people of Iraq, provided the Kurdistan Regional Government receives from federal budget the funds specified in Article 4.

(e) For the purposes of this article, commercial production means an average daily production over any consecutive twelve month period since January 1, 1998, of 20,000 barrels per day.

Article 4: Fiscal Arrangements

Section 1: Taxation:—The Kurdistan Regional Government and the Provisional Government of Iraq shall conclude an agreement regarding the applicability of federal tax laws in Kurdistan, which shall be binding when approved by the Kurdistan National Assembly and the Transitional Assembly of Iraq. Pending such an agreement, only taxes enacted by the Kurdistan National Assembly shall be valid in Kurdistan.

Section 2: Administration of Taxes:—The Kurdistan Regional Government shall be responsible for the administration of all taxation laws within the Kurdistan Region. It shall remit to the Treasury of the Provisional Government of Iraq all revenues (less the costs of administration and enforcement) from any applicable federal taxes.

Section 3: Block Grants:—For the purpose of governmental functions in the Kurdistan Region, the Kurdistan Regional Government annually shall receive, after permitted deductions, a sum of money that is a percentage of the total revenues of the Provisional Government of Iraq that is not less than the percentage the population of the Kurdistan Region is of the population of Iraq.

Section 4: Permitted Deductions:—For the purpose of this Article, "permitted deductions" means (1) Kurdistan's proportionate share (based on population) of Provisional Government expenditures for activities within the exclusive competence of the Provisional Government, (2) an amount not more than the revenues anticipated from federal taxes in Kurdistan where such taxes are applicable in all parts of Iraq except Kurdistan and (3) any revenues from the sale of petroleum retained by the Kurdistan Regional Government where the Kurdistan Region would retain more revenues from the sale of petroleum than any other region or governorate in Iraq.

Article 5: Kurdistan Region Ratification of Successor Laws to the Transitional Law

The Permanent Constitution of Iraq, or any successor law to this Transitional Law, shall be valid in the Kurdistan Region only if approved by a majority of the people of the Kurdistan Region voting in a referendum.

Article 6: Effective Date in the Kurdistan Region

This Transitional Law will come into effect in the Kurdistan Region when conforming changes are made in the Constitution and laws of the Kurdistan Region.

Iraq's Political Parties and the 2005 Elections

There were two parliamentary elections in 2005: on January 30 a 275-member Transitional National Assembly (TNA) responsible for drafting a permanent constitution was elected under a proportional representation system with all of Iraq being one constituency. Sunni Arabs mostly boycotted this election. On December 15 a 275-member Council of Representatives (COR) was elected under a proportional representation system with 230 members chosen from governorate-level constituencies and forty-five chosen countrywide. The electoral results are summarized by party and coalition as follows:

Major Shiite Parties and Coalitions

United Iraqi Alliance (al-Itilaf): As the dominant Shiite coalition, the United Iraqi Alliance (UIA) secured the largest number of parliamentary seats in both 2005 elections: it won 140 seats in January (ballot #169), and 128 seats in December (#555). The Alliance is led by two Shiite Islamist parties: the **Supreme Council for Islamic Revolution in Iraq,** whose senior leaders include Abdul Aziz al-Hakim and Deputy President of Iraq Adel Abdul Mehdi; and the **Islamic Dawa Party,** led by Prime Minister Ibrahim Jaafari. Other significant parties under the UIA list include the **Islamic Virtue Party (al-Fadhila),** a Shiite Islamist branch of the Sadrist Movement led by Muhammad al-Yaqubi and Nadim al-Jabri; and the **Iraqi National Congress** (INC), a secular Shiite party led by Ahmad Chalabi, which withdrew from the coalition before the December elections. In the December elections, supporters of radical Shiite cleric Moqtada al-Sadr were well represented on the UIA list with 30 elected. Senior independent figures on this list have included Hussein Shahristani; Qasim Dawud, former National Security Minister; and Mowaffak al-Rubaie, former National Security Advisor. The UIA and the Kurdistan Alliance were largely responsible for the constitutional terms accepted at the October referendum.

Al-Risaliyun (Upholders of the Message): The Risaliyun party emerged as one of two political entities to represent Moqtada al-Sadr in the December elections (#631). They won one seat in the COR and are expected to align with the UIA on most legislative issues.

National Independent Cadres and Elites (NICE): This Shiite Islamist party, led by Fatah'allah Ghazi Ismail (Fatah al-Sheikh), is comprised of Moqtada al-Sadr loyalists associated with his militia, the Mahdi Army. It ran in the January elections under ballot #352 and won three seats in the TNA.

Major Kurdish Parties and Coalitions

Kurdistan Alliance (KA): As the dominant Kurdish coalition, the Kurdistan Alliance won the second highest number of seats in both 2005 elections: 75 seats in January (ballot #130) and, under the name Kurdistani Gathering, won 53 seats in December (#730). Its main components are the two major Kurdish nationalist parties in Iraq: the **Kurdistan Democratic Party,** led by Massoud Barzani, President of the Kurdistan Regional Government; and the **Patriotic Union of Kurdistan,** led by Jalal Talabani, elected President of Iraq in 2005. The KA also includes Turcoman and Christian parties in the north.

Kurdistan Islamic Union (KIU): A moderate Sunni religious party tied to the Muslim Brotherhood, the KIU ran under the KA list in January 2005 but later withdrew to run independently (#561) in December. It won five seats in the COR.

Islamic Group of Kurdistan/Iraq (IGKI): This Kurdish Islamist party led by Muhammad Muhammad Qaader, ran in the January elections (#283) and secured two seats in the TNA. The party joined the Kurdistani Gathering in the December elections. The IGKI tends to support the Kurds on matters of federalism and religious Shiite parties on issues of moral concern.

Major Sunni Arab Parties and Coalitions

Iraqi Accord Front (al-Tawafuq): After the October 12, 2005, agreement that would mandate a constitutional amendment process, three major Sunni

Arab parties joined to form the Tawafuq bloc (#618), an anti-federalist, Iraqi and Arab nationalist coalition. Tawafuq consists of the Sunni Islamist **Iraqi Islamic Party,** led by Tariq al-Hashimi and associated with the Muslim Brotherhood; and the Sunni tribal **General Council for Iraqi People,** led by Adnan al-Dulaimy, and **Iraqi National Dialogue Council,** led by Sheikh Khalaf al-Ulayan. The coalition won 44 seats in the COR, significantly raising Sunni Arab representation after the general boycott in January left them with only 17 seats in the TNA.

Iraqi Front for National Dialogue (al-Hewar): The Hewar front (#667) was formed by secular nationalist Saleh al-Mutlaq to advocate a nonsectarian, anticonstitutional platform in the December elections—it won 11 seats in the COR. Al-Hewar's main components include Mutlaq's own **National Iraqi Front;** and the **National Front for the United Free Iraq,** led by Sunni Arab secular nationalist, Hassan Zeidan. The Front also includes Iraqi Christians.

Major Centrist Parties and Coalitions

Iraqi National List (INL): A secular, nationalist coalition led by former interim Prime Minister Ayad Allawi to contest the December elections, the INL secured only 25 seats in the COR (ballot #731), a significant drop from the 40 seats won by his January coalition, the **Iraqi List** (#285). The INL's main components include Allawi's own secular **Iraqi National Accord Movement (Wifaq),** also notably represented by former Minister of State and Deputy Chair of the Constitution Drafting Committee Adnan al-Janabi; **Iraqis,** a centrist Sunni tribal party led by former interim President Sheik Ghazi al-Yawar; the **Iraqi Communist Party,** led by Hamid Majid Mousa; independent notable Hajim al-Hassani, President of the TNA; and the **Independent Democrats Gathering,** led by elder statesman Adnan Pachachi, whose party ran independently in the January elections but failed to win a seat on the TNA.

National Congress Coalition: Ahmad Chalabi formed this bloc (#569) of multiethnic Shiites and Sunnis to advance a pluralist, federal platform in the December elections. It failed to win any seats.

People's Union: The main Communist coalition in the January elections, the People's Union won two seats under list #324, and consisted of leftist Sunnis and Shiites led by Hamid Majid Mousa and independent candidate Hikmat Daoud Hakim.

Major Minority Parties and Coalitions

Iraqi Turkmen Front (ITF): This ethnic-Turkmen, pro-Turkey movement based in Kirkuk and Erbil won three seats in the January elections (#175) as a coalition comprising the **Turkmen National Party,** the **Independent Turkmen Movement,** the **Islamic Movement of Iraqi Turkmen,** and others, under the leadership of Faruq Abdullah Abd al-Rahman. Predominantly Shiite, the ITF aligned with the UIA in the TNA. Led by Sadettin Ergec (Saad al-Din Arkaj), the Front ran alone in December and secured one seat in the COR (#630).

Al-Rafidain National List (Two Rivers List): Representing the Assyrian, Chaldean, and Syriac Christian communities in Iraq and the diaspora, the Rafidain list won one seat in both 2005 elections (#204 and #740 respectively) under the leadership of Younadem Kana, Secretary-General of the **Assyrian Democratic Movement.** The group supports a federal Iraq.

Yezidi Movement for Progress and Reform (Al-Ezediah): Primarily concerned with ensuring rights and recognition for the Yezidi minority in Iraq, this party ran in the December elections (#668) and secured one seat in the Ninewa governorate.

Cast of Characters

Mahmoud Ahmadinejad
President of Iran, 2005–

Ali Allawi
Iraqi Defense Minister, 2004
Iraqi Finance Minister, 2005–2006

Ayad Allawi
Founder of Iraqi National Accord
Prime Minister of Iraq, 2004–2005

Mohammed Atta
September 11, 2001, terrorist

Tariq Aziz
Deputy Prime Minister of Iraq,
    1979–2003
Iraqi Foreign Minister, 1979–1991

James A. Baker III
Secretary of State, 1989–1993

Ahmed Barmani
PUK Peshmerga
Iraqi Ambassador to Sweden, 2004–

Masrour Barzani
Head of Kurdistan intelligence
    service (Parastin)
Son of Massoud Barzani

Massoud Barzani
President of Kurdistan, 2005–
President of Kurdistan Democratic
    Party, 1979–

Mullah Mustafa Barzani
Founder and President of Kurdistan
    Democratic Party, 1946–1979

Nechirvan Barzani
Prime Minister of the Kurdistan
    Regional Government (KRG);
    KRG-Erbil, 1999–2006; unified
    KRG, 2006–

Gertrude Bell
British Oriental Secretary in
    Baghdad under Sir Percy Cox,
    1917–1925

Robert Blackwill
National Security Council Official,
    2004

Tony Blair
British Prime Minister, 1997–

Anne Bodine
U.S. Embassy Regional Coordinator,
    Kirkuk

Barbara Bodine
Coalition Provisional Authority
    Officer, 2003
U.S. Ambassador to Yemen,
    1997–2001

Stuart Bowen
Coalition Provisional Authority
    Inspector General, 2003–

Lakhdar Brahimi
United Nations Special Advisor to
the Secretary General for Iraq,
2004

L. Paul Bremer III
Coalition Provisional Authority
Administrator, 2003–2004

George H. W. Bush
President of the United States,
1989–1993

George W. Bush
President of the United States, 2001–

Robert Byrd
West Virginia Senator (D), 1959–
Senate Democratic Leader, 1977–1988

Andrew Card
White House Chief of Staff,
2001–2006

Jimmy Carter
President of the United States,
1977–1981

Naseer Chaderchi
Head of National Democratic Party

Ahmad Chalabi
Founder of Iraqi National Congress
Iraqi Deputy Prime Minister,
2005–2006

Sandy Charles
National Security Council Official,
1989–1992

Richard Cheney
Secretary of Defense, 1989–1993
Vice President of the United States,
2001–

Winston Churchill
British Secretary of State for the
Colonies, 1921

Bill Clinton
President of the United States,
1993–2001

Sir Percy Cox
British High Commissioner for
Mesopotamia

Ryan Crocker
Coalition Provisional Authority
Official, 2003

Larry Diamond
Coalition Provisional Authority
Official, 2004
Senior Fellow, Hoover Institution,
Stanford University

Edward Djerejian
U.S. Ambassador to Syria, 1989–1991

Sadoun Dulaimi
Iraqi Defense Minister, 2005–2006

Bill Eagleton
Coalition Provisional Authority
Official, 2003
Head of U.S. Interests Section in
Iraq, 1980–1984

Mohamed ElBaradei
Director General, International
Atomic Energy Agency, 1997–

Kenan Evren
President of Turkey, 1982–1989

Dante Fascell
Congressman from Florida (D),
1955–1993

Chairman of House Foreign Affairs
Committee, 1984–1993

Douglas Feith
Under Secretary of Defense for
Policy, 2001–2005

Noah Feldman
Coalition Provisional Authority
Official, 2003

Tommy Franks
Combatant Commander, Central
Command, 2000–2003

David Frum
White House Speechwriter,
2001–2002

Jay Garner
Head, Office of Reconstruction and
Humanitarian Assistance, retired
Lieutenant General

Dony George
Director of Iraqi Museum

April Glaspie
U.S. Ambassador to Iraq, 1989–1991

David Gompert
Coalition Provisional Authority
Official, 2004

Al Gore
Senator from Tennessee (D),
1985–1993
Vice President of the United States,
1993–2001

Richard Haass
Director for Middle East, National
Security Council, 1989–1993

Abdul Aziz al-Hakim
Head of SCIRI, Member of Iraqi
Governing Council

Muhammed Bakr al-Hakim
Ayatollah, SCIRI founder and leader

Nizar Hamdoon
Iraqi Ambassador to the United
States, 1984–1987

Tariq al-Hashimi
Vice President of Iraq, 2006–
Sunni Arab politician
Leader of the Iraqi Islamic Party

Hajim al-Hassani
Speaker of Transitional National
Assembly, 2005

Jesse Helms
Senator from North Carolina (R),
1973–2003

Saddam Hussein
President of Iraq, 1979–2003

Uday Hussein
Son of Saddam Hussein
Head of Iraqi Olympic Committee

Mohammed Ihssan
Kurdistan Regional Government
Minister of Human Rights,
2002–2006

Bayan Jabr
Iraqi Interior Minister, 2005–2006
Former head of Badr Corps

Ibrahim Jaafari
Prime Minister of Iraq, 2005–2006
Vice President of Iraq, 2004–2005
Dawa Party Leader

Najmaldin Karim
Kurdish-American neurosurgeon,
   President and Founder of the
   Washington Kurdish Institute

John Kelly
Assistant Secretary of State for the
   Near East, 1989–1991

Zalmay Khalilzad
U.S. Ambassador to Iraq, 2005–
Special Presidential Envoy and
   Ambassador to the Free Iraqis,
   2003–2004

Mohammad Khatami
President of Iran, 1997–2003

Abdul Majid al-Khoie
Moderate Shia cleric

Ayatollah Ruhollah Khomeini
De facto ruler of Iran, 1979–1989

Henry A. Kissinger
Secretary of State, 1973–1977
National Security Advisor, 1969–1974

Bill Luti
Deputy Under Secretary of Defense
   for Near Eastern and South Asian
   Affairs, 2002–

Ali Hassan al-Majid
Governor of Northern Iraq under
   Saddam
Cousin of Saddam Hussein, also
   known as "Chemical Ali"

John Major
British Prime Minister, 1990–1997

Kanan Makiya
Iraqi writer, author of *Republic of
   Fear* (1989)

Nuri al-Maliki
Prime Minister of Iraq, 2006–
UIA spokesman
Dawa politician

Mahmoud al-Mashhadani
Speaker of the Council of
   Representatives, 2006–
Sunni Arab politician

Robert McFarlane
National Security Advisor,
   1983–1985

Adel Abdul Mehdi
SPIRI leader, Vice President of Iraq,
   2005–
Iraqi Minister of Finance,
   2004–2005

Daniel Patrick Moynihan
Senator from New York (D),
   1977–2001

Saleh al-Mutlaq
Sunni Arab politician, Head, Iraqi
   Front for National Dialogue

Kendal Nezan
Chairman of the Kurdish Institute in
   Paris

Richard Nixon
President of the United States,
   1969–1974

Mahmoud Othman
Veteran Kurdish leader
Member, Iraqi Governing Council,
   2003–2004

Turgut Özal
President of Turkey, 1989–1993

Adnan Pachachi
Sunni-Arab politician, former
    Foreign Minister of Iraq

Claiborne Pell
Senator from Rhode Island (D),
    1961–1997
Chairman, Senate Foreign Relations
    Committee, 1987–1995

Thomas Pickering
U.S. Ambassador to United Nations,
    1989–1992

Colin Powell
National Security Advisor, 1988
Chairman of Joint Chiefs of Staff,
    1989–1993
U.S. Secretary of State, 2001–2005

Sami Abdul Rahman
Deputy Prime Minister of Kurdistan
    Regional Government, 1999–2004

Haywood Rankin
U.S. diplomat in Iraq, 1987

Robin Raphel
Coalition Provisional Authority
    Official
Former U.S. Ambassador to Tunisia

Latif Rashid
Patriotic Union of Kurdistan
    political leader
Iraqi Water Resources Minister,
    2004–

Kosrat Rasul
Peshmerga Commander
Prime Minister of Kurdistan
    Regional Government, 1994–2001

Ronald Reagan
President of the United States,
    1981–1989

Charles Redman
State Department spokesman, 1988

Condoleezza Rice
National Security Advisor,
    2001–2005
U.S. Secretary of State, 2005–

Brian Ross
ABC News Chief Investigative
    Correspondent

Mowaffak al-Rubaie
Iraqi National Security Advisor,
    2004–

Donald Rumsfeld
U.S. Special Envoy to Iraq,
    1983–1984
Secretary of Defense, 2001–

Moqtada al-Sadr
Iraqi Shia cleric and leader of the
    Mahdi Army paramilitary group

Muhammad Baqir al-Sadr
Grand Ayatollah
Iraq's most senior Shia cleric,
    arrested and murdered by
    Saddam Hussein in 1980

Barham Salih
Prime Minister of the Kurdistan
    Regional Government
    (Suleimania), 2001–2004
Deputy Prime Minister of Iraq,
    2004–2005, 2006–
Iraqi Planning Minister, 2005–2006

Richard Schifter
Assistant Secretary of State for
Human Rights, 1985–1992

Norman Schwarzkopf
Commander in Chief of U.S. Central
Command, 1988–1991

Brent Scowcroft
National Security Advisor, 1989–1993

Hussein Shahristani
Shiite political leader and member of
Iraqi Governing Council

Bruska Noori Shaways
Secretary General of the Iraqi
Ministry of Defense, 2004–

Rowsch Shaways
Speaker of Kurdistan National
Assembly, 2004
Vice President of Iraq, 2004–2005
Deputy Prime Minister of Iraq,
2005–2006

Eric Shinseki
Army Chief of Staff, 1999–2003

George Shultz
Secretary of State, 1982–1989

Ali al-Sistani
Grand Ayatollah, highest ranking and
most influential Shia cleric in Iraq

Walter Slocombe
Coalition Provisional Authority
Official, 2003
Under Secretary of Defense for
Policy, 1993–2001

Hero Talabani
Wife of Jalal Talabani, head of
KurdSat-TV

Jalal Talabani
Secretary General of Patriotic Union
of Kurdistan, 1975–
President of Iraq, 2004–

Qubad Talabani
PUK representative to the U.S., 2004–
Son of Jalal Talabani

Chris Van Hollen
Senate Foreign Relations Committee
Staff, 1988
Congressman from Maryland (D),
2003–

Sergio Vieira de Mello
United Nations Special
Representative in Iraq, 2003
United Nations Transitional
Administrator in East Timor,
1999–2002

Paul Wolfowitz
Deputy Secretary of Defense,
2001–2005
Under Secretary of Defense for
Policy, 1989–1993

Ghazi al-Yawar
Sunni-Arab politician
President of Iraq, 2004–2005
Vice President of Iraq, 2005–2006

Abu Musab al-Zarqawi
Jordan-born leader of al-Qaeda in
Mesopotamia

Babkir Zebari
Top Iraqi General, 2004–
Peshmerga Commander

Hoshyar Zebari
Iraqi Foreign Minister, 2003–

A Note on Sources

I have followed Iraq for twenty-six years, mostly for the U.S. government. This book is the product of that experience and my encounters with the people and the country. I began working on Iraq issues for the Senate Foreign Relations Committee with the outbreak of war between Iran and Iraq. During my years at the Committee (1979–1993), I worked on Iraq-related legislation and made trips to the country, as is related in this book. I developed professional contacts with many Iraqis that became personal friendships. I stayed in contact with my Iraqi friends even while I was embarked on unrelated assignments in Croatia and East Timor. While a professor at the National War College (1999 and 2001–2003), I taught a course on Turkey and Iraq and traveled to Iraqi Kurdistan, again as related in this book. Also from 1998 until 2003, I was a Board member of INDICT, a London-based nongovernmental organization with the purpose of bringing criminal cases against Saddam Hussein and the other top Iraqi leaders. In 2003, INDICT dissolved with most of our targets arrested or dead. Our files went to the new Iraqi authorities who included all our Iraqi Board members. Since Saddam's overthrow, I have been a frequent visitor to the country in a variety of capacities: as a consultant for ABC News, in the private sector, as a specialist in international law, and as an occasional contributor to the *New York Review of Books*. For a few months at the end of 2003 and the beginning of 2004, I did some compensated work for Kurdish clients.

Not entirely by chance, I was in Iraq at many critical turning points in the country's recent history. While at the Senate Foreign Relations Committee, I kept notes, wrote memoranda, and published reports about Iraq. The published Committee reports are *War in the Gulf* (1984, with co-authors), *War in the Persian Gulf: The U.S. Takes Sides* (1987, with co-authors), *Chemical Weapons Use in Kurdistan: Iraq's Final Offensive* (1988, with Christopher Van Hollen, Jr.), *Civil War in Iraq* (1991), *Kurdistan in the Time of Saddam Hussein* (1991), and *Saddam's Documents* (1992). In addition, the *New Republic* published in its April 29, 1991, edition my eyewitness account of the collapse of the 1991 Kurdish uprising, "Last Stand: A Report from Kurdistan." During my more recent trips, I kept journals and wrote for various publications, including the *New York Review of Books*.

In writing this book, I have also made use of the daily reporting in the *New York Times*, the *Washington Post*, the *Los Angeles Times*, the *Christian Science Monitor*, the *Boston Globe*, the *Financial Times*, and the *Guardian*, among other publications. The most useful Iraq-related daily blog is Informed Comment, a summary of major articles in the international and Arab-language press, pulled together and analyzed by University of Michigan Professor Juan Cole. I have also made use of articles, interviews, and reports on the Web sites of United States Institute for Peace, the Council on Foreign Relations, the Brookings Institution, and the American Enterprise Institute. Speeches, congressional testimony, and transcripts can be found on the Web sites of the aforementioned institutions as well as the White House, the State Department, the Department of Defense, the Senate Foreign Relations Committee, and the House International Relations Committee.

I drew on Jon Randal's superb account of the Kurds, *After Such Knowledge, What Forgiveness?: My Encounters with Kurdistan* for background material in Chapter 8, including the Kissinger double-cross of Barzani. I used Sandra Mackey's *The Reckoning: Iraq and the Legacy of Saddam Hussein* for its account of the Iran-Iraq War and Iraq's reaction to September 11 (Chapters 1 and 2). Samantha Power has a comprehensive account of the failed effort to impose sanctions for the genocide against the Kurds in her book, *"A Problem for Hell": America and the Age of Genocide* (Chapters 3 and 4). The Human Rights Watch publication that made use of the Senate Foreign Relations Committee documents is *Iraq's Crime of Genocide: The Anfal Campaign Against the Kurds*. In Chapter 7, I make extensive use of L. Paul Bremer III's revealing memoir, *My Year in Iraq: The Struggle to Build a Future of Hope* (written with Malcolm McConnell), and George Packer's *Assassin's Gate*. John Sawers's cable, cited in chapter 7, was first published in *Cobra II*, a superb and comprehensive account of the Iraq War by Michael R. Gordon and Bernard E. Trainor.

Useful books include

Anderson, Liam, and Gareth Stansfield. *The Future of Iraq: Dictatorship, Democracy, or Division?* New York: Palgrave Macmillan, 2004.

Bremer, L. Paul III, and Malcolm McConnell. *My Year in Iraq: The Struggle to Build a Future of Hope.* New York: Simon & Schuster, 2006.

Bulloch, John, and Harvey Morris. *No Friends but the Mountains: The Tragic History of the Kurds.* New York: Oxford University Press, 1992.

Bush, George Herbert Walker, and Brent Scowcroft. *A World Transformed: The Collapse of the Soviet Empire, The Unification of Germany, Tiananmen Square, The Gulf War.* New York: Alfred A. Knopf, 1998.

Catherwood, Christopher. *Churchill's Folly: How Winston Churchill Created Modern Iraq.* New York: Carroll & Graf, 2004.

Cockburn, Andrew, and Patrick Cockburn. *Out of the Ashes: The Resurrection of Saddam Hussein.* New York: HarperCollins, 1999.

Diamond, Larry. *Squandered Victory: The American Occupation and the Bungled Effort to Bring Democracy to Iraq.* New York: Times Books, 2005.

Dobbins, James, et al. *America's Role in Nation-Building: From Germany to Iraq.* Santa Monica, Calif.: Rand Corp., 2003.

Feldman, Noah. *What We Owe Iraq: War and the Ethics of Nation Building.* Princeton: Princeton University Press, 2004.

Gordon, Michael, and Bernard Trainor. *Cobra II: The Inside Story of the Invasion and Occupation of Iraq.* New York: Pantheon Books, 2006.

Helms, Christine Moss. *Iraq: Eastern Flank of the Arab World.* Washington, D.C.: Brookings Institution Press, 1984.

Henderson, Simon. *Instant Empire: Saddam Hussein's Ambition for Iraq.* San Francisco: Mercury House, 1991.

Human Rights Watch. *Iraq's Crime of Genocide: The Anfal Campaign Against the Kurds.* New Haven: Yale University Press, 1994.

Mackey, Sandra. *The Reckoning: Iraq and the Legacy of Saddam Hussein.* New York: W. W. Norton, 2002.

McDowall, David. *Modern History of the Kurds.* 3rd edition. London and New York: I. B. Tauris Co., 2004.

Nakash, Yitzhak. *The Shi'is of Iraq.* Princeton: Princeton University Press, 1994.

O'Leary, Brendan, John McGarry, and Khaled Salih. *The Future of Kurdistan in Iraq.* Philadelphia: University of Pennsylvania Press, 2005.

Packer, George. *The Assassin's Gate: America in Iraq.* New York: Farrar, Straus & Giroux, 2005.

Powell, Colin. *My American Journey.* New York: Random House, 1995.

Power, Samantha. *"A Problem from Hell": America and the Age of Genocide.* Basic Books, 2002.

Priest, Dana. *The Mission: Waging War and Keeping Peace with America's Military.* New York: W. W. Norton, 2003.

Randal, Jonathan C. *After Such Knowledge, What Forgiveness?: My Encounters with Kurdistan.* New York: Farrar, Straus & Giroux, 1997.

Schwarzkopf, Norman, and Peter Petre. *It Doesn't Take a Hero: The Autobiography of General H. Norman Schwarzkopf.* New York: Bantam, 1992.

Sciolino, Elaine. *Outlaw State: Saddam Hussein's Quest.* New York: John Wiley & Sons, 1991.

Woodward, Bob. *Plan of Attack.* New York: Simon & Schuster, 2004.

Web sites

Informed Comment: www.juancole.com

The American Enterprise Institute: www.aei.org

Senate Foreign Relations Committee: http://foreign.senate.gov/

House International Relations Committee: http://wwwc.house.gov/international_relations/

Iraq Body Count: www.iraqbodycount.net

Articles, briefs, and transcripts

Barnes, Fred. "The Postwar Corps." *Weekly Standard.* March 29, 2004.

Bremer, L. Paul III. "Operation Iraqi Prosperity." *Wall Street Journal.* June 20, 2003.

Cha, Ariana Eunjung. "In Iraq, the Job Opportunity of a Lifetime; Managing a $13 Billion Budget with No Experience." *Washington Post.* May 23, 2004.

Filkins, Dexter. "UN Envoy Wants New Iraq Government to Court Foes of Occupation." *New York Times.* June 3, 2004.

Freeman, Ambassador Charles. "A Shia Crescent: What Fallout for the U.S.?", Transcript of policy conference, Middle East Policy Council, Washington, D.C., October 14, 2005.

Galbraith, Peter. "Refugees from War in Iraq: What Happened in 1991 and What May Happen in 2003." *Policy Brief February 2003.* Migration Policy Institute. Washington, D.C., 2003.

Glanz, James. "Audit Describes Misuse of Funds in Iraq." *New York Times.* January 25, 2006.

Glanz, James, William J. Broad, and David E. Sanger. "Huge Cache of Explosives Vanished From Site in Iraq." *New York Times.* October 25, 2004.

Harnden, Toby, Aqeel Hussein, and Colin Freeman. "Iran 'Sponsors Assassination' of Sunni Pilots who Bombed Teheran; Iraqi President Offers Airmen Protection in his Native Kurdistan Where Some Dropped Chemical Weapons." *Sunday Telegraph*. October 30, 2005.

Johnson, Julie. "U.S. Asserts Iraq Used Poison Gas Against the Kurds." *New York Times*. September 9, 1988.

Knickmeyer, Ellen, and Omar Fekeiki. "Iraqi Shiite Cleric Pledges to Defend Iran; Sadr, with Powerful Militia, Vows to Respond to Attack by West on Neighbor." *Washington Post*. January 24, 2006.

Rieff, David. "Blueprint for a Mess." *New York Times Magazine*. November 2, 2003.

Sciolino, Elaine. "U.S. and Iraq Plan a Joint Inquiry." *New York Times*. May 20, 1987.

Slackman, Michael. "Guess Who Likes the G.I.'s in Iraq (Look in Iran's Halls of Power)." *New York Times*. January 29, 2006.

Wright, Robin. "Hussein Torpedoed CIA Plot Against Him, Officials Say." *Los Angeles Times*. September 8, 1996.

Zajac, Andrew. "Insiders Shape Postwar Iraq: Republican Ties Often Trumped Experience in Coalition." *Chicago Tribune*. June 20, 2004.

TV broadcasts

Vice President Richard Cheney Interview with Tim Russert, *Meet the Press*, NBC-TV, March 16, 2003.

Vice President Richard Cheney Interview with Larry King, *Larry King Live*, CNN-TV, May 31, 2005.

"Billions Wasted in Iraq?" *CBS News*, February 9, 2006.

Frontline interview with Norman Schwarzkopf, PBS-TV transcript at http://www.pbs.org/wgbh/pages/frontline/gulf/oral/schwarzkopf/7.html

Frontline interview with Richard Cheney, PBS-TV transcript athttp://www.pbs.org/wgbh/pages/frontline/gulf/oral/cheney/1.html

Frontline interview with Colin Powell, PBS-TV transcript at http://www.pbs.org/wgbh/pages/frontline/gulf/oral/powell/1.html

Frontline interview with Richard Haass, PBS-TV transcript at http://www.pbs.org/wgbh/pages/frontline/gulf/oral/haass/1.html

Acknowledgments

On March 31, 2004, I gave the first John Kenneth Galbraith Lecture, an event sponsored by the Cambridge Public Library and the American Academy of Arts and Sciences. In 1967, my father had written *How to Get Out of Vietnam*, a small book advocating a Vietnam policy in accord with U.S. interests in Vietnam and the realities on the ground. As a tribute to my father and because I saw parallels in the illusions that drove U.S. policy in both places, I gave my lecture the title "How to Get Out of Iraq." Anthony Lewis, the former *New York Times* columnist, was in the audience. He asked if he could contact Robert Silvers at the *New York Review of Books* about publishing the lecture and called me back that night to say that Silvers was interested. It appeared a few weeks later under the same title. Over the next fifteen months, I published three additional pieces on Iraq in the *NYRB*. Andrew Wylie, a friend and now my agent, contacted me to propose I write a book on the subject, and within days he had arranged a contract with Simon & Schuster.

I had the good fortune to have Alice Mayhew as my editor. She believed it was important to bring the case argued in this book to a wider audience in a timely fashion and made that happen. The book is much improved for her guidance and her many suggestions. Roger Labrie provided a fresh set of eyes and helped enforce a strict schedule of deadlines. Tom Pitoniak and Gypsy da Silva improved the text with careful copyediting. My thanks to Irene Kheradi, Jim Thiel, and Paul Dippolito, to Serena Jones, and to Victoria Meyer and Rebecca Davis. One of the many advantages of being an author at Simon & Schuster is that everyone is very nice.

Keith Bettinger and Andrew Galbraith assisted me with the research. I am particularly grateful to Keith for being available at all hours to check facts consequential and otherwise. Mona Iman prepared Appendix 2 on the Iraqi political parties and 2005 elections. James Galbraith and Jonathan Morrow reviewed the manuscript, offering suggestions on content, organization, and writing. On discovering that we had, rather separately, come up with a similar strategy for Iraq, Les Gelb and I co-authored two articles. This book is enriched by that collaboration. Jonathan Randal, Falah Bakir, Khaled Salih, Juan Cole, Harvey Rishikof, Brendan O'Leary, Joost Hilterman, and Chris Bassford responded generously to my questions or called my attention to material I would not otherwise have seen. And, a special thanks to Susan Lemke and Scott Gower of the Special Collections at the National Defense University Library, as well as to Sylvia Baldwin and Katherine de Freycinet.

This is a book about the peoples of Iraq drawing on my personal experience over twenty-five years. Massoud Barzani, Jalal Talabani, Nechirvan Barzani, Barham Salih, Rowsch Shaways, Latif Rashid, Kosrat Rasul, and Hoshyar Zebari have been extraordinarily generous with their time, with their hospitality, and in providing for my safety in Kurdistan, Baghdad, Mosul, and southern Iraq. Falah Bakir, a minister in the KRG, has doubled as an educator, logistician, and translator. Najmaldin Karim and Kendal Nezan introduced me to the Kurds as they have so many others in the United States and Europe. Ahmad Chalabi, Hameed Bayati, Mahmoud Othman, Mohammed Ihssan, Nabeel Musawi, Fuad Hussein, Kanan Makiya, Rend Rahim, Asad Gozeh, Bakhtiar Amin, and Laith Kubba are among those with whom I have been associated in the effort to document, and to bring to justice those responsible for, genocide and crimes against humanity in Iraq. I owe many others—peshmerga, drivers, the boatman who took me to and from Syria—a debt of gratitude for taking the risks that kept me alive and got me where I needed to go.

Over the years, ABC News has included me as part of its coverage of Iraq. My thanks to Ted Koppel, Peter Jennings, Brian Ross, Rhonda Schwartz, Chris Isham, Mark Litke, and Jill Rackmills. Judith Kipper, the Middle East scholar, made the connection to ABC and has educated me on the Middle East. While I am critical of the U.S. policies toward Iraq over the last twenty-five years, I am full of admiration for the men and women who faithfully carry them out, usually very aware of the shortcomings. My thanks to the many American diplomats, other government employees, and U.S. military who have helped me in Iraq over the years, especially Haywood Rankin, David Newton, Robert Finn, and Hamza Ulucay.

Claiborne Pell is a central figure in this book for his effort to stop Saddam's genocide against the Kurds. He was that rare public servant who focused on the result and never minded who got the credit. He was also a kind and generous boss who supported my work on Iraq unreservedly and therefore made possible the personal history told in this book. I also appreciate the support I received from other members of the Senate Foreign Relations Committee, especially Senator Daniel Patrick Moynihan, as well as from my fellow staff members including Mary Beth Markey, Chris Van Hollen, George Pickart, Jerry Christianson, Tom Hughes, Sandy Mason, John Ritch, Frank Sieverts, Ursula McManus, and Kathy Taylor. I am also deeply grateful to Liz Moynihan and Nuala Pell who have been steadfast in their friendship through the controversies described in this book.

Tens of thousands have died in Iraq's latest war, including three dear friends: Sami Abdul Rahman, Sergio Vieira de Mello, and Elizabeth Neuffer. They are gratefully remembered and very much missed.

This book is a family collaboration. Liv and Erik have cheered me on, even though Iraq has meant prolonged absences, delayed holidays, and a missed birthday. Tone made those absences possible, and also provided suggestions, fixed computers, and offered encouragement. Andrew, as noted, assisted with the research and accompanied me to Kurdistan. Jamie reviewed the manuscript while Alan and Katie ferreted out errors in the galleys. My parents, both authors, have long urged me to write a book and followed the progress of this one closely. All have my gratitude and love.

My father died after this book was finished but before final publication. Sentimentality, he believed, belongs in the private realm. Here I will only say that he inspired me, by example and in his words, to pursue a career devoted to mitigating the consequences of war and, now, to write about it. He often had the last word not because he was assertive but because he was right. For that reason, I conclude this book with the final paragraph of his last book, *The Economics of Innocent Fraud.* In a chapter entitled "The Last Word," John Kenneth Galbraith wrote:

> The facts of war are inescapable—death and random cruelty, suspension of civilized values, a disordered aftermath. Thus the human condition and prospect as now supremely evident. The economic and social problems here described, as also mass poverty and starvation, can, with thought and action, be addressed. So they have already been. War remains the decisive human failure.

Peter W. Galbraith
Townshend, Vermont

Index

About the Author

PETER W. GALBRAITH served as the first U.S. ambassador to Croatia. He is currently the Senior Diplomatic Fellow at the Center for Arms Control and Non-Proliferation and is a regular contributor to the *New York Review of Books*. He lives in Townshend, Vermont.